TREATING ANXIETY AND STRESS

TREATING ANXIETY AND STRESS

A Group Psycho-Educational Approach Using Brief CBT

Jim White
Greater Glasgow Primary Care NHS Trust, Scotland

JOHN WILEY & SONS, LTD

Chichester · New York · Weinheim · Brisbane · Singapore · Toronto

Other Wiley Editorial Offices

John Wiley & Sons, Inc., 605 Third Avenue,
New York, NY 10158-0012, USA

WILEY-VCH Verlag GmbH, Pappelallee 3,
D-69469 Weinheim, Germany

Jacaranda Wiley Ltd, 33 Park Road, Milton,
Queensland 4064, Australia

John Wiley & Sons (Asia) Pte Ltd, 2 Clementi Loop #02-01,
Jin Xing Distripark, Singapore 129809

John Wiley & Sons (Canada) Ltd, 22 Worcester Road,
Rexdale, Ontario M9W 1L1, Canada

Library of Congress Cataloging-in-Publication Data

White, Jim (Jim M.), 1957–
    Treating anxiety and stress : group psycho-educational approach using brief CBT /
Jim White.
        p. cm.
    Includes bibliographical references and index.
    ISBN 0-471-49306-6 (paper) ✔
    1. Anxiety—Treatment.   2. Stress management.   3. Cognitive therapy.   4. Group
psychotherapy.   I. Title.
    RC531 .W47 2000
    616.85'2230651—dc21
                                                                00-025306

British Library Cataloguing in Publication Data

A catalogue record for this book is available from the British Library

ISBN 0-471-49306-6

Typeset in 10/12pt Palatino by Dorwyn Ltd, Rowlands Castle, Hants
Printed and bound in Great Britain by Antony Rowe, Chippenham, Wilts
This book is printed on acid-free paper responsibly manufactured from sustainable forestry,
in which at least two trees are planted for each one used for paper production.

For Lilian

CONTENTS

List of Figures xi

List of Tables xii

About the Author xiii

Preface xv

Part 1: The Argument for Change 1

1. **Treating Anxiety: Delving beneath the Tip of
   the Iceberg** 3
   Introduction 3
   Prevalence 3
   Comorbidity 7
   Anxiety at the Primary Care Level 11
   Social Factors 13

2. **Treating Anxiety: The Gulf between Research
   Findings and Clinical Realities** 20
   Research Centres and Routine Clinical Practice:
   Different Worlds? 20
   Generalising from the Research Centre to the Clinic:
   The Pitfalls 21
   Diagnostic Systems 24
   The Issue of Comorbidity 25
   Treatment Outcome: The Effect of Comorbidity 27
   How Representative are Patients in Treatment Outcome
   Studies? 28
   Specific versus Non-specific Factors 30
   Time Considerations 35
   Conclusions 35

3. **Treating Anxiety: The Problems in Primary Care** 38
   Introduction 38
   Mental Health and Primary Care 38
   Developing a Primary Care Model 41

Dealing with Problems 41
Studies of Effectiveness in Primary Care: Heterogeneous
Samples 43
Studies of Effectiveness in Primary Care: Anxiety
Disorders 47
Anxiety Treatment as Part of an Interactive Service 50

PART 2: Issues in Devising and Setting-up the Group Therapy **55**

4. The 'Stress Control' Method **57**
Introduction 57
'Stress Control' 57
Providing a Rationale for the Approach 59
Diagnostic Issues 64
Therapy Issues 69

5. Setting up a Course **76**
Introduction 76
Assessment Issues 76
The Assessment Interview 77
Introducing the Course 78
Questions 82
The Key Messages 86
Is an Assessment Interview Necessary? 88
Special Circumstances 89
Spouses/Partners/Friends 89
Conclusions 89

6. Developing Materials for the Course **90**
The Importance of Written Material 90
Bibliotherapy 91
'Stress Control' 93
Therapist Manual 93
Self-help Manual 94
Conclusions 100

7. Preparing for the Course **101**
The 'Stress Control' Components 101
Step 1: Learning about Stress 101
Step 2: Describing your Stress 104
Step 3: Targeting your Stress 105
Step 4: Daily Diary 106
Step 5: Setting your Goals 106
Step 6: Clearing the Decks 106
Step 7: Quick Control 113
Conclusions 114

8. Running a Course **115**
Introduction 115
Selecting the Venue 115

Setting up the Room 1
Pre-session 11,
Group Size 119
Teaching Style 121
Teaching Aids 123
Session Format 124

PART 3: The Stress Management Course 129
  9. Learning about Stress 131
    Session 1: Introduction and Information 131
    Course Outline 132
    Step 1 Revisited: Learning about Stress 132
    The Session 134
    Conclusions 140

  10 Treating Somatic Anxiety 141
    Session 2: Step 8—Controlling your Body 141
    Step 8: Controlling your Body 142
    The Session 143
    Conclusions 149

  11. Treating Cognitive Anxiety 151
    Session 3: Step 9—Controlling your Thoughts . 151
    Step 9: Controlling your Thoughts 152
    The Session 154
    Conclusions 162

  12. Treating Behavioural Anxiety 163
    Session 4: Step 10—Controlling your Actions . 163
    Step 10: Controlling your Actions 164
    The Session 165
    Conclusions 174

  13. Treating Panic Attacks 175
    Session 5: Step 11—Controlling your Panic .. 175
    Step 11: Controlling your Panic 176
    The Session 177
    Conclusions 185

  14. Treating Insomnia 186
    **Session 5 (Continued): Step 12—Controlling your
    Sleep Problems** 186
    Step 12: Controlling your Sleep Problems 187
    The Session 187

  15. Treating Depression 192
    Session 6: Step 13—Controlling your Depression . 192
    Step 13: Controlling your Depression 193
    The Session 193
    Conclusions 200

16. **Completing the Jigsaw** **201**
    Session 6 (Continued): Step 14—Tying it all Together *and*
    Step 15: Controlling your Future **201**
    Steps 14 and 15: Tying it all Together *and*
    Controlling your Future 202
    Conclusions 207
Part 4: Evaluation and Future Developments **209**
    17. **Research Evidence** **211**
        Evaluation 211
        Controlled Evidence: The 1987 Study 211
        Longer-term Follow-up 213
        Recent Research 215
        Comparison with Other Treatment Outcome Studies 218
        'Stress Control' Run by Other Teachers 220
        Developments 221
        'Stress Control' 222
        Conclusions and Summary 223

References 224

Index 243

LIST OF FIGURES

5.1	The vicious and positive circles in stress	87
6.1	Worry cartoon	96
6.2	Fuel supply cartoon	97
7.1	Daily diary example	107
7.2	'Setting your goals' form	108–11
8.1	Seating arrangements (large group)	117
10.1	Relaxation diary	150
11.1	Court case diary	159
12.1	'Facing up' form	169
12.2	Problem-solving form	171–3
13.1	Panic diary	181
14.1	Sleep diary	189
15.1	Activity diary	198–9
16.1	'After the course ends' form	204–5
17.1	Mean change on STAI A-Trait (pre-therapy to six months follow-up)	219
17.2	Therapist hours per patient	219
17.3	Comparison between Glasgow and Oxford 'Stress Control' and Oxford individual therapy on BAI and BDI at individual assessment, start and end of treatment	221

LIST OF TABLES

1.1   *Lifetime prevalence of anxiety disorders in the National Comorbidity Survey*   4

17.1   *Students meeting criteria for clinically significant change on both BDI and A-Trait at six months, two years and eight years follow-up*   214

17.2   *Clinical efficiency scores*   220

ABOUT THE AUTHOR

Jim White is a consultant clinical psychologist in primary care working in Clydebank Health Centre. He has, over many years, attempted to develop cognitive–behavioural therapies to better meet the needs found in primary care settings. In particular, he has attempted to go beyond seeing the 'tip of the iceberg' by developing psycho-educational approaches designed to achieve the best compromise between clinical effectiveness for each individual and clinical efficiency—allowing greater numbers of people to receive appropriate treatment. His clinical and research interests lie mainly within the anxiety disorders.

PREFACE

The aim of this book is to describe a didactic, cognitive–behavioural group therapy approach to the anxiety disorders. 'Stress Control' is a robust six-session 'evening class' designed for either small or large group format—anything between six and 60 on each course. It is designed to be flexible to better meet the needs of routine clinical work. The therapy has, as its basic premise, the goal of 'turning individuals into their own therapists'. It differs fundamentally from much therapy in that the role of the therapist becomes that of the teacher while the patient becomes the student. Reconceptualising roles in this way helps the individual to take responsibility for change and to attribute change to the individual's own coping skills rather than to the skill of the therapist. It is mainly used as a 'complete' therapy but can be used adjunctively with individual therapy. It is designed for the treatment of heterogeneous anxiety disorders and assumes the presence of comorbid problems, some of which are tackled in the course. It attempts to teach individuals to understand their problems within both a psychological and social context.

The approach is clinically effective and efficient and has been empirically tested. It attempts, within a 'scientist–practitioner' framework, to achieve the best compromise between best practice and best value in providing help to a large number of people. It relies heavily on the written material that accompanies the course. Course topics can be varied according to the composition of the group.

I devised the idea of large-group didactic therapy in the mid-1980s, for two reasons. Firstly, as a young clinical psychologist in the National Health Service, my colleagues and I were (and still are) inundated with referrals from family doctors asking for help with people with severe, chronic, highly comorbid and well-entrenched anxiety disorders. Long waiting lists were the inevitable result. Even so, these individuals constituted only the tip of the iceberg. It was clear that by continuing with almost exclusive reliance on individual therapy approaches, we could do little to offer any help to the vast majority of individuals who were deprived of the chance to receive appropriate mental health treatment. Secondly, I assumed that even if I could not treat many patients, at least those I did treat would greatly benefit from therapy. However, it quickly became clear that individuals seen in routine clinical work often did not respond well to approaches developed in research centres.

This led to two conclusions: one, that I was a useless therapist and, two, that my patients were not doing it properly and, thus, must be to blame in some way for not getting better. Experience rapidly taught me that these conclusions were faulty (well, the second one anyway). The reason my patients did not get better was that the techniques I was using had, largely, been tested on almost perfect patients treated in almost perfect circumstances. The techniques failed to take into account the greater psychological and social complexities my patients presented with. They were not robust enough to cope with the limitations inherent in working in a busy, under-resourced clinical setting. Determined to devise a treatment more relevant to my patients' needs that would also allow me to reach much larger numbers of anxiety sufferers, I looked to combine my clinical experience with the many stimulating ideas particularly within the cognitive–behavioural theoretical and therapeutic literature. In essence, I argued against the goal of developing a 'Rolls–Royce' service, capable of carrying, in great style, the very few, when a 'Greyhound bus' service could reach the same goal but carry a lot more, in reasonable comfort and significantly cheaper. 'Stress Control' was the result and over 2000 people have now taken part in this approach.

This book presents a rationale for psycho-educational therapy along with practical guidelines for those interested in working in this way. It aims to integrate recent theoretical and empirical advances in our knowledge of anxiety, anxiety treatment and clinical realities. It looks critically at current practice both in research centres and clinical settings and describes an approach devised to blend the best from both worlds. It argues that the attempt to achieve a working compromise between a high-*quality* service, providing appropriate help for each individual, and a high-*quantity* service, providing appropriate help for as many as possible, can best be understood in the context of service provision as a whole. Offering didactic treatment groups not only allows larger numbers to be treated, and treated well, but as a result can ease pressure in other areas, e.g. allowing better use of scarce individual therapy time.

Part 1 offers an argument for change and provides a detailed background to this work. Chapter 1 looks at the prevalence of anxiety and associated disorders ranging from the community to clinical populations. Chapter 2 takes a critical look at research centre work and argues that, too often, the patients treated in such studies are not representative of the patients seen in clinical practice. Diagnostic issues, comorbidity and social factors are discussed. Chapter 3 examines current clinical practice and looks to provide a model of care particularly suited to outpatient health care settings.

Part 2 (Chapters 4–8) provides information on setting up and running didactic anxiety management courses including patient assessment, preparation and materials.

Part 3 (Chapters 9–16) offers detailed advice on running a flexible six-session course involving treatments for somatic, cognitive and behavioural anxiety along with panic, insomnia and depression. **Part 4** offers empirical evidence along with information on developing the approach.

'Stress Control' is used in examples throughout the book to allow an idea of how this didactic therapy works in practice. Although readers are encouraged to develop their own didactic approaches relevant to their own area of work, those interested in the 'Stress Control' approach can find the materials discussed in this book in 'Stresspac' (White, 1997a). All extracts from Stresspac are reproduced by permission of The Psychological Corporation © 1996 The Psychological Corporation Limited.

I am indebted to Avril Conacher and Richard German of the Marie Henderson library in Gartnavel Royal Hospital, Glasgow, for their helpfulness and efficiency. Paul McKeown of the Psychological Corporation kindly gave me permission to use extracts from 'Stresspac'. I would like to gratefully acknowledge my colleagues—David Westbrook, Derek Milne, Mike Scott and George Ralston—for their helpful comments on some of the chapters. My thanks also to my first Head of Department in Lanarkshire, Brendan Geraghty, who encouraged me to develop the service and to all the individuals over the years, in both Lanarkshire and Clydebank, who have taken part in 'Stress Control' courses. They have made these courses both stimulating and enjoyable and have provided so many insights and ideas that have subsequently found their way into the therapy. I want to particularly thank Mary Keenan (Ross) who was involved in 'Stress Control' from the very start and, as a superb co-therapist in the first 30 groups, influential in its development. Most of all, I would like to thank my wife, Lilian, for all the support and help she gave me while writing this book and my children, Kirsty, David and Neil, for their frequent visits to my study . . . to play football, to tell me what Homer was doing to Bart, to tell me why boys are so stupid, to try to get me to do their homework, to say 'yes' when their mum had just said 'no' or simply to help me by 'writing' some more words on the computer when I was not looking. I think I have erased all of them.

'STRESSPAC' MATERIALS

These materials—teacher manual, student book, supplements (agoraphobia, depression, panic attacks), handouts, diaries and self-assessment forms—can be computer-scanned or photocopied as required. The relaxation tape can also be duplicated. 'Stresspac' (which can also be used in individual therapy) is available from the Psychological Corporation.[1] A computer disc

---

[1] 24–28 Oval Road, London NW1 7DX. Phone 0171 267 4466.

of all the slides used on the course (140) in both Lotus Freelance Graphics and Powerpoint is available from the author.[2] These can either be prepared into transparencies for overhead projection, made into slides or shown via computer.

Jim White
October 1999

---

[2] Clydebank Health Centre, Kilbowie Road, Clydebank G81 2TQ, Scotland. Tel. 0141 531 6300; fax 0141 531 6336; email <jim@white555.fsnet.co.uk>; Web site <www.stresscontrol.org>.

Part 1

The Argument for Change

Chapter 1

TREATING ANXIETY: DELVING BENEATH THE TIP OF THE ICEBERG

INTRODUCTION

Anxiety is one of the most common problems in our society yet significant problems exist in the recognition and treatment of the disorder. Given the number of people suffering from it, appropriate treatment, where available, is doing little more than reaching the tip of the iceberg. Thus large numbers of individuals are deprived of help, resulting in long-term suffering for them and their families and significant costs to society. The limited work carried out in the field of prevention ensures that a new generation of anxiety sufferers will inevitably be created, thus adding to the current problems in mental health care provision of demand greatly exceeding supply. In Britain, long waiting lists for National Health Service treatment are the rule rather than the exception. In countries with other health care models, treatment may be limited to those well insured or wealthy enough to afford expensive therapy.

This chapter, by presenting evidence from a number of related fields—prevalence; comorbidity; anxiety at the primary care level; and social factors—will argue that only a radical rethink in how we provide mental health care can hope to alleviate the considerable suffering caused by these disorders.

PREVALENCE

Diagnostic criteria

Any disorder

The US National Comorbidity Survey (NCS), using DSM-III-R (American Psychiatric Association, 1987) criteria, reported that 29% of the large sample met criteria for at least one DSM-III-R disorder in the 12 months before interview; 48% met criteria at some stage in their lives (Kessler *et al.*, 1994). Half of all these lifetime disorders in the general population occur to people with a previous history of some other mental health disorder (Kessler, 1997).

Anxiety disorders: general

Anxiety disorders are the most prevalent psychological disorders (Brown and Barlow, 1992; Karno *et al.*, 1987). The Epidemiologic Catchment Area (ECA) Survey reported that 15% of the US population will suffer from an (DSM-III, American Psychiatric Association, 1980) anxiety disorder at some stage of their lives (Robins and Regier, 1991). NCS reported that 17% of the large community sample met criteria for an anxiety disorder in the previous 12 months. This compared to those who met criteria for substance use disorders (11%) or affective disorders (11%) (Kessler *et al.*, 1994).

Anxiety disorders: specific

While differing sampling methods used in ECA and NCS inevitably lead to differing outcomes, findings from both studies clearly show how common these conditions are. Table 1.1 shows the lifetime prevalence of some of the core DSM-III-R anxiety disorders reported in the NCS (Kessler, 1997).

Table 1.1.   Lifetime prevalence of anxiety disorders in the National Comorbidity Survey

Anxiety disorders	Lifetime prevalence	
	%	SE
Generalised anxiety disorder	5.2	0.4
Panic disorder	3.6	0.3
Social phobia	13.3	0.7
Simple (specific) phobia	11.3	0.6
Agoraphobia	6.8	0.3
Post-traumatic stress disorder	7.6	0.5
Any anxiety disorder	28.7	1.0

The British Psychiatric Morbidity Survey

In an attempt to improve information and understanding about mental health, the Department of Health recently reported that one in six adults between 16 and 64 had suffered from some type of neurotic disorder[1] (ICD-10 criteria, World Health Organization, 1992) in the week before

---

[1] Neurotic disorders defined as: mixed anxiety and depressive disorder; generalised anxiety disorder; depressive episode; phobias; obsessive-compulsive disorder; and panic disorder.

interview (Jenkins *et al.*, 1998). Mixed anxiety and depressive disorder made up almost 50% of this figure, generalised anxiety disorder (GAD) about 20% and depressive episode 13%. The four most common neurotic symptoms were fatigue (27%), sleep problems (25%), irritability (22%) and worry (20%). Alcohol dependence in the previous year was found in 5% of the sample while 2.5% had a drug dependency. Thirty-two per cent of those meeting criteria for a neurotic condition reported difficulties in activities of daily living. Prevalence of neuroses in a homeless sample was, predictably, higher: 38% in those living in hostels, 60% in night shelter residents and 57% among those sleeping rough.

The authors concluded that 'the very high prevalence of neurosis, some of which is very severe and associated with suicidal risk, means proper attention must be given to the education and training of primary care teams about mental health [and] to the primary/secondary care interface' (p. 7). They also noted the importance of early detection and development of preventative interventions (see Jenkins and Ustun, 1998). This is given greater impetus by the finding in the ECA survey that over half of all panic disorder sufferers had pre-existing symptoms of generalised anxiety for a median duration of between 8 and 10 years prior to the onset of panic disorder (Eaton *et al.*, 1998).

Primary health care settings

International data

The DSM-IV Field Trial for Mixed Anxiety–Depression (Zinbarg *et al.*, 1994; American Psychiatric Association, 1994), looking at the distribution of specific mental health problems in the USA, Australia and France, found 11.9% and 13% of the 666 sample had GAD and social phobia, respectively, as their principal diagnosis in primary care settings. In addition, 8% were diagnosed as having an anxiety disorder, not otherwise specified (NOS). This study looked at the number of people presenting, in primary care, with severe impairment caused by anxiety and depression but not necessarily meeting definitional thresholds for Axis I anxiety or mood disorders. It found these problems to be at least as common as patients with definable Axis I disorders, suggesting the need for this new diagnostic category. An international multi-centre[2] World Health Organization collaborative study in primary care (Ustun and Sartorius, 1995) showed that 24% of patients in general health care had a current well-defined mental disorder while 9% had subthreshold but clinically significant disorders. Depressive conditions were found to be the most frequent (12.5%), followed by anxiety disorders (12%), of which by far the most common was GAD (7.9%).

[2] Turkey, Greece, India, Germany, Holland, Nigeria, Britain, Japan, France, Brazil, Chile, USA, China, Italy.

US data

Individuals suffering from anxiety form one of the largest groups using US medical and mental health services (Marsland *et al.*, 1976; Boyd, 1986). Shear *et al.*, (1994a) found 10% and 11% of a US primary care sample met criteria for GAD and panic disorder (PD) respectively. Olfson *et al.* (1996) reported that more than one quarter of their primary care sample in California reported subthreshold psychiatric symptoms that, although not meeting DSM-IV criteria, still resulted in significant impairment in work, family and social function. Regier *et al.* (1993) reported that anxiety sufferers use primary care medical facilities as often as they use mental health services, while Fifer *et al.* (1994) found 33% of over 6000 primary care patients showed heightened symptoms or disorders of anxiety.

British data

Approximately one-quarter to one-third of all general practitioner (GP) consultations are for mental health problems (Sharp and Morell, 1989; Shah, 1992). Looking at conspicuous morbidity alone, mental health problems (primarily anxiety and depression) are the second most common reason for consulting a GP. These individuals also have increased rates of consultation to medical and surgical outpatient departments and general hospital admissions over many years (Jenkins, 1998). Screening routine primary care patients using the Hospital Anxiety and Depression scale (Zigmond and Snaith, 1983) resulted in 51% being 'probable cases' and 28% as 'cases' of psychiatric disorder (Dowell and Biran, 1990), with anxiety and depression being by far the most common (Lloyd and Jenkins, 1995). This ties in well with self-report data where, in the previous year, 56% of the sample described themselves as suffering a 'moderate' or 'large' amount of stress (Bridgewood *et al.*, 1996).

Clinical psychologists based in primary care settings consistently report anxiety problems to be the most common difficulty referred to them by GPs. Jerrom *et al.* (1986) recorded 69% of their sample (n = 236) as suffering 'anxiety and stress'. Espie and White (1986a) reported that, of 1085 patients seen in a primary care psychology service, 70% could also be similarly classified. McPherson *et al.* (1996) noted that 51% of patients referred for help with 'emotional disorders' had an anxiety disorder while 10.6% had depression and 10.3 mixed anxiety–depression. Within these broad categories, the most commonly diagnosed problem was 'generalised anxiety'. Turvey (1997) classified 30% of 13,057 patients as such while 21% of Espie and White's (1986a) sample complained of generalised anxiety. Similar results emerged from US primary care studies (Barlow *et al.*, 1996).

A similar picture is emerging with counsellors. Harvey *et al.* (1998) reported that 40% of patients referred to person-centred counselling in primary care complained of an anxiety disorder. Friedli and King (1996) point to anxiety as being one of the most common problems dealt with, although

Friedli *et al.* (1997) in their controlled study reported that patients with depression constituted around 50% of all referrals to the counsellor, with only 20% of the sample being referred for help with anxiety. This possibly reflects local health care factors such as the skills and interests of particular therapists and GPs.

COMORBIDITY

Comorbidity refers to the co-occurence of at least two different disorders in the same individual. Removal of the hierarchical exclusion criteria that obtained in DSM-III has resulted in greater interest in looking at patterns of comorbidity and the possible influence on response to treatment. Indeed, Kendall and Clarkin (1992) saw the study of comorbidity as 'the premier challenge' facing mental health professionals in the 1990s, while Brown and Barlow (1992) believed that the conceptual advances that may result from comorbidity research would profoundly affect the clinical science. Comorbidity directly challenges the concept of homogeneity within individual diagnostic categories. It may also weaken the foundations of categorical systems that assume discontinuity and qualitative differences between disorders. High levels of comorbidity would suggest poor discriminant validity among the disorders. As Blashfield (1990) noted, high levels of comorbidity may indicate that current diagnostic systems may be artifactually distinguishing phenomena that would be more parsimonious if combined. The ECA study found that 54% of respondents with a lifetime history of at least one DSM-III disorder were found to have a second diagnosis as well (Robins and Regier, 1991). Similar findings (56%) were found in the NCS (Kessler, 1997).

Comorbidity within the anxiety disorders

Sanderson *et al.* (1990) investigated patterns of comorbidity in 130 patients with DSM-III-R anxiety disorder patients. Seventy per cent of the total sample received at least one additional Axis I diagnosis. Broken down by principal diagnosis, 91% of GAD, 83% of obsessive-compulsive disorder (OCD), 69% of panic disorder with agoraphobia (PDA), 58% of social phobia and 53% of simple (specific) phobia patients were given at least one additional diagnosis. For the sample as a whole, the most common additional anxiety disorder diagnoses were social (29%) and simple phobia (32%). However, at the clinically significant level, GAD was the most frequently assigned additional diagnosis. The authors concluded 'that there is a strong tendency for anxiety disorders to cluster together, and that there are consistent patterns of co-occurrence' (p. 310). They also noted that key features of various anxiety disorders such as panic attacks, intrusive thoughts, social fears and excessive worry seem to exist, to varying degrees, in most patients presenting with a principal diagnosis of almost any of the anxiety disorders. They concluded that 'the typical practice of describing patients with one principal diagnosis is inadequate to convey the overall pattern of psychopathology in the majority of patients. A more useful classification system may well ascertain the presence of a trait or negative affect or an anxious personality and then rate the presence of a variety of anxious or depressive features . . . resulting in a diagnostic pattern that would have substantial implications for treatment and course' (p. 312).

Moras and Barlow (1992) found 50% of a large sample of carefully diagnosed anxiety disorder patients had at least one additional anxiety or depressive disorder. GAD was the most commonly assigned additional diagnosis (23%). When degree of severity was taken into account, comorbidity rates rose to 79%. GAD and PDA were associated with the highest comorbidity rates, simple phobia with the lowest. GAD was strongly associated with social phobia, panic disorder (with or without agoraphobia) and mood disorders; PDA, particularly at severe levels, with social and simple phobia, GAD and, most of all, a mood disorder.

Borkovec *et al.* (1995), studying 55 DSM-III-R GAD patients, found 78% received at least one additional diagnosis. Thirty-one per cent received more than one. Social and simple phobia were most commonly assigned. The results are limited as the sample (for a treatment outcome trial) excluded patients meeting criteria for panic, major depression or substance abuse disorders.

These reports may help explain the relatively poorer diagnostic reliability found with GAD as, in addition to the lack of specific behavioural markers, GAD is rarely found without comorbid disorders. The presence of other disorders has been shown to complicate the process of diagnosis (Chorpita *et al.*, 1998).

The US NCS (Kessler *et al.*, 1994), reported that 79% of individuals diagnosed as having a DSM-III-R anxiety disorder at some stage of their lives had at least one additional comorbid disorder. They noted that the vast majority (89%) of those with severe 12-month disorders occurred in the 14% of the sample with a lifetime history of three or more disorders. They concluded that while mental health problems are common in the USA, the significant burden of mental health problems are to be found in a highly comorbid group comprising about one-sixth of the population.

Anxiety and depression comorbidity

Depressive disorders are more likely to co-occur with anxiety disorders than with any other disorder, with nearly half the cases of depression and anxiety comorbid at the same time in the same primary care patient (Sartorius *et al.*, 1996). Sanderson *et al.* (1990) found that 33% of their anxiety disorder sample noted above met criteria for a mood disorder (either major depression or, more commonly, dysthymia). Kessler *et al.* (1996), reporting on the US NCS, found that 68% of a primary anxiety disorder group had a secondary major depressive disorder, while 84% of those with a lifetime GAD diagnosis also had a lifetime mood disorder (Judd et al., 1998). Andrade et al. (1994) reported the lifetime comorbidity of PD/PDA and major depression to be 11 times higher than expected by chance. Borkovec et al. (1995) reported that 49% of a GAD sample met criteria for past depressive episode. Similar results emerged from a multinational study (Merikangas et al., 1996) that showed panic disorder and social phobia particularly strongly related to comorbid depression.

Kendler (1996), taking a genetic epidemiological approach to comorbidity, studied a cohort of female twins, and suggested that the same or highly similar non-specific genetic factors contribute to the predisposition to both GAD and major depression ('same genes, (partly) different environments'). These may be associated with environmental risk factors such as, in the case of GAD, stressful life events based on danger and, in the case of major depression, life events based on loss. In terms of the temporal sequence of comorbid anxiety and depression, anxiety disorders are often found to precede depression (Rohde et al., 1991; Wittchen and Essau, 1989), although Coryell et al. (1992) found the opposite. Kessler et al. (1999c) found an elevated risk of mood disorders emerging for many years after the onset of social phobia. Angst et al. (1990) found that those patients diagnosed with pure anxiety tended to develop additional depression, while those with pure depression tended to retain that single diagnosis over the years. Comorbidity of these disorders is associated with greater severity (Scheibe and Albus, 1994), with an exacerbation of primary disorders often accompanying the onset of secondary disorders (Kessler and Price, 1993). Wittchen and Essau (1989) found that patients with a mixed anxiety/depression were more severely impaired in psychosocial functioning than those with a pure depression, while the Kessler et al. study found that socially phobic depressives had twice as many impairments and two-thirds more episodes as depressives without social phobia.

Anxiety and alcohol abuse comorbidity

The NCS reported that anxiety, depression and alcohol disorders are the most common syndromes (Kessler, 1997). The high co-occurrence represents a significant health care issue. A range of studies suggests a high degree of comorbidity with between 25% and 45% of alcohol-dependent patients also meeting criteria for an anxiety disorder—often PDA or social phobia (e.g. Bowen et al., 1984; Chambless et al., 1987). When a lower threshold for anxiety is used, the rate approaches 60% (e.g. Smail et al., 1984). Anxiety disorder patients have current or past comorbid alcohol abuse or dependence rates of between 15% and 25% (Bibb and Chambless, 1986; Thyer et al., 1986). The NCS found that those with addictive disorders had the greatest delay between onset of the disorder and entry into treatment, thus providing fertile ground for other problems to grow (Olfson et al., 1998).

Although no clear temporal relationship was reported for GAD, panic and mood disorders, the emergence of phobic disorders (social, specific and agoraphobia) appeared to precede the onset of alcohol problems in a multinational study, thus providing some evidence for a self-medicating hypothesis (Swendsen et al., 1998). Although some evidence suggests that anxiety may be a consequence rather than a cause of alcohol abuse (Allan, 1995), recent NCS data suggest that alcohol use disorders are usually temporally second. Earlier anxiety and mood disorders are stronger predictors of alcohol dependence than alcohol abuse among women than men (Kessler et al., 1997c). However, the specific mechanisms of these associations remain unclear and complex.

Anxiety and personality disorder comorbidity

Oldham et al. (1995), looking at comorbidity of Axis I and Axis II (personality) disorders, found a strong relationship between anxiety disorders and (cluster B) borderline and (cluster C) avoidant and dependent personality disorders. Mauri et al. (1992) found that 50%, 41% and 34% of panic disorder, generalised anxiety disorder and recurrent depressive disorder patients respectively met criteria for an Axis II personality disorder. Panic patients had a greater variety of personality disorders but, again, cluster C diagnoses—especially avoidant and dependent—predominated. Mavissakalian et al. (1995), reporting on a DSM-III GAD sample, found an Axis II comorbidity rate of 37%—with avoidant disorder being most commonly assigned. Sanderson et al. (1994) found 50% of a DSM-III-R GAD sample to have a personality (mainly avoidant and dependent) disorder.

Scott et al. (1995), treating DSM-III-R GAD, PD and major depression patients, found that half of the sample met criteria for an Axis II personality disorder—typically cluster C avoidant and dependent personality disorders. Chambliss et al. (1992) found agoraphobics to have a 92% comorbid rate with mainly cluster C disorders. Klass et al. (1989), comparing DSM-III-R anxiety disorder patients with (AnxPD) and without (Anx) an additional personality disorder diagnosis, found that AnxPD patients received significantly more diagnoses of current dysthymia and past major depression, were more likely to receive diagnoses of low-frequency disorders and had significantly lower rating of current adaptive functioning.

Data from 'Stress Control' patients

Seventy-one patients with a principal diagnosis of GAD (DSM-IV criteria) were assessed with both the Anxiety Disorder Interview Schedule IV (Brown et al., 1994) and the Structured Clinical Interview—Personality Disorders section (Spitzer et al., 1990, DSM-III-R criteria) prior to taking part in 'Stress Control' courses. Fifty-two per cent met criteria for an Axis II personality disorder—mainly fairly evenly spread across the cluster C disorders. These two groups—GADs with (GAD/PDs) and without (GADs) Axis II diagnoses—were then compared on a range of measures as well as response to treatment. All GAD/PDs and 88% of GADs had at least one additional Axis I diagnosis. GADs had, on average, 2.4 Axis I diagnoses, GAD/PDs had 2.7. GADs were more likely to have social or specific phobia comorbid disorders, while GAD/PDs were much more likely to have a mood disorder. GAD/PDs had a longer duration of the problem (7.2 v. 4.8 years), although determining a specific onset for both groups was difficult (White, 1997b).

ANXIETY AT THE PRIMARY CARE LEVEL

Consultation rates

Hassall and Stilwell (1977) suggested that, due to longer consultation times, 30% of all consultation time is taken up by patients complaining of common emotional problems—more than patients suffering from severe mental illness (Corney et al., 1996). National morbidity statistics show that, with the exception of those suffering from respiratory disorders and cardiovascular problems, this group makes most demands on GPs' time (Corney, 1997). Jenkins et al. (1998) showed that individuals with a 'neurotic' complaint were twice as likely as those without to have consulted their GP in the two weeks prior to interview.

General practitioner perceptions

Over a 20-year period, three-quarters of women and half of all men had consulted their GPs about a mental health problem (Shepherd, 1991). GPs, in general, do not feel equipped to deal with this population either in terms of training or in the amount of time they have at their disposal (McLeod, 1992). Salmon et al. (1988) reported that problems with a large psychological component led to dissatisfaction in the GP. Bennett et al. (1978) reported that GPs cite termination of consultation to be a particular source of difficulty with such patients. Yet GPs are highly likely to be the sole health provider to the vast majority of these patients (between 90% and 95%—Espie and White, 1986b; Goldberg and Huxley, 1992).

Characteristics of the 'neurotic' group

Defining 'high attendance' in women as more than 10 GP consultations per year, Corney and Murray (1988) found it to be significantly associated with psychiatric morbidity, young age, lower socio-economic group, concomitant physical symptoms and psychotropic medication use within the previous 12 months. These women also used other agencies to a greater degree.

Reviewing a sample of neurotic primary care patients first reported 11 years earlier by Mann *et al.* (1981), Lloyd *et al.* (1996) found that initial General Health Questionnaire (GHQ) (Goldberg and Williams, 1988) score was strongly associated with high GHQ score at 11 years, chronic course of psychiatric illness and high consultation rates. Almost half the sample had a chronic course over the 11 years with over half meeting 'caseness' at the assessment point. There was also evidence that death from natural causes was significantly higher than would be expected. Social and personality factors were not related to clinical outcome or course over the 11 years. The authors concluded by stating that the findings highlight the need for early identification and more efficient systems for managing these patients. Jenkins *et al.* (1998) also noted that around 50% of their neurotic sample suffered from long-standing physical complaints compared to 30% of the non-neurotic group. This may reflect the effect of secondary problems associated with anxiety and depression, i.e. drinking or smoking more.

Problems identifying or diagnosing anxiety and depression in primary care

Approximately half of all patients presenting with a mental disorder in primary care settings are not appropriately diagnosed (Fifer *et al.*, 1994; Shear and Schulberg, 1995). Sartorius *et al.* (1996) found less than half of their international sample was recognised as having a mental health diagnosis by the primary care team. In Britain, the annual rate of *conspicuous* psychiatric morbidity, i.e. that identified by the GP in primary care, has been reported as 101 per 1000 population. When combined with the *hidden* morbidity (e.g. identified through the use of screening instruments), this figure rises to 230 per 1000 (Royal College of General Practitioners, 1986).

Fifer found that, of the 33% of US primary care patients who met criteria for anxiety symptoms and possible anxiety disorders, less than half (44%) had been identified by the primary care physician. Of this sample, 48% had more than one anxiety disorder with panic (with or without agoraphobia) and post-traumatic stress disorder (PTSD) the most common problems. Katon (1984) reported that 89% of panic disorder patients initially presented to their doctor with somatic complaints that were misdiagnosed as a physical condition. Castro (1993) estimated that only 20% of those with a diagnosable mental health disorder gets into treatment, while Regier *et al.* (1993), reporting on the ECA study, found that only one-third of those meeting criteria for an anxiety disorder were involved in any form of psychological or pharmacological treatment. Goisman *et al.* (1993) found that of the 38% of anxiety disorder patients receiving treatment, 93% of these were receiving medication as the primary approach. This was often prescribed inappropriately (Shear and Schulberg, 1995). As Barlow *et al.* (1996) noted, many individuals with anxiety disorders are being inadequately treated in primary care settings.

Failure to attend primary care

An additional problem relates to the fact that many patients do not present for help to primary care facilities in the first place. In the USA, only 32% of anxiety disorder sufferers seek treatment and half of these go directly to secondary care facilities (Barlow *et al.*, 1996). This highlights the fact that most US states operate a different primary care system from Britain, where the vast majority of secondary care patients are directly referred for specialist help by their GP. Katerndahl and Realini (1995) found that only 59% of individuals experiencing panic attacks had sought help for the problem, while Katon *et al.* (1987) suggested that 30% of primary care patients had experienced at least one panic attack in the previous year. The British Psychiatric Morbidity Survey (Jenkins *et al.*, 1998) found that one-quarter of those diagnosed as having a neurotic disorder had not sought help from their GP (or other professional) as they felt no one would or could help.

SOCIAL FACTORS

Economic costs

Based on ECA mental health data, Dupont *et al.* (1993) reported that, in 1990, direct (health care) and indirect (lost productivity) costs amounted to $46 billion, representing 32% of the total mental health cost. The figure also represents a 38% increase over 1985 figures, suggesting a rapid increase in costs. Similarly, Greenberg *et al.* (1999), using data from the NCS, reported an annual economic burden of anxiety disorders in the United States to be approximately $63.1 billion in 1998. Kessler and Frank (1997) looked at days lost from work or 'cut-back' days, i.e. when the individual was unable to do as much work as usual owing to the mental health disorder. They found that the presence of comorbidity involving at least two of the three categories of anxiety, affective and substance use disorders resulted in the highest number of days lost (49 per month per 100 workers) and cut-back days (346 per month per 100 workers). These findings suggest that over 15 million days and over 110 million work cut-back days are lost annually in the USA. The authors suggest that, humane reasons aside, there are very good economic reasons to make appropriate treatments widely available.

British data on 'neurotic' disorders in UK general practice in 1985, reported conservatively, a cost of £373 million, equivalent to 9% of the annual total spent on GP services. In addition, £219 million was spent on these problems in hospital treatment (Croft-Jeffreys and Wilkinson, 1989). These disorders accounted for one-third of days lost from work due to ill-health (Jenkins, 1985). More recent data from the Institute of Management suggest that 270,000 people take time off every day because of work-related stress. In terms of sick pay, lost productivity and National Health Service (NHS) costs, this represents a cumulative annual cost of around £7 billion (Charlesworth, 1996).

Turner *et al.* (1995) reported that costs for individuals receiving mainly cognitive–behavioural therapy approaches, for GAD (average 23 hours therapy), PD (27 hours) and Social Phobia (29 hours) were $2181, $2599 and $2695 respectively—large sums especially if not covered by appropriate health insurance. These figures may be underestimates as it is not clear if they include the numerous booster sessions (14–24). The impact of managed care in health care delivery systems such as health maintenance organisations (HMOs) in the USA is likely to significantly reduce these figures for many sufferers. It is notable that British NHS figures for the same disorders treated in routine clinical work are significantly smaller; e.g. Turvey (1997) reported the majority of anxiety disorder patients being treated in seven or fewer appointments, representing the implicit attempt to marry clinical effectiveness and time economy.

Social costs

The common mental disorders—principally anxiety and depression—are possibly the most costly to society (Weich, 1997). There is a wealth of evidence pointing to a higher prevalence for anxiety and depression (among other problems) among manual workers (Kessler and Frank, 1997) and in inner city areas where social deprivation is greatest.[3] Brown (1992) found an annual prevalence of clinical (i.e. severe) depression of 10–15% among women in Camberwell, a working class area in London, with half of these cases persisting for at least one year. NCS and ECA data from the USA, consistent with previous research, suggests that rates of almost all psychiatric disorders, particularly anxiety disorders, increases as socio-economic status decreases (Kessler *et al.*, 1994; Robins and Regier, 1991). Yet roughly 16% of the US population have no health insurance (Frank and McGuire, 1994) and many others have limited mental health care cover. The public health care system is unable to provide sufficient help to those members of society with the highest rates of disorders. However, in comparing the USA and Ontario, Olfson *et al.* (1998) report that those most socially disadvantaged do not receive treatment more quickly in the Canadian Province health care system that, in theory, provides easier access to care for the poor.

A recent report on deprivation and health (Information and Statistics Division, National Health Service in Scotland, 1998) showed not only a significant relationship between social deprivation and incidence of cancer, coronary heart disease and stroke, but also a significantly greater incidence (and GP contact rates) of both anxiety and depression among the poorest sections of society than among those in most affluent areas—roughly three times higher in the case of anxiety in women. Similar results were found in the NCS (e.g. Wittchen *et al.*, 1994). These physical and mental health

---

[3] Social deprivation includes low income and financial hardship, unemployment, poor housing and lack of education.

problems may often be linked, producing low physical and mental health quality of life persisting over time (Sherbourne *et al.*, 1996). Women, in general, are twice as likely to experience common mental disorders such as anxiety and depression than men (Paykel, 1991; Wittchen *et al.*, 1994). Working-class women are more at risk of depression than middle-class women (Brown and Harris, 1978), with environmental rather than biological factors more likely to be responsible (Paykel, 1991).

The British Psychiatric Morbidity Survey (Jenkins *et al.*, 1998) found unemployment, relationship status (single, divorced, or widowed), and living status—especially single parents—to be associated with higher levels of neurotic disturbance. As an example of this, unemployed people are about twice as likely to suffer a neurotic disorder than those in work (Kessler *et al.*, 1987a). Lack of control over one's life—arguably more common in socially deprived areas—and having fewer social supports also contribute to mental distress (Newton, 1988; Bennett and Murphy, 1997). The association between social deprivation and increased mortality may also be mediated by psychosocial factors (Wilkinson, 1992). Many of these factors may be interactive or bidirectional and may also interact with biological and other predisposing factors—unemployment may lead to a vicious circle where self-esteem drops, anxiety and depression rise, leading to lowered confidence about seeking a new job etc.; single parents, owing to financial pressures or lack of child-minders, may have fewer opportunities to have a social life, thus increasing social isolation and maintaining depression, etc. The survey found that alcohol dependence was nearly twice as common and drug dependence five times as common among those who were unemployed as among those who were working.

Social and psychological interactions

In a series of papers based on data from the NCS, Kessler and colleagues report on the social consequences of mental health problems, particularly those with onset in teenage years, i.e. the time when individuals are making decisions that will often have life-long repercussions. The implication is that the presence of a disorder is more likely to result in individuals making detrimental decisions, negatively affecting their future well-being. While socio-demographic processes strongly influence the areas noted below, there has been, until recently, a dearth of studies looking at psychological factors.

Disorder onset and first treatment contact

Patients generally do not reach secondary care services until their problems have become well entrenched. Comparing first treatment contacts in the USA and Ontario, Olfson *et al.* (1998) found that while panic sufferers had the highest probability of first-year treatment, those with phobia and addictive disorders had the lowest. Importantly, they also found a strong inverse relationship between age at onset and first treatment contact, with those in their thirties much more likely to seek and obtain treatment quickly. In the case of depression, those with a first onset between 30 and 54 were 14 times more likely to receive treatment within one year of onset compared to those with an onset prior to age 13.

There was no evidence that the Ontario system, based on universal public health insurance cover, provided quicker access to treatment. Kessler *et al.* (1997a) also found that those with lower levels of need but higher perceived need for treatment were more likely to be in treatment than those with greater need. Kessler *et al.* (1999b) reported that nearly half of those in treatment in the year prior to assessment did not qualify for any of the disorders assessed in the NCS. Kessler *et al.* (1999a) found that although, in general, individuals in the USA with GAD, PD and Major Depression do seek and receive help, there is an average delay of between six and 14 years across these disorders.

Individuals taking part in early 'Stress Control' courses had, on average, a current problem duration of six years, thus allowing the build-up of secondary maintaining factors such as demoralisation (White *et al.*, 1992).

Education

Kessler *et al.* (1995) found evidence that the presence of an early-onset mental health disorder (commonly anxiety disorders among females and conduct disorders in males) was a strong predictor of failure to complete high school. Those with such a disorder were twice as likely not to graduate than those without. These figures suggest that 7.2 million people in the USA prematurely terminated their education owing to these factors. Failure to do well at school is likely to have life-long implications for the individual as educational success is an important factor in determining occupational achievement, financial security and lifestyle behaviours that affect well-being and health.

Teenage parenthood

Teenage parents are at higher risk of poor employment opportunities, lower educational attainment and more unstable relationships. Women who have children while in teenage years are more likely to receive welfare and to have difficulty in coming off such benefit. There is substantial evidence that, generally, children are adversely affected by having teenage parents. The NCS data support the conclusion that teenagers with mental health problems (commonly anxiety, affective, addictive and conduct disorders) are three times as likely to become teenage parents as those without a disorder (Kessler *et al.*, 1997b).

Marriage and marital stability

There is strong evidence suggesting that married people have better health, financial security and social support than those not married, while divorce is associated with future anxiety and depression problems, financial insecurity, physical illness and lower levels of general satisfaction in life (Aseltine and Kessler, 1993). However, compared to those who marry later, teenage marriage is associated with future difficulties including marital instability, poorer economic resources, poorer educational attainment and child care difficulties (Teti *et al.*, 1987).

Kessler *et al.* (1998) reported that those with an early-onset mental disorder (anxiety, affective and substance use disorders) were more likely to marry by the age of 18 than those without. They also found that these teenagers had a greater risk of divorce than others. Those with a teenage-onset anxiety disorder, in particular, are about half as likely to be currently married, at the point of NCS assessment, than those with no early-onset disorder. This study also found that those with early-onset disorders who did not marry by this age were less likely to marry later compared to others.

It seems plausible that those with mental health problems benefit from stable marital relationships and suffer when these relationships are disrupted. It is possible that the direct effects of the mental health problems can create interpersonal difficulties, thus increasing the risk of divorce (Kessler and Forthofer, 1999).

Socio-economic status

Looking at male employment, Jayakody *et al.* (1998) reported that men who experienced an early-onset anxiety disorder are about three times more likely to be unemployed than those with no early-onset disorder. This negative effect is mediated by the fact, as noted above, that early-onset mental health disorders also diminish the likelihood of being married and having good educational attainment. This study also found that, in the absence of an early-onset disorder, the probability of men having a recent mental health disorder was 8%. If they had experienced an early-onset anxiety disorder, it was 21%. Even for those in employment, Kessler (1999) noted that, in every year of their working lives, they will earn on average $2500 less than those who had no early onset.

These findings call for the greater integration of psychological, economic and sociological factors in developing more robust models of psychological and social interactions. Taking into account the lowered probability of early-onset sufferers getting into appropriate treatment quickly compared to those with later life onset (Olfson *et al.*, 1998), it is imperative that more work should be carried out in this area to improve detection of problems and availability of help.

Treatment considerations

Many research centre studies do not take social and economic factors into account and, indeed, may exclude possible subjects specifically because of social circumstances, thus decreasing the representativeness of their samples. In routine clinical practice in health care systems based on insurance and private practice, it may be that those with greatest social disadvantages are least likely to enter treatment. This may lead health care workers to neglect social variables in planning health care needs. As a psychologist working in one of the most socially deprived areas in Scotland, much of the literature seems woefully inadequate in describing the daily realities faced by many of my patients who can often report social and financial difficulties that play a large part in explaining why they feel the way they do. Mental health research has, largely, focused on intrapsychic models rather than seeing these within a wider perspective that may also contain such factors as unemployment, poor housing, bad neighbourhoods, poverty, education, articulacy and family issues. As Wilkinson (1996) states, the scale of income differences and the condition of a society's social fabric are crucially important determinants of the real subjective quality of life among modern populations.

In addition, current models often do not take into account important cultural differences that play an important part in determining how the disorder manifests. Thus conditions such as koro or susto cannot be understood without understanding the culture, and treatment rationales must be consistent with this. Even in Western cultures, subcultural factors may play significant roles. Street et al. (1997) found that 14% of a Hispanic population in the USA suffered from anxiety and affective disorders that could not be captured by the DSM system. Similarly both cultural and educational factors had to be taken into account in understanding the expression of anxiety in African Americans (Heurtin-Roberts et al., 1997). There is too often a suspicion in, for example, therapy transcripts that, apart from being well motivated and self-starting, the patient's cultural background is very similar to that of the researcher, i.e. articulate, well educated and middle class.

SUMMARY AND CONCLUSIONS

- Anxiety disorders and mixed anxiety–depression are extremely common problems whether using explicit diagnostic criteria or more subjective criteria.
- There appear to be fairly consistent patterns of comorbidity, with GAD least likely to be found in a 'pure' state. At the clinical level, GAD, panic and social phobia are most commonly assigned as comorbid disorders. Mood and Axis II disorders are commonly found with anxiety disorders.
- Those suffering from such conditions often report a chronic course and use primary care services extensively.
- GPs feel themselves poorly equipped to deal with this population.
- Many patients who could benefit from psychological approaches slip through the net in primary care either because they do not attend for assessment and subsequent referral or because they are missed or misdiagnosed by primary care workers.
- Patients are being referred too late—after problems have been allowed to solidify and secondary problems appear.
- A significant number of those suffering from these conditions do not seek out treatment owing to a belief that no appropriate help is available.
- Social and psychological factors can interact with lifelong consequences.
- The numbers greatly outstrip our current ability to meet the demand. Secondary care services are currently only seeing the tip of the iceberg.

ACTION

- More effort should go into the earlier detection of, and help for, these problems in primary care. The 'filter' system suggested by Goldberg and Huxley (1992) offers one possible model.
- GPs should be helped to create appropriate, practical preventative interventions.
- Patients who do not respond to initial primary care help should be quickly referred to mental health professionals.
- Resources, as currently utilised, cannot support significant increases in referrals. Thus more efficient methods of dealing with larger numbers should now be a priority for mental health professionals in primary care. As it is unrealistic to assume that resources will significantly increase, this quest will inevitably focus on more cost-effective approaches and the move away from one-to-one therapies at least for some patient groups.

Chapter 2

TREATING ANXIETY: THE GULF BETWEEN RESEARCH FINDINGS AND CLINICAL REALITIES

RESEARCH CENTRES AND ROUTINE CLINICAL PRACTICE: DIFFERENT WORLDS?

There are three basic questions that can be asked about any treatment (Howard *et al.*, 1996): Does it work under experimental conditions? Does it work in practice? Is it working for this patient? Those who mainly ask the first question too rarely ask the second and third. Those who ask the third may not ask the first. Relatively few clinicians attend the prestigious conferences where the vast majority of papers, focused on the first question, are given by academics and are listened to by academics. Similarly the prestigious journals overwhelmingly feature research centre papers (for obvious reasons). These papers are often held to be of little relevance to routine clinical work. The current interest in 'evidence-based practice' in research centres does not excite the average clinician. The 'best available' information has major constraints for the care of individual patients as these data show comparative efficacy of treatment for an 'average' randomised patient with little or no data on cogent clinical features such as severity, comorbidity and other clinical nuances (Feinstein and Horwitz, 1997). As Beutler *et al.* (1996) noted: 'science and practice have only a passing acquaintance' (p. 197).

It is dispiriting to find that evidence presented in the first edition of the *Scientific Practitioner* (Barlow *et al.*, 1984) that research had little influence on practice is reiterated in the second edition (Hayes *et al.*, 1999). Thus the gulf between research and practice continues to echo into the new millennium with no hint that the gulf is narrowing. Thus Cohen (1976) noted that 40% of US mental health professionals felt that no research existed that was relevant to their practice, while Bergin and Strupp (1972) quoted Matarazzo: 'Psychological science per se doesn't guide me one bit . . . My clinical experience is the only thing that has helped me in my practice to date' (p. 340). When clinicians were asked to rate the usefulness of various sources of information, research publications often appeared near the bottom (Morrow-Bradley and Elliott, 1986). These authors found particular criticism of research that failed to address clinically meaningful questions about therapist qualities and the therapist–patient relationship—variables held to be important by the clinicians surveyed. In the 1990s, and particularly addressing the difficulties imposed by Managed Care, Campbell (1996), Beutler *et al.* (1996) and Hayes (1998) pleaded for greater integration of science and practice, while clinicians still reported getting their clinical ideas from trial and error, workshops or colleagues rather than from the research literature (Cohen, 1976; Hoshmand and Polkinghorne, 1992).

In order to look at why well-designed research with high levels of external validity should be carried out with clinically representative populations, this chapter will look at eight related areas: generalising from the research centre to the clinic: the pitfalls; diagnostic systems; the issue of comorbidity; treatment outcome: the effect of comorbidity, how representative are patients in treatment outcome studies?; specific versus non-specific factors; time considerations and conclusions: research centre versus clinical realities—bridging the chasm.

GENERALISING FROM THE RESEARCH CENTRE TO THE CLINIC: THE PITFALLS

The gap between research and practice

A distinguished American clinician and researcher wrote an article entitled 'Why don't my patients do as well as the ones in the outcome studies?' (Persons, 1994). In the article she made some cogent arguments why this should be, e.g. many patients in these studies do not actually get better and that what patients want from a clinician may not be simply the reduction/ removal of symptoms. Yet the article highlights the view among too many clinicians that what they do is neither as effective nor as prestigious as the work their academic colleagues do.

Although Milne *et al.* (1990) found a healthy interest among clinicians in carrying out research and audit projects, the modal frequency of publications among British NHS clinical psychologists was zero. This impedes transmission of clinically relevant work to other clinicians. Research, although paid lipservice to, is often not encouraged by either managers or other clinicians. Even where it is encouraged, e.g. within the NHS research and development strategy, the barriers an individual must go through from initial idea to write-up can be daunting, particularly for the inexperienced clinician/researcher. While trying to keep up to date with developments in their field, carrying out clinically relevant research often poses great difficulties to even the most motivated workers (see Jones, 1994).

It could be argued that too many academics are, in general, selling clinicians short by carrying out research of limited clinical significance because of their emphasis on scientific rigour at the expense of 'real-life' problems. The degree of control needed to produce internal validity to their work too often results in that work being too unrepresentative, specialised or narrow to travel well to clinical settings. Conversations with research centre workers has often highlighted an astonishing lack of awareness of the way clinicians work and the complexity of problems they routinely deal with. Clinicians, listening to the confident views of conference speakers, may wish the speaker would come and work in their clinical setting for a week, see the patients they treat and handle the number of patients they treat daily and then see if the views are still expounded so confidently. Barry Wolfe of the National Institute of Mental Health recorded this anecdote from a workshop he attended on the behavioural treatment of social and simple phobias: 'After listening to several of the world's leading authorities talk about how they can successfully treat simple phobias in one to five sessions, I finally asked with great exasperation, "I don't know what kinds of patients you are seeing, because it is so unusual for the patients I see to be treated successfully in so few sessions." One of the participants replied "Barry, you are overlooking the first law of research: don't use real patients" ' (Wolfe, 1994, p. 161). Whether merely intended as a humorous aside, many clinicians may feel this too often describes much research work.

Researchers typically communicate with other researchers and investigate problems that researchers face, while clinicians, as previously noted, learn from each other. As a result, as Barlow *et al.* (1984) noted, 'few procedures are practised with theoretical purity, to the great advantage of millions seeking help from psychotherapy' (p. 34). Clinicians are more likely to be eclectic—mix-and-matching differing approaches according to clinical experience and intuition. Prochaska and Norcross (1983) found more clinicians (30%) rated their approach as 'eclectic' than they rated any other approach and used interventions in which they had little recent training. However, with little cross-fertilisation between science and practice, clinicians may be using techniques that have no theoretical base or are based on pseudo-science (Hayes, 1998). A good example of this may be eye movement desensitisation and reprocessing (EMDR: Shapiro, 1995). In the absence of theoretical or therapeutic justification (Lohr *et al.*, 1998), this technique has been taught to over 23,000 clinicians in eight years (see Rosen *et al.*, 1998, for a discussion of 'Power Therapies').

In addition, fads and fashions influence research more than we would like to believe. This may partially be affected by the aims of government and grant-awarding authorities. However, it is also instructive to look through old conference programmes to see the keynote addresses, workshops and symposia given by leading researchers. 'Hot' topics mysteriously disappear, to be replaced by new 'hot' topics that do not seem to be obvious developments from the old ones. We must also accept the gulf that exists within clinician and researcher groups; e.g. cognitive–behavioural therapy (CBT) researchers attend CBT conferences, while psychodynamic researchers attend psychodynamic conferences, often to discuss the same patient groups.

Clinicians, likewise, typically congregate with like-minded colleagues. These also operate as separate worlds.

Research versus clinical values

Seligman (1993) described researchers as 'simplophiles'. They routinely exclude complex problems (or problems with comorbid disorders) from research, while clinicians—'complophiles'—routinely deal with complex cases where comorbidity, socio-economic and medical problems are the rule rather than the exception. Researchers will be given extensive (up-to-date) training in the treatment under consideration; clinicians will be expected to keep up to date with developments in many areas without the time or funding to adequately do so. Researchers often have an in-built bias (the 'allegiance effect')—cognitive therapy centre workers comparing their favoured approach with another psychological approach are both likely to be more skilled in cognitive therapy and more enthusiastic. As many of the originators of techniques then test them, the 'allegiance effect' is activated and results in less experienced, more neutral therapists failing to achieve the same results with the techniques. Thus approaches, although successfully tested, do not become widely disseminated to clinicians and therefore do not become available to patients (Barlow and Lehman, 1996).

Research therapists, often postdoctoral, will be expert in a specific treatment with a specific population but possibly only in that treatment and only that population. They will often be restricted to a therapy increasingly likely to be manualised. Clinicians, who rarely administer theoretically pure interventions (Norcross and Goldfried, 1992), will be expected to be jack of all trades but will be able to draw on their wide-ranging experience and flexibility to develop the intervention if the therapy is not producing the hoped for change.

Researchers will be more interested in the overall effect; the clinician will be more interested in the effect on the individual. Researchers often want to fix a targeted problem; clinicians are more likely to seek improvement in general functioning. Researchers will extensively assess patients particularly with regard to DSM diagnoses; clinicians will regard diagnosis as less important than the presenting concerns of the individual. In addition clinicians will not mistake *statistically* significant change on questionnaires for *clinically* significant change; e.g. has the patient's quality of life improved?

Researchers are likely to see only a fraction of the number of patients a clinician sees and have sufficient time between patients to reflect on the session and prepare for the next. Clinicians, in addition to heavy and varied caseloads, are also likely to work in less than perfect settings and be expected to carry out a range of other duties during clinic time, e.g. complete paperwork, phone other patients, talk to medics. Clinicians in the NHS are likely to be under pressure to improve throughput, i.e. reduce therapy time as much as possible (Division of Clinical Psychology, 1997). These pressures do not lend themselves to calm reflection on research issues or clinical practice. The need to achieve *internal validity*—the extent to which a causal relationship can be discerned among variables—has often been achieved to the detriment of *external validity*—the extent to which the causal relationship can be generalised to the kind of patients routinely seen by clinicians. Finally, much research looks at whether treatment A or treatment B is best at treating problem C. Clinicians are more likely to be interested in the question posed by Paul in 1967: 'What treatment, by whom, is most effective for this individual with that specific problem, under which set of circumstances?' (p. 111). More than 30 years on, the answers remain almost as elusive as they were then.

DIAGNOSTIC SYSTEMS

DSM

Particularly in the research community, the DSM system has achieved an extraordinary level of acceptance (Hickey, 1998). The American Psychiatric Association's classification system has, throughout its various editions, sought to systematically improve precision and expansion of the various classification categories. Each edition is larger than its predecessor—DSM-I (American Psychiatric Association, 1952) listed 60 types and subtypes of disorder; DSM-IV (American Psychiatric Association, 1994) lists 417. DSM-I had three anxiety categories; DSM-IV has 12. As Albee (1990) notes, 'clearly the more of the ordinary human problems in living that are labelled "mental illnesses", the more people will be found who suffer from at least one of them—and, the cynic might add, the more conditions that therapists can treat and for which they can collect health insurance payments' (p. 372).

New diagnostic entities are added in each edition, e.g. mixed anxiety–depressive disorder. Occasionally some disappear, e.g. DSM-III-R's passive aggressive personality disorder is removed to the 'criteria sets and axes provided for further study' in DSM-IV (where mixed anxiety–depression is placed). Some diagnoses are significantly altered. A good example is generalised anxiety disorder (GAD). In DSM-II (American Psychiatric Association, 1968) this diagnosis was subsumed under the broad heading of 'anxiety neurosis'. In DSM-III, GAD was defined as a 'residual' category; i.e. even if a patient met criteria for GAD, the diagnosis could be made only if that patient did not meet criteria for any other anxiety disorder. By DSM-III-R and DSM-IV, the category had become, by dint of accumulating research and empirical evidence, more clearly conceptualised although reliability in diagnosing the condition remains more difficult than other anxiety disorders (Barlow and DiNardo, 1991).

This heuristic system, through the operationalisation of diagnostic criteria, allows clinicians and researchers a common language for communication. It has, however, been criticised for being overly descriptive, too medically orientated and providing an extension of a medical approach to behavioural disturbance. The implicit disease model overemphasises symptom reduction as the principal outcome measure in therapy. In particular, it implies qualitative distinctions between patients with different diagnoses where quantitative distinctions may more accurately reflect the reality (e.g. Zubin, 1978; Eifert, 1996; Persons, 1986). A major concern for clinicians is the suggestion that there is greater homogeneity within diagnoses than actually exists. This may encourage researchers to limit their enquiries to particular diagnostic groups, thus often severely limiting the ability to generalise research centre work to the clinic, where such 'pure' patients are rarely seen. The next section looks at this issue.

THE ISSUE OF COMORBIDITY

Theoretical and treatment implications from comorbidity

The evidence presented in Chapter 1 seems to attest that comorbidity, particularly at severe levels—both within and outside the anxiety disorders— seems to be the rule rather than the exception. Yet research into anxiety treatments has tended to concentrate heavily on specific diagnostic problems rather than taking a dimensional approach. Patients who have comorbid conditions are often excluded for this reason (see below). In addition, treatments, although often involving some form of exposure, cognitive restructuring or coping strategies, increasingly tend to be specific to each anxiety disorder (e.g. Wells, 1997).

Many workers now argue that these divisions are largely artificial and that comorbidity points us to the fact that the similarities between the various anxiety disorders (and other disorders) are more important than the differences (see Andrews, 1996b, for a detailed analysis). This group—'the lumpers'—look for the commonalities, e.g. shared vulnerabilities, while 'the splitters' look for the differences between the various disorders. There remain real tensions between the 'splitters' and 'lumpers': on the one hand, as a result of further understanding about the structure of the anxiety disorders, a renewed interest in the old 'umbrella' category of 'anxiety neurosis', abandoned after DSM-II, but which could return in DSM-V, possibly as 'negative affect disorder' (Barlow, 1998); and, on the other, work looking at a greater understanding of subtypes within diagnoses (e.g. panic disorder, Biber and Alkin, 1999; agoraphobia, Chambliss and Goldstein, 1988). The truth may lie in between these two poles (see below and Chapter 4). The theoretical and therapeutic implications are immense. If general vulnerability factors are of greater importance than separate aetiological factors, the current emphasis on developing separate treatments for separate anxiety disorders would be much less appropriate. More positively, it may also lead to innovative, robust and pragmatic treatments being developed suitable for a range of current disorders.

General vulnerability factors

Andrews (1996b) pointed to the importance of long-term vulnerability factors—trait/neuroticism and coping factors—in explaining aetiology in both anxiety and depression. Kendler (1993), as noted above, postulated that many of the anxiety disorders appear to share the same genes in part or in whole, thus suggesting the concept of a general vulnerability factor. He also reported that the genes involved in GAD and major depression were likely to be the same and that they contributed 30% of the variation found in these disorders. These genetic factors operate in a non-specific fashion (Kendler, 1996).

As Andrews pointed out, the implications for treatment would include the need to tackle common vulnerability factors in addition to tackling specific symptoms. Preventative programmes would be of particular importance. 'Splitters' make the argument that, particularly where good behavioural markers are available, good interrater diagnostic reliability exists for most of the anxiety disorders—with the exception of panic disorder without agoraphobia, severe panic disorder with agoraphobia, Post-traumatic stress disorder (PTSD) and GAD (kappa coefficients of 0.43, 0.44, 0.46 and 0.57, respectively (Brown and Barlow, 1992)[1]—providing evidence supporting the validity of the DSM classification system for most of the anxiety disorders (e.g. DiNardo et al., 1993).

Barlow and colleagues have recently suggested a middle position in the argument. While accepting the existence of a general higher-order trait vulnerability factor common to all anxiety disorders ('negative affectivity'), these workers provided evidence of first-order factors allowing the reliable discrimination of specific disorders with different foci of attention (e.g. Zinbarg and Barlow, 1996). Barlow and his co-workers have gone on to suggest that an important factor contributing to the findings of high levels of comorbidity within the anxiety disorders (with the exception of specific phobia) relates to the core feature of GAD—anxious apprehension—with the focus of apprehension varying from disorder to disorder, and panic disorder (PD). These factors represent characteristics present to some extent in all the anxiety disorders (see Brown, 1996). Indeed, Rapee (1991b) referred to GAD as being the 'basic anxiety disorder' whose presence creates a vulnerability factor for the emergence of other anxiety disorders. These issues will be looked at in Chapter 4. While further studies are needed to unravel these issues, the phenomenon of comorbidity can no longer be overlooked by researchers and clinicians when developing new treatments. While this has, on the whole, not happened yet, data are beginning to emerge about the effects of comorbid conditions on, usually, focused anxiety treatments.

---

[1] More recent work suggests better GAD diagnostic reliability using DSM-IV/ADIS-IV (Barlow and Wincze, 1998). Diagnostic agreement also increases in GAD as severity of the condition increases (Chorpita et al., 1998).

TREATMENT OUTCOME: THE EFFECT OF COMORBIDITY

Few anxiety disorder treatment outcome studies have evaluated comorbid conditions or their effect. Often patients with comorbid conditions (e.g. mood and substance abuse) are actively excluded from these trials. As Brown and Barlow (1992) pointed out, including patients in a trial without consideration of comorbidity gives the illusion of homogeneity when the sample may well be heterogeneous. However, recently some attempt has been made to look at this crucial issue. Data from the National Comorbidity Survey (NCS) suggest that the co-occurrence of two or more disorders is more likely to result in severe impairment in social and occupational functioning (Kessler, 1997).

A recent study suggests that the co-occurrence of major depression does not adversely affect outcome in individual cognitive–behavioural treatment for panic disorder with or without agoraphobia although patients with comorbid depression had higher levels of both panic and depression (McLean *et al.*, 1998). It is difficult to generalise from this study as exclusion criteria included meeting criteria for any other Axis I disorder.

Wittchen and Essau (1989) found that those patients with a mixed anxiety/depression had more management problems than those with a pure depression. It was also related to a chronic, unfavourable course in 44% of patients compared to 26% of the pure depression patients. Pini *et al.* (1994) found depression symptoms to be more severe, persistent and recurrent when found along with an anxiety disorder compared to a pure form of depression.

Borkovec *et al.* (1995) looked at the effect of cognitive–behavioural treatment on comorbid conditions in GAD. Although limited by the factors noted in Chapter 1, this study found that successful treatment for GAD produced a significant reduction in comorbid conditions.

Sanderson *et al.* (1994), looked at the effect of comorbid personality disorder in cognitive therapy for GAD. Sixteen of the 32 patients met criteria for a PD. Although the presence of a PD did not affect outcome, it was significantly associated with higher drop-out—seven of the 10 drop-outs had a PD diagnosis. Similar results were reported by Dreesen *et al.* (1994). Reviewing GAD outcome studies, Durham and Allan (1993) reported that patients with coexisting clinical and personality disorders and chronic social stresses are likely to do poorly.

Scott *et al.* (1995), treating a clinically (heterogeneous) representative sample using CBT group work, found that the presence of a personality disorder diagnosis was associated with elevated Beck Anxiety Inventory (BAI) and Beck Depression Inventory (BDI) scores at pre- and post-therapy and follow-up (six and 12 months). However, these differences were significant only for patients with a principal diagnosis of depression but not for those with GAD or panic disorder.

Brown *et al.* (1995) examined 126 panic disorder patients undergoing CBT. Fifty-one per cent of patients had a pretreatment comorbid depressive condition. Comorbidity did not greatly affect short-term (three-month) outcome and comorbidity rates at this point reduced to 17%. The authors suggested, among other possibilities, that the reduction in (untreated) co-morbid disorders may suggest the treatment was successfully addressing processes common to all anxiety and mood disorders. However, by 24 months follow-up, comorbidity had increased to 30% and was no longer significantly different from pretreatment levels. This was despite the fact that patients maintained post-therapy gains in the panic condition over the follow-up period. It was noted that patients with comorbidity at post-treatment were more likely to seek additional treatment over the two-year follow-up period.

Attempting to explain why treatment of the principal disorder might also reduce comorbid disorders, Brown and Barlow (1992) suggested generalisa-tion may occur when patients use their newly learned coping skills in areas not covered by the treatment. They also suggested that as anxiety and mood disorders share certain overlapping features, change in these features in the principal disorder would automatically affect the presentation of comorbid disorders. Borkovec et al. (1995) noted, drawing on the 'lumpers and split-ters' debate, that certain psychological processes may be basic to most or all anxiety disorders. Thus the same basic mechanism (or mechanisms) may be shared by these disorders. A treatment, e.g. for PD that impacts on that basic mechanism, would affect any other disorder sharing that mechanism.

HOW REPRESENTATIVE ARE PATIENTS IN TREATMENT OUTCOME STUDIES?

Using GAD as an example, this section looks at five main outcome studies: Barlow et al. (1992), Butler et al. (1991), Borkovec and Costello (1993), Dur-ham et al. (1994) and White (1997b).

Exclusion criteria

All studies excluded entry if there was evidence of psychosis, current substance or alcohol abuse or a medical condition contributing to the anxiety. Beyond these, exclusion criteria varied greatly, thus making comparisons difficult.

Barlow excluded patients if they were suicidal, if concurrent psycho-therapy had lasted less than six months and was focused on anxiety man-agement, if they had begun benzodiazepines or beta-blockers within the last three months or tricyclics or monoamine oxidase inhibitors (MAOIs) within the previous six months.

Butler excluded patients if they met criteria for any phobic disorder, major depressive disorder, if their generalised anxiety centred on a fear of another panic attack, if they were taking antidepressant medication or had received psychological treatment for anxiety within two years. Of the 161 patients referred, 104 were excluded from the study.

Borkovec excluded patients if panic disorder criteria were met, if they were taking antidepressant medication, there was evidence of severe depression or substance abuse. Of the 508 individuals assessed, 442 were excluded for not meeting criteria.

Durham and White, both using British NHS populations, used much less stringent exclusion criteria: no patient was excluded if an Axis I or II disorder was present or if they were taking currently psychotropic medication.

Comorbidity issues

Brown *et al.* (1998) have shown that GAD has the highest degree of overlap with other DSM-IV disorders and was often found to be comorbid with panic disorder and social phobia. It also showed particularly high levels of comorbidity with mood disorders. As noted in the previous chapter, the NCS showed that 84% of individuals with lifetime GAD also had a lifetime mood disorder. The presence of a comorbid mood disorder also typically resulted in a significant increase in help-seeking behaviour and psychosocial dysfunction (Judd *et al.*, 1998). These findings provide indirect support for the observation that GAD and major depression share a common genetic diathesis (Kendler, 1996). Comorbidity seems to be a fundamental characteristic of GAD; thus the 'purer' studies may involve patients who are unrepresentative of GAD patients in general (although see Brawman-Mintzer *et al.*, 1993). Based on comorbidity evidence (above), the Barlow, Durham and White samples appear to be much closer to routine clinical populations. White's population included over 50% who met criteria for an Axis II personality disorder. This group was much more likely to meet criteria for major depression and to be taking antidepressant medication (ADM). In general, they were more symptomatic than GAD patients without an Axis II disorder. Thus they would be more likely to be excluded from the university-based studies. In addition, 95% of the whole sample (n = 71) met criteria for at least one additional Axis I disorder. Twenty-five per cent of Durham's sample were taking ADM and thus would be excluded from some other studies.

The evidence seems clear that these five studies, although sharing a principal diagnosis of GAD, are quite distinct and generalising from the research centre to the clinic is fraught with problems. However, these factors are often entirely overlooked in comparison studies, e.g. Fisher and Durham (1999). Even ignoring Axis II data, using Axis I comorbidity and other data from the White (1997b) study, only two of the 71 patients would probably have gained entry to the Butler study and three to the Borkovec study.

Social factors

Although seldom quoted in papers, the social circumstances of patients may be of great significance. All patients in the White study lived in a socially deprived area in the west of Scotland where high unemployment, poor housing, high levels of crime and low social amenities are the norm (see Durham and Allan, 1993, regarding the effect of social stressors). While DSM-IV offers the chance to detail multiaxial assessment, Axis IV (Psychosocial and Environmental Problems) is so vague as to be virtually useless. Although Axis II (Personality Disorders) data are increasingly recorded in treatment outcome studies, Axis III (General Medical Conditions) and Axis IV are almost never reported.

Eighty-four per cent of Borkovec's sample, noted above, replied to news advertisements. It seems implausible that many individuals from socially disadvantaged areas would be confident enough to actively seek treatment from prestigious research centres due to a perceived gulf between them and such establishments. This would particularly be the case with those suffering from GAD—individuals who often describe their problems in trait terms and who often assume little can be done for them. Butler and Booth (1991) have shown that demoralisation is a common secondary problem in such patients seen by clinicians, further suggesting that research trial patients differ in significant ways from routine clinical samples.

This raises the possibility that patients in research studies are better motivated and self-starting than those found in routine treatment settings, especially given the amount of questionnaires, diaries, homework assignments, etc. patients will complete in research settings. Clinicians do not find patients keen to do this in routine therapy. Scott and Stradling (1997), in a clinic-based PTSD study, found that only one of 14 patients completed the image habituation procedure for homework in the manner described by its authors. They further note that not one of the eight PTSD outcome studies reviewed by Otto *et al.* (1995) reported compliance rates with homework and only two detailed the numbers of potential patients who were excluded or who refused to participate.

Most clinical interventions would automatically take such realities into account in designing appropriate help and perhaps modify the expectations of treatment outcome if social/medical/psychological factors could not be significantly altered. Ideas from community psychology may be more relevant for many patients with social difficulties than simple reliance on one-to-one interventions looking almost exclusively at intra-psychic phenomena and primarily aiming at symptom reduction (e.g. see Orford, 1992).

As the evidence from comorbidity makes clear, there is great danger in generalising from these cleaned-up populations to the complex patients clinicians are more used to treating. It is little wonder that clinicians largely ignore findings from these studies (Cohen *et al.*, 1986; Beutler *et al.*, 1993).

SPECIFIC VERSUS NON-SPECIFIC FACTORS

Comparative trials

There is growing evidence supporting the Dodo's verdict that 'everyone has won so all shall have prizes' (Luborsky *et al.*'s 1975). Smith and Glass (1980), conducting a meta-analysis, reported that a range of theoretically and thera-peutically distinct approaches achieved similar outcomes irrespective of the disorder treated or the therapy. Similar findings, suggesting that different forms of therapy have major common elements, have been reported by Sloane *et al.* (1975), Luborsky and Digeur (1993), Orlinsky and Howard (1986) and Crits-Christoph (1992), although some trials suggest that dir-ective approaches may be more beneficial than indirective (Rachman and Wilson, 1980; Shapiro and Shapiro, 1982; Andrews, 1996a).

In a primary care study, comparing patients diagnosed as having either GAD, panic disorder or dysthymic disorder and randomly assigned to either drug treatment, cognitive–behavioural treatment or self-help, Tyrer *et al.* (1993) found few differences at two-year follow-up. Similar results, also in primary care, were found by Barkham *et al.* (1996), who compared CBT and a psychodynamic approach with depressed patients. In a massive study, Seligman (1995) reported similar findings from 7000 responses to the Consumer Reports (1995) therapy survey. Although limited by significant methodological weakness and based on only 4% of the originally contacted sample, this study, looking at what actually happens on the ground, suggested that no specific therapy modality did better than any other for any problem and that psychologists, psychiatrists and social workers did not differ in their effectiveness, although they were superior to marriage counsellors and family doctors (see also Scott and Freeman, 1992). These results confirm previous clinical trials and naturalistic studies (e.g. see Jacobson and Christensen, 1996). However, only 54% of respondents in the Consumer Reports study reported that therapy had helped 'a great deal'. These results contrast with those in a review of empirically supported treatment for adult disorders (DeRubeis and Crits-Christoph, 1998), where evidence was presented that efficacy of be-havioural and cognitive–behavioural treatments was particularly marked in comparison to other treatments, especially in the anxiety disorders. However, as the authors note, most of the studies reviewed involved care-fully screened patients treated in university-based settings who were un-likely to be representative of clinical populations (see also Roth and Fonagy, 1996).

Looking specifically at anxiety, Durham *et al.* (1994), comparing CBT and psychodynamic treatment for GAD and using highly experienced therapists, found CBT to be significantly more effective. However, possibly of greater interest was their (largely neglected) finding that surprisingly good results were obtained by junior psychiatrists with no previous experience of psy-chological techniques who were rapidly trained in the use of Anxiety Man-agement Training (Suinn and Richardson, 1971).

A recent review of GAD treatment outcome studies found Applied Relax-ation to perform at least as well as cognitive–behavioural approaches in a condition, centred on chronic worry, where cognitive therapy should be the obvious treatment of choice (Fisher and Durham, 1999). Even in a field where cognitive approaches have been shown to be highly successful, Shear *et al.* (1994b) showed that a non-prescriptive approach can also be effective.[2] Similarly the National Institute of Mental Health (NIMH) study (Shea *et al.*, 1992) suggested that cognitive therapy, interpersonal therapy, imipramine and placebo medication all performed at about the same relatively mediocre degree, although a statistical reanalysis suggested that imipramine was superior to the psychotherapies (Klein and Ross, 1993). When the sample was split, both interpersonal therapy and imipramine performed better than cognitive therapy with severe depression (see Jacobson and Hollon, 1996), although DeRubeis *et al.* (1999), in an analysis of four randomised trials, including NIMH, found no differences between tricyclics and cognitive therapy for severe depression. A recent meta-analysis of mild to moderate depression treatments suggested no difference between cognitive therapy, behaviour therapy or (mainly tricyclic) antidepressants (Gloaguen *et al.*, 1998).

In a carefully designed components analysis of cognitive therapy for depression, Jacobson *et al.* (1996) compared the behavioural activation component of CBT (BA), the cognitive component focusing on the modification of automatic thoughts (AT) and the full CBT version including a focus on the modification of core schema (CT). At post-therapy, there was no difference between the three conditions, with BA and AT being as effective as CT at altering both negative thinking and dysfunctional attributional styles. Two-year follow-up data yielded a similar picture, with the three conditions being virtually identical on every criterion measure, i.e. the full CT package was no better than either of its component parts; indeed the trend, if anything, favoured the behavioural approach. The authors raise interesting questions about the mechanisms of change and the long-term effectiveness of cognitive approaches as only 25% of those entering cognitive therapy recovered at post-treatment and maintained gains at two-year follow-up (Gortner *et al.*, 1998). They further point out that in order to justify its existence cognitive approaches, applied in individual therapy, must significantly outperform less expensive treatments that can be carried out by less qualified therapists (Jacobson and Gortner, 2000).

Even when significant differences are found, the results from randomised controlled trials can be easily misinterpreted. Perhaps the most significant problem with RCTs (randomised controlled trials) is the common finding of only minor differences between treatments A and B, resulting in the claim that treatment A is the treatment of choice. The fact that perhaps significant numbers of patients also benefited from treatment B would suggest that either there is more than one road to the same goal, that different people respond differently to the same or different therapies or that non-specific factors, inherent in both treatments, are of importance.

---

[2] Since reconceptualised as an 'emotion-focused' treatment (Shear *et al.*, 1995).

Non-specifics

It seems obvious that all therapies contain both specific and non-specific factors (see Oei and Shuttleworth, 1996). The idea that common factors are of importance in explaining the similarity of findings in comparative trials has become increasingly voiced by many workers. Garfield (1995) suggested common variables such as, among others, the therapeutic relationship, explanations, perceptual and cognitive change, the creation of hope, homework assignments and the opportunity for emotional release. Frank and Frank (1991) suggested four common non-specific elements: an emotionally charged confiding relationship, a healing setting, a rational conceptual scheme (or 'myth') offering a plausible explanation for the patient's problems and a ritual or procedure that involves both patient and therapist that is believed by both to be the means of restoring the patient's health. These factors combat demoralisation by lessening the patient's sense of alienation, strengthening the therapeutic relationship, providing inspiration and positive expectation in the patient, providing new learning experiences, arousing emotions showing individuals that they can cope with feared emotions, enhancement of self-efficacy and providing opportunities for the patient to practise new behaviours.

'Tactics' and 'deep strategy'

Seligman (1998) rightly pointed out that the term 'non-specific' is a derogatory misnomer. He suggested two classes: 'tactics' and 'deep strategies'. The former may involve, for example, attention, rapport, alliance, tricks of the trade and acceptance of the problem. The latter would include installing hope to a demoralised patient and 'the building of buffering strengths'. Common to all competent therapists is the strategy to help patients build a variety of strengths rather than simply aim to remove the damage. Seligman suggested these strengths may include 'courage, interpersonal skill, rationality, insight, optimism, honesty, perseverance, realism, capacity for pleasure, putting troubles in perspective, future mindedness and finding purpose' (p. 3). Research into these 'non-specifics' would allow us to better understand the results of comparative trials and the so-called placebo effect. By operationalising these strengths, more effective therapies may be produced. Unfortunately this goes against the empire-building often found among the adherents of particular approaches. However, this 'first past the post' approach is no longer tenable.

Therapist–patient factors

Therapist factors

Other issues relevant to the debate include the skill and experience of the therapist (see Beutler *et al.*, 1994; Luborsky *et al.*, 1997; Kingdon *et al.*, 1996).

Blatt *et al.* (1996), looking at the NIMH Treatment of Depression Collaborative Research Program, found that the most effective therapists were more psychologically minded, eschewed biological interventions in routine practice and expected treatment to take longer than less effective therapists. Luborsky *et al.* (1997) noted that effective therapists achieved similar results with different caseloads.

The skill of experienced clinicians is knowing how to take an approach tested in a research setting and make it fit the individual sitting beside them. A skilled clinician knows when to push, when to sit back and wait, when to use humour, etc. It is the combination of the scientist and the artist that makes a good clinician. The humanistic triad of genuineness, warmth and empathy is important if we want to engage, in structured therapy, patients who enter our rooms demoralised and with low expectation of positive outcome—difficult to measure yet, intuitively, obvious.

Patient factors

Similarly, diagnostic systems neglect the individuality of those given the same diagnosis (see Roth and Fonagy, 1996)—factors relatively overlooked in, for example, the report on empirically validated psychological treatments (Task Force on Promotion and Dissemination of Psychological Procedures, 1995). While difficult to evaluate, clinicians understand that they take to some patients and not to others; that some patients take to them and some do not; that patients often seem to improve for highly idiosyncratic reasons. If asked to recommend a therapist among colleagues, most clinicians would have very clear preferences who that therapist should be and who it should not be, even though all are trained to the same high level. Castonguay *et al.* (1996) found that patient improvement in cognitive therapy for depression was predicted by two common factors: the therapeutic alliance and the patient's emotional involvement (experiencing).

There is a difficulty with approaches such as the Task Force that attempted to educate the public on psychotherapies of proven efficacy. The idea that there can be a 'treatment of choice' for a certain condition endorses the homogeneity concept of individuals given the same principal diagnosis. There is growing evidence that different people respond differently to different procedures (something any experienced clinician would never doubt). Addis and Jacobson (1996), in an offshoot study from the Jacobson *et al.* (1996) study reported above, found that patients who endorsed existential reasons for depression had better outcomes with CT and worse outcomes with BA. Relationship-orientated reasons were associated with poorer outcome in CT. Beutler *et al.* (1991), in another depression outcome study, reported that directive treatments (cognitive therapy and focused expressive psychotherapy) were maximally effective among externalising patients with low defensive (resistance) traits. Non-directive treatment (supportive/self-directive) was maximally effective among those who were highly defensive (resistant) and internalising.

Therapist–patient interactions

Therapists and patients are not robots. Relationships may be central to therapy yet largely overlooked in the increasingly manualised, rigid therapy approaches advocated by researchers (see Horvarth *et al.*, 1993). Beutler and colleagues are currently working on an interactive model including *patient and problem dimensions* (e.g. complexity of problem, level of distress, functional impairment, coping style, resistance level), *therapist factors* (such as sex, skill and experience) and *treatment variables* (e.g. theoretical model, therapist directiveness, therapy focus and treatment modality) (see Beutler *et al.*, 1996). Such work, although complex, is likely to yield insights into therapy that randomly controlled trials cannot access.

TIME CONSIDERATIONS

Research studies generally include only those outcome measures relating to clinical *efficacy* (the results achieved in the trial—often changes in questionnaire data). Yet, within any health care system, an increasingly important part of a therapist's work is how best to achieve a compromise between clinical *effectiveness* (therapy outcome in routine practice) and clinical *efficiency* (bringing about the greatest change per unit time). A highly clinically effective therapy may be a clinically inefficient one if it takes a lot of time to do. This will be of major concern to clinicians in poorly resourced, pressurised clinics and yet it is a question rarely tackled by researchers (although see Clark *et al.*, 1999—see Chapter 4). Omitting assessment sessions, the Borkovec GAD study detailed above entailed 14 hours' therapy. While low by US therapist standards—Turner *et al.* (1995) reported on a national survey of methods where an average of 23 hours (plus 14 booster sessions) for GAD treatment in clinical settings prevailed—this figure would represent a very high investment for what would appear to be more straightforward problems than are usually met in routine clinical work.

It will be of interest to see whether the strictures placed on therapists by Managed Care in the USA significantly affects the Turner figure and, if so, whether researchers pay more attention to the issue of efficiency.

CONCLUSIONS

Research centre versus clinical realities: bridging the chasm

With health care systems increasingly emphasising the importance of evidence-based practice, there is a danger that clinicians will quote research centre studies and then be found wanting due to the likelihood that poorer results will be obtained because of the differences noted above. Weisz *et al.* (1992), studying children and adolescents, found that a meta-analysis of clinically representative samples suggested no improvement compared to significant change noted in research centre studies. Shadish *et al.* (1997), in a meta-analysis of heterogeneous samples, found a more positive result from clinically representative patients. However, out of over 1000 studies looked at, only 56 met their criteria for lowest level of clinical relevance; only one met the most stringent. This reinforces the point that much of the research published by clinicians is methodologically weaker than it should be. It is imperative that the experience and flexibility of the clinician are married to the research skills of the scientist to produce robust research findings with clinically relevant populations. Measurement of clinical efficacy, efficiency and effectiveness must all be looked at. DeRubeis and Crits-Christoph (1998) and Roth and Fonagy (1996), reviewing empirically supported treatments, note that little of such work was available for inclusion in their reviews. As Raw (1993) pointed out, researchers, who do the least clinical work, have a disproportionate role in defining the clinical field.

Becoming 'scientist–practitioners'

As Jones (1998) reminds us, within clinical psychology at least, there has been a traditional tension within the profession between the desire to help people and the scientific approach to the discipline yet, as Goldfried and Wolfe (1998) noted, what is the purpose of outcome research if not to inform the practising clinician? The 'scientist–practitioner' model (Barlow *et al.*, 1984; Hayes *et al.*, 1999) offers the chance to amalgamate the best from each camp and, in the process, produce methodologically sound, clinically relevant robust research. Barlow described three interrelated roles for clinicians: as consumers of new research findings; as evaluators of their own interventions using empirical methods; and as researchers, producing new data from their own settings. This may result in significantly different trends than are presently seen at the research centre level—Hughes (1997) pointed to an increasingly voiced scepticism among clinicians about cognitive therapy especially in the treatment of depression. Perhaps this scepticism reflects some of the issues noted above.

Two significant developments, in Britain and the USA, may help to foster much-needed change in this area. In a refinement of the scientist–practitioner approach, Milne and Paxton (1998), assessing possible models of professional practice deriving from the research and development strategy in the British NHS, suggested three levels: the *'empirical clinician'*, a consumer of research characterised by an emphasis on the application of validated procedures; the *'evaluative clinical scientist'*, who undertakes pragmatic and implementation work; and, at the highest level, the *'clinical scientist'*, responsible for innovation and development of new approaches that can then be validated and, if found beneficial, entered into routine clinical practice.

In the USA, managed health care may develop from focusing on cost containment to 'quality purchasing', where empirically supported treatments that have been shown to best marry efficiency and effectiveness will have the competitive edge (Strosahl *et al.*, 1998; Calhoun *et al.*, 1998).

Goldfried and Wolfe (1998) looked to the next generation of research which they feel will be characterised by 'the collaboration between researcher and practitioner; the need to study theoretically integrated treatments; the use of process research findings to improve our therapy manuals; the use of clinical case replications; the need to focus on less heterogeneous, dimensionalised clinical problems; and finding a better way of disseminating our research findings to the practising clinician' (p. 147).

There is a clear danger in allowing the gulf between researchers and clinicians to continue. Collaboration, with each benefiting from the others' particular skills, must be the way forward—the clinician's experience and wide-ranging skills married to the researcher's specialised knowledge and methodological sophistication can help develop the best compromise between clinical effectiveness and clinical efficiency. Although there are significant practical difficulties involved with the development of these new approaches, clinicians themselves can and should be much more heavily involved in research. 'Stress Control' is one attempt to do so.

SUMMARY AND CONCLUSIONS

- There exists a long-standing gulf between clinicians and researchers. The gulf weakens the impact of both groups.
- DSM and other classification systems suggest homogeneity within diagnostic groups and discontinuity between groups. Neither is accurate.
- There is mixed evidence concerning the presence of comorbid disorders on treatment outcome. There is some evidence that comorbid disorders significantly improve without being directly targeted. These findings are limited by a dearth of methodologically sophisticated empirical studies in this area.
- The major implication from comorbidity and other issues dealt with in this chapter is that the cleaned-up samples often reported in the outcome literature are unrepresentative of 'real' clinical populations. This significantly restricts the relevance of these studies in routine clinical settings.

ACTION

- Researchers and clinicians must recognise the unsatisfactory nature of the current situation. By working together with our complementary skills, more relevant, robust techniques can emerge and improve routine clinical practice.
- Treatments should aim at achieving the best compromise between clinical effectiveness, efficiency and efficacy.

Chapter 3

TREATING ANXIETY: THE PROBLEMS IN PRIMARY CARE

INTRODUCTION

The preceding chapters have shown that anxiety problems are extremely common. At the clinical level, they tend to be severe, chronic and are associated with high levels of comorbidity. The treatment outcome literature is often found wanting as it typically has not been conducted on clinically representative samples. The implications are that:

1. clinicians currently are seeing only the tip of the iceberg;
2. the techniques developed in research centres, tested on patients who appear to be almost hand-picked and treated in almost optimal circumstances, may not be the most clinically effective or even appropriate for the types of problems typically seen at the clinic level;
3. if we are to help larger numbers of people, we need to develop more clinically efficient approaches that are also clinically effective.

This chapter looks at current practice at the primary care level. Much of this evidence comes from clinical psychology within the British NHS as this primary care model, where clinicians work closely alongside referring family doctors, has been in place for some time. By understanding the problems, the solutions may become clearer and point the way to better practice. The chapter divides into six sections: mental health and primary care; developing a primary care model; dealing with problems; studies of effectiveness in primary care: heterogeneous samples; studies of effectiveness in primary care: anxiety disorders; and anxiety treatment as part of an interactive service.

MENTAL HEALTH AND PRIMARY CARE

Clinical psychology and primary care

GPs operate as the central figures in NHS health care delivery. They act as gatekeepers to the range of specialist physical and mental health services available within the NHS. Thus the vast majority of individuals with psychological problems will initially consult their GP. They will, often after medication and simple advice have been attempted, be referred to specialist mental health care workers: clinical psychologists, community psychiatric nurses, psychiatrists, counsellors, etc. Community Mental Health Teams (CMHTs), although, in theory, focused on treating the severe and enduring mental health problems such as psychotic disorders, often offer a range of services to this population— from sophisticated cognitive–behavioural or, less commonly, psychodynamic, interventions to less formal 'anxiety management' and group approaches such as relaxation classes. Although practices vary across the country, many anxiety disorder patients are likely to be referred either to counsellors, often based in the GP practice, or directly to clinical psychology primary care services. These may be based in the GP practice, local health centre or in a psychology department in a local hospital.

Clinical psychologists are trained to doctoral level (previously to masters level). Salaries are paid in full by the government-funded NHS. Treatment is provided free of charge to all patients. Services are organised geographically, e.g. large psychology departments, within a mental health or primary health care trust, may cover a city but be broken down into smaller localities where only a few psychologists may work. Current recommendations are for one full-time psychologist to cover a population of 30,000 (Division of Clinical Psychology, 1998). Achieving this target will vary considerably across the country.

The advantages of the system are that psychologists can develop good working relationships with the GPs in their locality. This can help the GP in deciding which patients should be referred and helps provide continuity of care. Psychologists often have freedom to develop a service best fitted to their skills and interests; thus psychology services may often vary considerably even within the same department. The main advantage to NHS services is that all members of the community, irrespective of wealth or social standing, should have equal access to a highly qualified therapist. As psychological morbidity for common disorders such as anxiety and depression is inversely related to social status, this means that social difficulties coexisting with psychological problems often have to be taken into account in planning interventions.

Disadvantages include, largely, lack of choice in which therapist the individual sees and, consequently, lack of choice in which therapeutic approaches are available. The prospective patient may be largely passive in this system. The locality therapist(s) may lack skills in certain areas and, if a therapist leaves the post, the service in a locality can be significantly weakened due to inadequate cover while the post remains vacant. However, the most significant barrier to immediate help is the inability, using current service models, to deal with the imbalance between demand and supply.

Waiting lists

Given the prevalence of anxiety and other common disorders and the reliance on one-to-one therapies as the main therapeutic tool used in therapy settings, long waiting lists are inevitable. In 1993, a British Psychological Society survey estimated that 44% of patients referred would wait at least six months for a first appointment. Fifteen per cent would wait over one year. At any one time, around 28,000 people were on psychologists' waiting lists (Division of Clinical Psychology, 1993). A more recent survey suggested that, on average, patients were waiting 17.5 weeks for a first appointment (Division of Clinical Psychology, 1997). These figures hide significant variation. Newnes (1993) reports waiting times of between four weeks and three years across the Mersey region.

It seems likely that these figures hide a much greater problem. Clinicians are seeing only the tip of the iceberg. The length of the waiting list may be determined to some extent by the perception of those who refer. If waiting times come down, GPs will refer more patients. If it goes up, they will refer fewer. This has implications for developing new strategies in primary care as clinicians may, if they do not address these issues, end up seeing more and more patients while failing to reduce their waiting list. Indeed, Westbrook (1995) suggests that, like death and taxes, waiting lists will always be with us. A study in Glasgow reported that patients and GPs most frequently reported long waiting time to see a clinical psychologist as a sign of a poor service (McAuliffe and McLachlan, 1992). Long waiting times were one of three main causes of dissatisfaction with the mental health service in Edinburgh (Jones and Lodge, 1991).

Waiting list approaches

Various solutions for controlling waiting lists have been proposed. Some examples include: offering patients one or two appointments soon after referral and prior to being placed on a waiting list (Geekie, 1995); predicting therapeutic need from the referral letter (Westbrook, 1991); using self-help packages for patients on the list (White, 1995a, 1998c); referring on more readily and restricting access to the service (Startup, 1994) and curtailing treatment length (Westbrook, 1993).

However, as McPherson (1998) pointed out, there is a danger in developing short-term strategies whose main focus is simply to 'deal with the waiting list'. While important, services should, as their main aim, develop to better meet the needs of the population seen at the primary care level. At the same time, and bearing in mind the limited resources that will always pertain in public sector mental health, work must focus on helping the large number of people who currently are deprived of any contact with a mental health professional. There has been a growing consensus, both in Europe and the USA, that therapists have to develop innovative long-term approaches to deal with these problems (e.g. Robertson and Sheldon, 1992; Botella and Garcia-Palacios, 1999; Barlow *et al.*, 1996).

DEVELOPING A PRIMARY CARE MODEL

The Trethowan Report on psychological services (Trethowan, 1977) strongly advocated that clinical psychologists could make a positive contribution in primary care. It suggested the setting up of pilot studies on patients referred directly by GPs. Johnston (1978) suggested that, compared to hospital-based psychologists, primary care workers could foster greater continuity of care of patients; could improve communication between psychologists and members of the primary care team; could intervene earlier, thus avoiding the entrenchment of severe difficulties and reduce stigma for the patients. Perhaps of greatest importance, she suggested that the move into primary care would lead to the development of new therapeutic approaches relevant to problems presenting in primary care. These hopes failed to materialise. The move from secondary to primary care largely took place in a theoretical, organisational and resources vacuum—a 'feet first and fingers crossed approach' (Griffiths, 1985). This has resulted in mental health therapists often taking approaches developed in and for very different health care systems and attempting to make them fit primary care settings without taking into account the unique characteristics and demands in primary care. The next section looks at this issue.

DEALING WITH PROBLEMS

The ubiquity of anxiety disorders

In a survey of psychological therapies used in an NHS Trust, anxiety management was, by far, the most common specific approach offered across a range of professions (Cureton and Newnes, 1995). There has been a tendency, perhaps because anxiety disorders are so frequently referred, to see them among the easiest to deal with. As such, they are often dealt with inappropriately, for example, non-mental health therapists, who may not have the appropriate training, providing 'anxiety management courses' without any great understanding of the complexities involved in these disorders. The individual's failure to improve may reinforce a self-image as a 'failure' and deter that individual from seeking more appropriate therapy. The referring GP, especially if operating within a quota system with the psychology department, may decide against re-referral to allow others to 'have their turn'. We must not lose sight of how difficult anxiety problems remain in terms of treatment outcome. This is particularly true of generalised anxiety disorder, with only about 50% of carefully screened patients attaining normal functioning after treatment in optimum conditions (see Durham and Allan, 1993).

The limitations of cognitive therapy

Even as far back as 1984, Teasdale *et al.* noted that 'cognitive therapy in its present form may be too complex and time-consuming to become widely available in a National Health Service short of resources' (p. 405). This trend towards complexity has continued (Snaith, 1992). As there is unlikely to be a significant increase in the number of highly qualified mental health professionals within the NHS, should we drop cognitive therapy and develop other more efficient approaches? Jacobson and colleagues point to the similar results obtained in depression using either complex schema-focused cognitive therapy and the more basic behavioural activation part of cognitive–behavioural therapy (CBT) (Gortner *et al.*, 1998). This has significant implications with regard to using less qualified therapists. However, as mentioned in Chapter 1, CBT may be more malleable than other approaches. What has not been adequately looked at is how far we can shape these techniques to meet routine clinical demands. This may be because many researchers have not adequately considered the issue of efficiency in recent cognitive therapy manuals (e.g. Wells, 1997). Yet the possibility exists that the flexibility of this approach may prove its greatest asset in routine clinical work. Scott, working in inner-city Liverpool, has produced evidence that while the essential Beckian model for depression (Beck, 1981) does not work well in group format in this setting, a modified version, more relevant to local culture and needs, can be used successfully (Scott and Stradling, 1990). 'Stress Control' is another such attempt.

Given that demand will always outstrip supply, therapists must make best use of limited therapeutic time. Prior to developing services, we must ensure that patients and referring agents understand and want these services. One major issue in primary care work has been patient drop-out and failure to appear, resulting in wasted therapist time.

Failure to attend

Grunebaum *et al.* (1996), reporting on a US psychiatric outpatient clinic at a university-affiliated primary care clinic, found fully 50% of patients missed appointments. Madden and Hinks (1987) found that 17% of NHS outpatients failed to attend for their first appointment, 23% by the second appointment, with 35% dropping out eventually. Similar high rates (33%) are reported by Hughes (1995). Grunebaum and colleagues found three predictors of failure to attend: patients with milder problems, those with greater resistance to seeing a psychiatrist and those who had to wait longest.

As a way of improving attendance at the first appointment, therapists have suggested the importance of teaching about 'good referring' (Skaife and Spall, 1995); the introduction of a triage system and speeding up administration time (Grunebaum *et al.*, 1996); developing 'opt-in' systems that now usually also involve information booklets and self-assessment packs (e.g. Anderson and White, 1996; Fox, 1997) and giving responsibility for referral to the patient (Seager *et al.*, 1995).

McCaskill and McCaskill (1983) suggest that those patients who have realistic expectations and favourable attitudes to therapy tend to remain in treatment and have better outcome. Sledge *et al.* (1990) report drop-out rates are halved when the likely duration of therapy is specified from the outset. The evidence also points to the difficulty in generalising from the often idiosyncratic reasons for failing to opt-in. Offering explicit therapy options and providing information about these prior to attendance would seem to constitute good practice in this area (see Anderson and White, 1996).

Innovation in the treatment of anxiety

Any innovation in primary care must seek to achieve the best compromise between quality of service provided and quantity of patients treated. Probably the majority of therapists remain convinced that one-to-one therapy comprising frequent sessions remains the gold standard in terms of quality, justifying the extra cost in terms of time. However, an increasing number of developments start with the premise that other approaches may offer equal or better-quality approaches. However, any development must be seen in the context of the service as a whole. This will be looked at later in this chapter.

STUDIES OF EFFECTIVENESS IN PRIMARY CARE: HETEROGENEOUS SAMPLES

Because of the problems associated with the research trials reported in the previous chapter, this section concentrates on research carried out in clinical settings. Although there is a plethora of studies of primary care work, most are uncontrolled and suffer from various methodological weaknesses, including lack of diagnostic clarity, small sample sizes, poor randomisation, high attrition rates, use of unrepresentative or unreliable measures and inadequate follow-up. Thus internal validity has been sacrificed at the expense of external validity—a mirror image of the criticisms directed against researchers in Chapter 2. This seriously limits the conclusions that can be drawn. As King (1997) points out, controlled trials are difficult to do in this setting for a range of reasons. This section reviews primary care studies carried out in Britain with different professions.

Community psychiatric nurses

Gourney and Brooking (1994) reported on a controlled trial involving 177 heterogeneous non-psychotic patients who were randomly referred to community psychiatric nurse (CPN) 'counselling' intervention, continuing GP care or a waiting list. No differences emerged between the CPN- and GP-treated groups. Fifty per cent dropped out of the CPN intervention. There was no evidence that referral to a CPN saved GP time. The authors concluded by suggesting that CPNs refocus their activity on people with serious mental illness and acquire skills in techniques of proven effectiveness, e.g. behaviour therapy.

Community nurses

Following on from a study (Mynors-Wallis *et al.*, 1995), showing GPs to be equally effective as psychiatrists in using a problem-solving approach with major depression patients, Mynors-Wallis *et al.* (1997) compared GP treatment as usual with nurse treatment with heterogeneous anxiety and depression patients. Post-treatment results suggested no difference in clinical outcome between the two conditions, although problem-solving-treated patients had fewer days off work.

Behaviour nurse therapists

Ginsberg *et al.* (1984) found behavioural psychotherapy with a mixed anxiety and depression group to be equally effective as GP care. Marks (1985) found nurse therapists to be superior to GP care in dealing with mainly phobic and obsessive-compulsive disorder patients at one year follow-up. However, a significant proportion of potential patients (55%) were excluded at screening, being deemed unsuitable for behaviour therapy, thus limiting ability to generalise from the results.

Community mental health team

Goldberg *et al.* (1996) reported on the treatment of anxiety and depression problems by either a hospital-based psychiatric service or a community mental health team. Clinical and social outcomes were similar but those treated in the community were seen quicker, had greater continuity of care and were more satisfied with the service. The community team treatment was more cost-effective.

Psychiatrists

Catalan *et al.* (1991) compared problem-solving and GP treatment as usual. Problem-solving patients showed significantly greater improvement at post-therapy and 16 weeks follow-up. The authors suggested that this simple approach could be offered to patients with poor-prognosis emotional disorders in primary care.

Person-centred counselling

The number of counsellors (usually person-centred) has dramatically risen in primary care over the last five years. One-third of GP practices currently employ a counsellor (Friedli and King, 1996). There is no evidence that the availability of counselling reduces referral to clinical psychology or psychiatry (Cape and Parham, 1998). Evidence for the effectiveness of counselling is sparse and often of poor quality (Harvey *et al.*, 1998; Corney, 1997; King and Friedli, 1996). However, evidence from controlled trials is now becoming available. Ashurst and Ward (1983) reported no significant differences between counselling and routine GP care groups at one year follow-up. Boot *et al.* (1994), again comparing counselling and routine GP care, reported greater improvement in the counselling group. Caution must be applied in interpreting the findings from both these studies owing to serious methodological problems.

Friedli *et al.* (1997) compared 6–12 sessions of non-directive (Rogerian) counselling with routine GP care for emotional disorders. Although patients preferred counselling to GP care, there were no differences on a range of measures. Harvey *et al.* (1998), comparing generic counselling and usual GP care, on clinical and economic measures, found significant change in both conditions at four months follow-up but no difference between the conditions. No clear cost advantage was associated with either intervention.

Clinical psychologists

Uncontrolled studies

Espie and White (1986a, 1986b) found that although 75% of a mainly anxiety population reported at least slight change following behavioural therapy, only 43% reported at least moderate or marked change. Anxiety disorders were associated with greatest change. Similar results were found by Jerrom *et al.* (1986), who noted 52% of their sample reporting 'definite benefit' following behavioural treatment.

One recent study of long-term follow-up (mean of 22 months) routine NHS CBT work is of interest (Westbrook and Hill, 1998). Results suggested that patients treated with cognitive–behavioural techniques were able to maintain post-therapy gains although 59% of the sample had further help, mainly from their GP.

Turvey (1997) reported on 13,057 patients treated over eight years in an adult clinical psychology service. Generalised anxiety was the most common problem treated. Bearing in mind the limitations inherent in such studies, 68% of treated cases improved. Panic disorder had the best outcome, followed by generalised anxiety. The presence of anger or depression negatively affected anxiety treatment outcome.

Controlled studies

Earll and Kinsey (1982) randomly allocated consecutive heterogeneous referrals either to behavioural treatment or GP treatment as usual. Although
the behaviour therapy group improved more by discharge, these differences
disappeared by seven months follow-up. Robson *et al.* (1984), in a better-
designed study, found a similar pattern although they noted that one-
quarter of a clinical psychologist's salary could be paid for by savings to the
drugs bill.

Milne and Souter (1988), employing a double baseline assessment with 22
heterogeneous primary care patients, found no change during the waiting
period, followed by significant improvement at post-therapy and maintained at one year follow-up. This study of behavioural therapy also showed
clear economic benefits to primary care psychology treatment in terms of
reduced drugs costs, GP consultations and hospital referrals.

Conclusions

The evidence reviewed above has to be treated with caution owing to the
methodological weaknesses commonly found in such studies. However, the
impression is formed that routine outcome with emotional disorders, as
would be expected, is poorer than that suggested by the carefully controlled
outcome studies based in research centres. They leave no room for
complacency.

Most clinical psychology research work at the primary care level has
moved on from these large heterogeneous studies in primary care in favour
of more carefully designed studies focusing on particular diagnostic groups
(e.g. Sharp *et al.*, 1997) or comparing different treatment modalities (e.g.
White, 1995a) and the resulting more optimistic findings suggest this is the
appropriate route to take. It may be that person-centred therapists will
obtain more informative results if they do likewise. Adopting a pragmatic
approach, it may be appropriate for highly skilled, (relatively) highly paid
but scarce mental health professionals such as clinical psychologists to employ a triage model, with less severe patients being treated by less qualified,
less well paid but more abundant clinicians such as (person-centred) counsellors. The latter, possibly adding to their skills with further training in
cognitive–behaviour techniques, would be supervised by the psychologist.

However, clearly, if our services to patients are to improve, mental health
professionals should avoid getting into turf wars with other professional
groups. We must work more closely together and share our skills. There is
good reason for not becoming arrogant. Christensen and Jacobson (1994)
report that, comparing professional and non-professional help (e.g. self-help
groups, self-help books, para-professionals), there often appears to be few
differences in outcome. The positive implication is that there are perhaps
many relatively unexplored possibilities to develop our services and produce less expensive, more effective, wider-ranging and robust approaches

for a much larger number of patients than can currently be dealt with. It is possible that, in the future, professional therapists will draw back from treatment administration and adopt a more consultative, supervisory role. The next section looks at specific primary care interventions with anxiety disorders.

STUDIES OF EFFECTIVENESS IN PRIMARY CARE: ANXIETY DISORDERS

Individual therapy

Jannoun *et al.* (1981, 1982), in methodologically weak studies, reported that Anxiety Management Training (AMT) (Suinn and Richardson, 1971) was effective with generalised anxiety patients. Blowers *et al.* (1987) randomly allocated 66 patients to AMT, non-directive counselling or to a waiting list control. Both AMT and counselling were superior to the waiting list but there was no difference between the two treatment conditions. The authors suggest that non-specific factors operating across conditions may help explain the findings. Lindsay *et al.* (1987) compared CBT, AMT, benzodiazepine medication and a waiting list. The two psychological treatment groups produced greater change but could not be differentiated. Patients in the drug condition may not have received optimal dosage of lorazepam.

Power *et al.* (1990) compared CBT for generalised anxiety disorder with placebo medication and diazepam. Large variation in response to all three treatments emerged. CBT showed significant change over time; however, no significant differences emerged between the three conditions. Sharp *et al.* (1997), studying panic disorder with or without agoraphobia in a primary care setting, randomly allocated patients to either CBT, fluvoxamine antidepressant medication (ADM), placebo medication, CBT plus ADM and CBT plus placebo. Patients in the conditions involving CBT did particularly well. This study is important as it shows that high-quality research can be carried out in primary care with representative patients.

Group therapy

'Traditional' groups

Such groups are common in primary care settings. From experience, clinicians often run groups primarily to reduce waiting lists and not because they see group therapy as a treatment of choice for therapeutic reasons. They are often based on AMT or cognitive–behavioural formats and employ techniques focusing on a 'three-systems' (cognition, somatics and behaviour) model (Lang, 1978), e.g. relaxation, exposure, cognitive restructuring. Sessions can vary between six (Jupp and Dudley, 1984) and 20 (Eayrs *et al.*, 1984).

Jupp and Dudley (1984), in a descriptive paper of group anxiety management, presented information on three groups. The content involved information provision, 'positive thinking', target setting, exposure and relaxation. Six weekly group sessions involving seven generally anxious patients were undertaken. Questionnaire and therapist ratings showed significant improvement.

Eayrs et al. (1984) reported on a pilot study designed to compare a relaxation group and a 'coping skills package' for generally anxious patients. Coping skills included progressive relaxation, anxiety management training, positive self-talk, targeting and self-monitoring. With the exception of one measure, there were no differences between the two groups. The authors suggested that the multi-component package may have been too difficult for some patients to understand within a six-session format. It may also be that this package lacked an internal consistency.

Trepka et al. (1986) compared individual therapy with two types of group treatment: an anxiety support group involving 12 unstructured sessions during which the seven patients were given the opportunity to discuss problems, and a more structured anxiety management course (five patients). This involved 11 sessions during which relaxation, self-hypnosis and graded exposure were taught. Neither approach had a clinically significant effect on anxiety symptoms as post-therapy reductions had disappeared by one year follow-up. Individual therapy was somewhat more successful.

Powell (1987) reported on 47 patients treated in six anxiety management groups, of whom only one-third were defined as 'generally anxious'. Coping skills such as deep and cued relaxation, respiratory control, rational self-talk and distraction were used. Results suggested a decrease in the negative effect of anxiety in daily life. Although anxiety symptoms fell significantly, they remained moderately high. A similar finding was reported by Campbell et al. (1993). Ormrod (1995), looking at long-term outcome in a 'quick and dirty' evaluation of group cognitive–behavioural anxiety management training, found post-therapy trait anxiety and depression gains were maintained at both a short-term follow-up (between six months and two years) and longer term (two to five years).

While the above studies suffer from the common methodological problems often imposed by primary care realities—lack of control groups, diagnostic uncertainties, inappropriate measures, confounding of treatment variables, eclectic mix of theoretically incoherent treatments—they do suggest that anxiety management groups are an appropriate primary care approach. It would be beneficial, however, for these clinic-based studies to adopt a more rigorous methodology while retaining the necessary degree of external validity. Models of well-designed approaches would include group treatments of social phobia (Heimberg et al., 1993) and panic disorder (Telch et al., 1993).

A more sophisticated primary care study by Scott et al. (1995) in a primary care study compared a waiting list control and a seven-session cognitive group therapy for generalised anxiety disorder (GAD), panic disorder and major depression patients (all DSM-III-R). This approach was based on a 12-session group treatment for depression that was previously shown to be as effective as—and thus more efficient than—individual cognitive therapy for depression (Scott and Stradling, 1992). Half the sample (of 96) had at least one personality disorder (mainly DSM cluster C). Results, to one year follow-up, indicated that the approach was effective for the depression and GAD patients but not the panic patients.

Common active ingredients

It is interesting that many authors point to non-specific factors as being important in explaining positive outcome. Jupp and Dudley emphasised the role of information provision; Eayrs *et al.* commented that one of the most frequently mentioned aspects of the group was the opportunity to share problems with others 'who were in the same boat'. They also noted that the group itself was an integral part of the treatment, i.e. the medium of the group provided opportunities for observational learning, modelling, role-playing and rehearsal and offered 'moral support' from other group members. Campbell *et al.* also noted the importance of 'peer support'. Ormrod found group members rated 'meeting people with similar problems' and 'learning about anxiety' as the most helpful components of the groups. These findings echo the views of Yalom (1975), who suggested the gaining of hope and finding that you are not alone among a range of 'curative factors'. Powell concluded his study by suggesting that as 'information' and 'meeting people with similar problems' were the most valued aspects of his treatment package, these factors should be given more consideration by therapists. He also suggested that therapists should place less emphasis on individual therapy and move towards the position of educators and organisers of self-help services.

Innovation in group work

The above studies, although emphasising the role of information provision, remain within the classical group therapy tradition—i.e. individuals are expected to actively contribute to the group through personal disclosure. Other approaches to group work suggest new avenues to therapy.

Butcher and de Clive-Lowe (1985) reported on a series of adult education evening classes entitled 'Strategies for Living', a twelve-session course offering practical help in reducing anxiety and coping with life crises. During the eight theoretical and practical sessions, participants were encouraged to sit behind desks and take notes. The four group discussions emphasised the sharing of experience and personal problem solving. Little information was given about the 23 participants and the outcome measure was not informative. The course was judged to be a success by the authors.

More recently, Brown *et al.* (1998) reported on a comparison between large-scale, day-long stress management workshops open to the general public and small stress management groups for referred NHS patients. The day-long groups were run as part of a 'Healthy Birmingham 2000' campaign. There were between 20 and 24 participants in each workshop, based in a leisure centre and led by a team of four psychologists. The small groups contained, on average, six participants and were run by two therapists. Both approaches emphasised cognitive–behavioural principles.

When change scores on the trait anxiety measure were compared, no differences emerged, with both approaches being successful. A subgroup comparison, of those in the large and small groups with higher levels of anxiety, again showed no difference, suggesting that this format is robust enough to deal with a range of anxiety sufferers. While lacking in methodological rigour—it was impossible to gather diagnostic data from those attending—the authors concluded that such an approach is a realistic alternative to traditional group therapy. The approach, run at weekends, was convenient for those in work, as it may have been easier to attend for one full day rather than six weekly meetings. It may involve less stigma, and thus boost attendance and help engender a positive attitude—something found to correlate highly with improved outcome in GAD (Durham and Allan, 1993).

ANXIETY TREATMENT AS PART OF AN INTERACTIVE SERVICE

The river analogy

A man is standing, upstream, on the riverbank. He falls in. Although other people knew that he was at risk of falling in, there was no one there to try to prevent it. He calls for help. People throw him a lifebelt to keep him afloat but they do not know how to get him out of the water. He slowly floats downstream. The man tries to get out of the river on many occasions but fails each time. He soon realises that although he can see that the riverbank is tantalisingly close, he does not possess the skills necessary to reach it and that he has no control over his journey downstream. This soon instils a sense of hopelessness and ends any further attempts to escape from the water. Various flotsam and jetsam stick to him, weighing him down, and this makes it harder to keep his head above the water. Eventually, he drifts far downstream where an individual finds him and teaches him to swim. This gives him the confidence to give up the lifebelt and swim into the shallow waters. Owing to the amount of water his clothes have absorbed, the amount of attached flotsam and jetsam and his loss of belief in himself, it proves a very time-consuming and difficult job getting him back on to dry land.

Even although we are steadily gaining knowledge about vulnerability factors for these disorders (e.g. Chorpita and Barlow, 1998), little health promotion or early intervention work is done in most countries even although there are some excellent examples of such work (e.g. Dadds *et al.*, 1997). At the early stages of disorders, individuals frequently attend their family doctor. Often therapy at this stage—drugs or person-centred counselling—may help but will not teach the skills required to re-establish a sense of self-control even although there are simple CBT strategies family doctors could use (e.g. White *et al.*, 1999). Anxiety sufferers typically, inconsistently and often unsuccessfully, try their own methods of relaxation, cognitive restructuring and exposure, leading to feelings of demoralisation (Butler *et al.*, 1987). Those who are most demoralised respond least well to therapy (Butler and Anastasiades, 1988). As they drift, individuals appear to develop comorbid disorders. Anxiety may develop gradually, e.g. evidence from the Baltimore Epidemiologic Catchment Area (ECA) study suggested that about 50% of those meeting criteria for panic disorder with or without agoraphobia have had anxiety of one kind or another prior to meeting panic criteria. Similarly, anxiety often appears to precede depression (Rohde *et al.*, 1991). This suggests that early intervention, using core psychological techniques, could prevent a serious and disruptive disorder (Eaton *et al.*, 1998). By the time they reach the clinician, problems have become entrenched and complex and the quality of the individuals' lives (and, probably, those around them) badly affected.

Developing a comprehensive service

Clinicians working in the NHS or in conjunction with health care delivery systems such as health maintenance organisations (HMOs) or even working in a specialised anxiety treatment unit, e.g. along the lines suggested by Chambless and Hollon (1998), may feel they always have to seek a compromise between providing a high-*quality* service to the individual and providing help to a large *quantity* of individuals. The difficulty will be in deciding at which point the compromise should be made. In addition, the service, e.g. in an NHS setting, will be expected to provide therapy for a large number of problems, at differing levels of severity and meet different needs of the individuals requesting help. However, improving both the quality of service provision and the quantity of patients seen within that system without increased financial resources need not be mutually incompatible. Putting an effective didactic therapy in place for common disorders allows many people to be taken out of the individual therapy service, thus making more of this scarce commodity for those most in need of it.

This service should be interactive—changing any component will affect all the others. Thus changes to anxiety management procedures must be seen within the context of the service as a whole. The rest of this section looks at a significant widening of service provision within the NHS from the almost exclusive one-to-one approaches for individuals with significant problems favoured by most therapists to a multi-level service. It assumes that significant increases in staffing will not occur unless financial savings in other areas, e.g. decreased direct costs (drug bills and decreased referrals to hospital) and decreased indirect costs (e.g. time off work), can be clearly demonstrated.

A multi-level, multi-purpose service

In order to tackle some of the issues in the river analogy, a comprehensive service provision should involve work at different levels and tackle different goals. Clinicians often adopt a generic approach to primary care work—a *jack of all trades* rather than a *master of some*. Referrals are typically placed in the waiting list and dealt with consecutively. While superficially a fair system, it fails to optimise the use of the inevitable scarce therapy time available and fails to exploit the particular skills and interests of the individual clinician. It also means, given that the GP referral letter tells us little about the need of the individual (Westbrook, 1991), that severe cases are dealt with in the same way as the less severe. It also prevents those whose needs could be dealt with using less time-intensive approaches from obtaining quicker and appropriate help. Removing these individuals from the waiting list would automatically cut waiting time for those most in need of it. White (1998d) has outlined a possible seven-level service. These levels are: (1) prevention/health promotion, (2) working through and with other professional, community and self-help groups, (3) use of bibliotherapy, computer-, internet- and video-based therapies, (4) walk-in/advice clinics (e.g. White, 1998b), (5) specialist clinics, e.g. sleep clinics, postnatal depression, (6) anxiety (and associated problems) management groups and (7) individual therapy for those who cannot benefit from, or do not wish to take part in, other approaches.

This system would require to be flexible. Patients with different needs could be better accommodated—some could concentrate on symptom reduction approaches, some could prevent more serious problems developing, some could use the service as a lifeline that they use from time to time when most in need of it and some could stay on the periphery using the self-help approaches made easily available to them. Patients could move from level to level depending on need. They may start with less intensive approaches and move to more intensive if they are not progressing. Those who have completed, for example, individual therapy could return for booster sessions, e.g. with computerised therapy or the advice clinic. Others could be involved at various levels of the system simultaneously, i.e. attending the anxiety management course, receiving individual therapy for a severe comorbid disorder and attending an aerobic therapy class with a trainer.

The model offers choice; e.g. as part of the assessment, individuals could be offered a menu of appropriate approaches and, in consultation with the therapist, choose the approach(es) they felt would be most suitable—a 'horses for courses' approach. It would allow clinicians working in a generic team to develop specialist skills, e.g. in a PTST early intervention clinic. These services could operate within and across localities or city-wide to maximise local clinical skills, i.e. experts in specific problems could be peripherally involved in the system, responsible for the management of a triage system and for training others.

Chapter 4 outlines in greater detail how didactic anxiety management fits into this model.

SUMMARY AND CONCLUSIONS

- Waiting lists constitute a problem in NHS settings depriving access to appropriate help to all but a minority of mental health problem sufferers.
- Attempting short-term solutions—'to do something about the waiting list'—may be, paradoxically, stopping therapists looking for more useful developments to their services.
- Methodological weaknesses limit the conclusions that can be drawn from many of the studies carried out in primary care.
- Controlled evidence, where it exists, may have important implications for training or allocation of different mental health professionals.
- Group approaches may offer a reasonable compromise between clinical efficiency and effectiveness.
- Any group approach must be considered within the wider service context.

ACTION

- Waiting lists must be reduced in order to allow patients quick access to therapy.
- Managing services more effectively may help in this, e.g. operating opt-ins, providing information packs.
- Developments must not simply aim at short-term efficiency solutions to waiting lists, e.g. seeing more patients in the same time.
- We should be devising approaches that offer the best compromise between quality of service and quantity of patients seen. Group therapy offers one such approach.
- In developing new treatments, clinicians should not neglect the potentially powerful role of non-specific factors as part of the therapeutic intervention.
- Therapists must also allocate resources to help the huge number of people who could potentially benefit from therapy but who are unable to obtain a referral due to the log-jam at the secondary care level.
- Training must be provided to a range of professionals to help them gain conceptual as well as therapeutic skills. Generic 'anxiety management' is no longer good enough.
- Research in this area must be methodologically more sophisticated while retaining clinical relevance and robustness.

Part 2

Issues in Devising and Setting Up the Group Therapy

Chapter 4

THE 'STRESS CONTROL' METHOD

INTRODUCTION

Improving the quality and quantity of service provision

The evidence from Part 1 suggests that only a minority of individuals suffering from anxiety and related disorders are currently receiving appropriate psychological help. Group therapy offers one possible way to allow far larger numbers to access appropriate treatment. This chapter looks at the 'Stress Control' approach. It divides into four: 'Stress Control'; providing rationales for the approach; diagnostic issues; and therapy issues.

'STRESS CONTROL'

'Stress Control' is a six-session didactic cognitive–behavioural 'evening class'. It aims to:

- teach students about anxiety and associated problems—depression, panic and insomnia;
- teach self-assessment skills to allow individuals to learn how these problems affect them;
- teach a range of techniques designed to enable individuals to tailor their own treatment with minimal therapist contact.

It emphasises a psycho-educational format in which the individual does not require to discuss personal information. The aim of the course is to 'teach individuals to become their own therapists'. The therapeutic relationship is significantly altered. The therapist becomes the teacher and patients reconceptualise their role more as students.[1] It is a flexible approach run by one or more teachers and run with student numbers between six and 60. A detailed

---

[1] The terms 'student' and 'teacher' will now be retained throughout when discussing this approach.

student manual accompanies the course. The course invites students with a wide range of clinical and other problems to participate. It is designed to meet as many as possible of the heterogeneous needs often found in primary care.

Although here described in the six-session format I have always used, the number of sessions can be increased or decreased according to teacher and student needs. Some of the topics can be removed from the course if the students do not require them. Similarly, more topics could be added. For example, if used in a medical setting with students with a similar medical condition, a session specifically aimed at the psychological factors associated with that condition may be useful. Flexibility is the watchword with this approach.

Although there are clear advantages in starting at the first session, students can join the course at any stage. The book will teach them the overall approach, while each session is taught in a 'stand-alone' format. This allows rapid entry following assessment. Students then complete the sessions they missed in the next course. With a rolling programme, i.e. a new course starts as soon as an old one ends, this helps provide continuity. Other advantages include allowing students to break for holidays, work commitments, illness, etc. without having to miss important sessions. A rolling programme also allows students to rejoin courses at any stage in the future without difficulty.

The therapeutic model emphasises an educational approach to emotional problems. Although the roles of teacher and student differ significantly from those of therapist and patient, a strong therapeutic alliance is important. The approach is structured and problem-orientated and looks to develop general skills that individuals can use in a wide range of situations. No longer defined as illnesses, the problems should be readily understood by the sufferer. As Salkovskis (1995) points out, this is highly normalising and, if used correctly, empowering as individuals understand that many others would experience the same distress.

'Stress Control' aims to identify and modify the perceptions involved in anxiety. It also looks at other maintaining factors, e.g. avoidance, and thus includes behavioural techniques such as exposure. However, the rationale for the use of these behavioural techniques is not simply that they produce habituation but rather, within a cognitive framework, they function as experiments to collect information that disconfirms fears whereby, individuals with agoraphobic problems, for example, are asked to go to the supermarket to gather information related to their threat-related perceptions of what will happen to them in such a situation. They are then taught to gradually relinquish their safety behaviours. As it is suggested that their efforts to avoid disaster are actively reinforcing the problem, individuals may be asked to make no attempt to avoid losing control or even asked to try to lose control. This reality-testing is aimed at disconfirming these threat-laden predictions and thus allows individuals the chance to reappraise the meanings they subscribe to their symptoms.

Understanding the theory also directly points towards the therapy, thus patients are also empowered by actively taking responsibility for change instead of being passively treated by the 'expert'. This highlights the importance of information provision inherent in the model. Thus the approach emphasises the importance of teaching new, and unlocking old, resources in the individual rather than providing professional 'expert' solutions.

A critical feature of 'Stress Control' is its positive emphasis on the building of strengths rather than the negative removal of weaknesses. Any therapy should actively reinforce the message of what individuals *can do* not what they *cannot*. I frequently find myself full of admiration for the individuals I see in the clinic who, although often badly afflicted by anxiety, can still achieve so much in their difficult daily lives. They continue to raise their families, work, look after neighbours, etc. despite all that life has thrown at them. Allowing the student to recognise these strengths rather than just their perceived failures can allow them to begin the process of personal reconceptualisation that can help anxiety and depression reduction.

PROVIDING A RATIONALE FOR THE APPROACH

The theoretical rationale

'Stress Control' therapy has been broadly developed within the cognitive–behavioural therapy (CBT) framework most associated with Beck (e.g. Beck *et al.*, 1985) and Meichenbaum (e.g. Meichenbaum, 1985). Evolving from neobehaviourism and social learning theory, CBT emphasises that learning is not a passive phenomenon but involves the active acquisition of complex skills; that thinking, behaviour, emotion and somatics are all causally related and that emotions such as anxiety result from our *perception* of the situation in which anxiety arises; i.e. cognitions may not cause the anxiety but play a powerful role in its maintenance. This suggests that an observer can only understand the anxiety of another by understanding the idiosyncratic meanings the individual ascribes to the situation. Meaning can only be understood within the context of that individual life, e.g. previously learned assumptions, attitudes and biological factors as they interact with the current situation.

In the context of anxiety, the important perceptions or interpretations relate to *danger*. Once a situation is perceived as dangerous, an 'anxiety programme' is activated involving autonomic arousal (fight/flight/freeze/faint)—to prepare to combat the danger; inhibition of ongoing behaviour and selective scanning for threat—to better concentrate on the danger, and to better understand and anticipate the nature of it. Focusing on the source of danger results in the enhancement of the threat and suppresses information incongruent with it. While this has good survival value when the danger is obvious, e.g. if threatened by an armed mugger, in clinical anxiety the perceptions are likely to be unrealistic and overestimations of the degree of danger inherent in a given situation. Clark and Beck (1988) list four errors involved in this:

- overestimating the probability of a feared event;
- overestimating the severity of the feared event;
- underestimating coping resources (what you can do to help);
- underestimating rescue factors (what others can do to help you).

These estimations relate to the underlying beliefs and assumptions (schemas) that activate the danger perceptions. These lead the individual to see danger in, to others, innocuous situations and increases the sense of vulnerability and lack of control in these situations. Perceptions lead to more anxiety, anxiety to more danger-related perceptions, until vicious circles help maintain the problems. In addition, the individual attempts to prevent feared outcomes by altering behaviour, e.g. carrying out certain rituals to avoid something terrible happening to loved ones, or sitting in the end seat in the back row of the cinema to make escape easier if necessary. These behaviours may lead to an immediate reduction in anxiety (thus reinforcing the action) but also stops the individual from testing the reality of his or her fears, e.g. nothing bad may happen in the absence of the ritual. The hyper-sensitivity in feared situations forces individuals to selectively attend to information that confirms their fears, e.g. in social phobia that everyone thinks they are boring after noticing someone in the group yawning. At the same time they are unable to look for alternative possibilities, e.g. the person is tired, the room is hot, others seem to be enjoying being with them.

While CBT is open to criticism with lack of clarity about its active ingre-dients and whether it is 'better' than other approaches, it provides a flexibility critical for running such a course. Recent work by Clark (1999) offers valuable insights into maintenance and treatment factors in the anxiety disorders.

The therapeutic rationale

No health care organisation will ever be able to afford to employ enough therapists to adequately meet the demand if one-to-one therapies continue to dominate. At this point, many therapists aim at a quality service— providing excellent treatment to a few while remaining virtually blind to the issue of quantity, i.e. offering at least some help to the vast majority who are currently deprived of access to a mental health professional. While this is a respectable approach, it neglects to take into account the facts, noted in Chapter 3, that one-to-one therapies in health care settings often fall far short of excellence and that other more cost-effective approaches may indeed enhance therapy effects rather than dilute them. Therapists must question whether the preservation of such sacred cows impedes the formation of better ways of working.

Therapists must not only look carefully at research findings and modify them to better meet the needs of these clinical populations but, if developing any new approach, look at these pragmatic issues and aim at what is possible. Clinicians should concentrate on their greatest asset—one given little importance in the research literature—extensive clinical experience that will have taught them how best to implement therapies and to motivate demoralised patients.

The preventative rationale: the river analogy revisited

Group work, although often still used downstream (White *et al.*, 1992, 1995), offers the possibility of working upstream where problems should be easier to treat. It can be aimed at preventing the individual falling in in the first place. Prevention of secondary disorders can also be seen within this rationale (Kessler and Price, 1993). Stopping the individual progressing downstream will, eventually, relieve pressure on the downstream service. Pragmatically, a course flexible enough to mix individuals at different stages of their journey downstream would best meet the manifold needs in primary care.

The social support rationale

Therapists perhaps overemphasise the importance of the therapeutic contact. To many patients, therapy may just be one small part of a hectic life. Once therapy ends, the world that may have caused and maintained the individual's problems may still exist. Offering therapy in a flexible evening class setting allows students to invite partners, friends or parents to accompany them. While lending some support if attendance alone would be too stressful, it offers the opportunity for the other person to learn more about the condition, to get on the same wavelength and to learn how to help the students in their quest to control the stress. Those accompanying the student may realise that coping strategies they are employing may be reinforcing problems. They may also, either as a result of living with the student or for other reasons, be under stress themselves and may wish to take part in self-help treatment. This may decrease stress levels at home, thus helping the student. Coyne *et al.* (1987) reported that 40% of adults living with a depressed individual were themselves distressed enough to meet a standardised criterion for referral for specialist help. Coyne emphasised the importance of seeing an individual's problems within a more generally distressed interpersonal context.

The relapse prevention rationale

Westbrook and Hill (1998) reported that 59% of patients given individual therapy in an NHS setting required further help following discharge (mainly medication and other GP help). Individuals may consider themselves failures for requiring further help. If they require further specialist help, re-referral is often time-consuming. Indeed, many GPs, aware of waiting times, may be reluctant to re-refer patients who are not exhibiting high levels of distress. However, it can be helpful for students who have a greater degree of self-knowledge to have the opportunity to return to the course before problems build up. The knowledge that the course is available at any time and that a return to it can be seen as a positive act that will be actively welcomed by the teacher may help reinforce students' sense of control.

The carousel rationale

Related to the above, many people seen in primary care cannot expect to fully get over their problems either because of social/family factors, personality factors, or simply because we know many anxiety disorder sufferers do not get significantly better with current treatments. Thus, the course can, when required, operate as a 'carousel' with students able to join and leave at any point and return to it at any stage in the future. The decision to return to the course for booster sessions to help cope with a difficult life must be seen as a positive one and not an admission of failure. This may be particularly relevant to those with problems relating to generalised anxiety disorder (GAD), a chronic problem often with repeated acute-on-chronic episodes (Lader, 1998).

The 'standing still' rationale

Most clinicians have, among their caseloads, long-term anxiety patients they have made no headway with but cannot discharge through fear of the consequences of leaving the individual with no mental health contact. Anxious individuals with particularly chaotic lives, perhaps those with secondary personality disorders, are frequently passed from clinician to clinician in primary care with no one making much of an impact. These individuals may use the course to make minor improvements in their lives or simply to help them keep their lives stable for a period of time. These individuals must be very carefully assessed to ensure they can benefit from the course and also that they will not prove to be a disruptive influence. The course should not be used as a 'dumping ground'.

The triage rationale

'Stress Control' is a straightforward approach using simplified cognitive–behavioural techniques. A teaching manual is available in the 'Stresspac' materials. Teaching is fully supported by teaching aids such as slides, handouts and, if required, videos. There seems no reason why such an approach need be carried out by a highly trained professional. Although no data exist as yet, future research will look at appropriately qualified therapists assessing suitable individuals for courses run by less qualified, less expensive teachers.

The economic rationale

Therapy, from a qualified therapist, is expensive. Turner *et al.* (1995), looking at a range of therapies used by US clinicians, quotes average costs of $2181 (range $700–6500) for GAD treatment and $4370 (range $1200-12,000) for obsessive-compulsive disorder (OCD). It is not clear if these include the costs of booster sessions (14 for GAD, 29 for OCD). These costs would seem to preclude the opportunity of therapy for people from the poorest sections of society where these problems may be particularly prevalent. In addition, in the USA, there is concern that some contracted provider organisations may be imposing as little as a four-visit limit as a result of cost-cutting measures by managed-care companies (American Psychological Association Monitor, 1998). Although not a good reason to choose one treatment method over another, pragmatically, managed-care companies, if they are influencing what treatment can be provided, may look more favourably at group approaches. There is some evidence that the new health care marketplace in the USA may place greater emphasis on therapies that can achieve both clinical and cost-effectiveness (American Psychological Association Monitor, 1999; Cummings, 1995).

In terms of organisational costs, clinicians in the NHS in Britain, aware of constant financial constraints, have generally looked at achieving the best compromise between quality of service and quantity of patients treated. Group work offers a clinically efficient approach.

The Greyhound bus rationale

Related to the above, many therapists strive to offer a Rolls-Royce service to patients in their journey from point A to point B. Whether it actually operates as a Rolls-Royce is very much open to debate but it does allow only a few to take the trip. The 'Stress Control' approach argues that a Greyhound bus, with significantly greater capacity, can travel the same route in much the same time, in reasonable comfort and at little expense. It also offers the opportunity of meeting many fellow passengers and the trip can be retaken with the minimum of fuss at any stage.

The choice rationale

Mental health providers should adopt a 'horses for courses' approach, recognising that people with similar mental health problems may prefer, and may benefit from, different treatment interventions. While the clinician should provide guidance as to what is appropriate, patients may benefit from having a menu of choice. In the British NHS such choice does not exist to any great extent. Previous work providing information about anxiety in local newspapers and public lectures on self-help approaches attracted a group of people who, although as severely anxious as a clinical population, did not want to receive individual treatment from the NHS. Instead they preferred to learn ways of coping themselves (White, 1992). This group, perhaps substantial (Jenkins *et al.*, 1998), may be more open to didactic self-help approaches.

The service development rationale

As argued previously, developing one part of the service has implications for all the other parts. By providing a high-volume didactic course for the most common problems referred to the service, scarce individual therapy time is released for those most in need of it. By reducing waiting lists (a highly likely consequence of providing such courses) all patients are seen and assessed earlier and appropriate help put in place. By relieving pressure to constantly 'do something' about the waiting list, stress is removed from clinicians, resulting in the luxury of greater time to stand back and think about further service developments.

DIAGNOSTIC ISSUES

The structure of the anxiety disorders

There is a clear dichotomy between research group trials that tend to concentrate on specific anxiety disorders rigorously diagnosed (e.g. Telch *et al.*, 1993) and uncontrolled clinical trials that tend to minimise the importance of specific anxiety disorder diagnosis (e.g. Ormrod, 1995). Group approaches can marry practical concerns, e.g. the ability to meet the requirements of as many patients as possible, with theoretical issues such as the importance of devising a method compatible with current knowledge on appropriate treatment. For the following theoretical and pragmatic reasons, 'Stress Control' accepts a wide range of problems.

A hierarchical model

Zinbarg and Barlow (1996) presented evidence suggesting that the question of whether anxiety is a unitary or multidimensional construct is overly simplistic. Taking a dimensional rather than categorical approach, they noted the existence of two structural levels in anxiety. One, a general higher-order factor named negative affectivity (NA), represented a trait diathesis common to all anxiety disorders (and perhaps also to major depression and dysthymia). This acts as a non-specific vulnerability factor. The second distinguished five lower-order factors (panic, agoraphobia, social anxiety, obsessions–compulsions and general anxiety) appearing to differentiate between the various anxiety disorders in the DSM system. Thus a hierarchical model is posited with NA acting as a general factor, with more specific factors giving rise to the various anxiety disorders. Identifying the various disorders will depend on finding the key feature resulting in different foci of anticipatory anxiety or worry. Similarly, Krueger *et al.* (1998), attempting to make greater sense of comorbidity findings, produced evidence of DSM disorders being reliable, covariant indicators of stable underlying 'core psychological processes', although their two-factor model, where some DSM disorders reflect both internalising and externalising problems, differs from Barlow's model.

Generalised anxiety

Rapee (1991a) noted that a trait construct, generalised anxiety (GA), is present in all individuals to a greater or lesser degree. High levels of GA will be a fundamental presenting characteristic found in all anxiety disorder sufferers, with the possible exception of specific phobia (Barlow and DiNardo, 1991). Rapee asserted that two basic constructs are likely to be important in the maintenance of high GA: biased perceptions of threat and general perceptions of uncontrollability.

Rapee viewed GAD as a relatively pure form of high GA with a probable large overlap. Thus GAD has been described as the 'basic' anxiety disorder (Rapee, 1991b) with anxious apprehension, the key diagnostic feature of GAD, serving as a vulnerability factor in the development of a wide range of emotional disorders. Anxious apprehension is defined as 'a future-orientated mood state (composed of primarily high negative affect) associated with a sense of uncontrollability, and a self-focused attentional shift. In other words . . . a state of persistent overarousal associated with a preparatory and hypervigilant style concerning negative events that one may or may not be able to cope with or control' (Brown and Barlow, 1992, p. 837). Within the anxiety disorders, anxious apprehension is ubiquitous, with the focus of apprehension varying from disorder to disorder, e.g. poor performance and negative evaluation in social phobia. Further support for this model was found by Brown *et al.* (1998), where GAD was shown to have the highest degree of overlap with other DSM-IV disorders and to have a strong correlation with the non-specific NA dimension. Related to this, Akiskal (1998) suggested that GAD is an exaggeration of a normal personality disposition that can be termed 'generalised anxious temperament'.

In addition, Barlow (1991) pointed to the core features of Panic Disorder similarly being present in all the anxiety disorders, with panic attacks occurring across the various anxiety and depressive disorders.

The tripartite model of anxiety and depression

Related to the above model, Clark and Watson (1991), in arguing for a new diagnostic category of mixed anxiety–depression, produced psychometric data supporting the view that the 'anxious and depressed syndromes share a significant non-specific component that encompasses general affective distress and other common symptoms, whereas these syndromes are distinguished by physiological hyperarousal (specific to anxiety) versus the absence of PA [positive affect] (specific to depression)' (p. 331). Brown et al. (1998) suggested that autonomic arousal may be limited mainly to panic disorder and agoraphobia, while GAD is characterised by motor rather than autonomic symptoms. However, this distinction is blurred as many GAD sufferers do have panic attacks but do not qualify for panic disorder (Sanderson and Barlow, 1990). In addition, the presence of negative affectivity, acting as a risk factor for both anxiety and depression, suggests poor prognosis for targeted treatments (Clark, L.A. et al., 1994). Several writers, assessing the temporal sequence of comorbid anxiety and depression, frequently find that anxiety disorders precede the onset of depression (e.g. Rohde et al., 1991; Alloy et al., 1990). These findings further strengthen the view of taking these shared commonalities into account in devising appropriate and robust treatments.

Treatment factors

Considering the above, any intervention based on tackling GA, NA and panic may result in a greater sense of personal control irrespective of the particular focus of that anxious apprehension. Drawing on the comorbidity literature discussed in Chapter 2, Brown and Barlow (1992) noted that learning coping skills in one major area, e.g. GAD, allows patients then to apply these skills to other anxiety (and other) disorder areas not specifically tackled by the intervention. In studying the higher-order NA trait, Brown and Barlow (1992) pointed to the significant overlap at the symptom level among the various anxiety disorders. Thus improvements in one disorder would probably lead, without specific targeting, to improvements in any other.

In addition, Borkovec et al. (1995) suggested that 'certain psychological processes may be basic to all emotional disorders even if secondary processes specific to different disorders exist. If this is the case then most anxiety and depression problems share, at a fundamental level, the same underlying psychological mechanism (or mechanisms): discrete, qualitatively different disorders with distinct aetiologies would not exist in the way implied by diagnostic systems. Treatments that affect basic mechanisms would impact on any disorder sharing that mechanism' (p. 482). Tackling the basic anxiety disorder—GAD—and, in particular, worry, may lead to more efficient emotional processing, resulting in the removal of a significant maintaining factor in anxiety and, thus, to the emergence of adaptive new learning (Borkovec, 1994). These views may help explain the findings that comorbid diagnoses often improve following treatment for another specific anxiety disorder (Borkovec *et al.*, 1995). In terms of NA, successful outcome may relate to the successful treatment of different features of an underlying syndrome or tacking processes common to all the various disorders.

Added to this, although specific techniques exist for all the anxiety disorders, there are clear overlaps between treatments as all tend to involve exposure either to internal or external anxiety-provoking situations and some form of cognitive restructuring tackling the overestimation of threat risk and catastrophic perceptions of the impact of feared events.

Anxiety disorders

For the reasons noted above, the 'Stress Control' course is regarded as particularly suitable to any patient with an identifiable anxiety disorder. The main exception is specific phobia as GA is unlikely to be present at a high level and for whom highly effective quick treatments already exist (Ost, 1989a). More problematic is OCD. Although in many ways similar to GAD, OCD is rarely found as a comorbid disorder with it (Brown, 1998). In the relative absence of worrying over minor matters, those with OCD have generally been excluded from 'Stress Control'. However, as all the anxiety disorders may share the same diathesis (e.g. biological or trait vulnerabilities), it may be worthwhile to research this area.

Other diagnostic groups

Although no research data are available, it seems plausible to include individuals with both mixed anxiety–depression and mild/moderate depressive conditions but only where anxiety also plays a prominent role. A wide range of adjustment disorders, very commonly found at the primary care level but often not referred for specialist mental health care, are suitable for the course.

Individuals not meeting Axis I diagnostic criteria

Although diagnostic information is an important factor in determining who should be given a place on the course, other factors should be taken into account. As mentioned previously, heterogeneity is the rule in most mental health primary care settings.

Axis II disorders

While the 'Stress Control' course should never be used for individuals with primary cluster A and B personality disorders, many individuals with cluster C disorders are likely to present to primary care clinics (and frequently attend their GP). Those with dependent and avoidant disorders in particular may be appropriate for the course. Realistic expectations of the likely degree of change should be clearly given before the course.

Axis III disorders

Primary care therapists are likely to see many individuals with problems thought to have a strong psychological component referred either by the GP or directly from outpatient medical clinics. For example, individuals with irritable bowel syndrome, a condition often found with GAD (Tollefson *et al.*, 1991) are often referred to 'Stress Control' as part of their treatment—similarly, those suffering from serious medical conditions that are highly likely to cause psychological distress, e.g. cancer, diabetes, coronary disease or those awaiting an operation for a life-threatening condition. While specialised counselling may be available at the hospital (see Mostofsky and Barlow, 2000) such individuals can often benefit from more generalised stress management techniques.

Axis IV disorders

A large group of individuals present with realistic stress problems and who want to find better ways of coping with them. Recent examples include a single parent dealing with a child with spina bifida, an individual going through bankruptcy proceedings, a woman looking after her husband who has advanced Alzheimer's and a man awaiting trial and possible imprisonment.

In addition, many people in the socially deprived area where I work have to cope with daily difficulties/dangers, e.g. fear of going outside because of physical threats, living in overcrowded, poorly constructed housing, trying to raise their families on welfare, or engaged in insecure, poorly paid, menial jobs offering no sense of satisfaction or achievement. Options for change for these people are generally severely limited. As with those individuals noted above, in the absence of or in addition to any more pertinent help, they often report that attending the course was appropriate and useful. In these cases, the aim is not necessarily to reduce symptoms but to help them cope more effectively with stressors that will remain in their daily lives.

The course used as an adjunct to individual therapy

Some patients may benefit both from attending the course and, simultaneously attending for individual therapy. An individual with post-traumatic stress disorder could attend the course for help with the increased arousal symptoms, for example, while individual therapy time could concentrate on more focal aspects of the condition, for example, the re-experiencing of, and avoidance of stimuli associated with, the trauma. This would help save therapy time and, thus, increase scarce individual therapy time for others who need it. Any individual with a severe anxiety or mood disorder and alcohol dependence, for example, could attend for both group and individual approaches.

The courses may be an appropriate adjunctive therapy to drug and possibly individual cognitive approaches for those suffering from a psychotic disorder. Moorey and Soni (1994) note that 40% of those with a stable, chronic schizophrenic disorder showed heightened incidence of anxiety symptoms. With some evidence that anxiety may precede an acute exacerbation (Herz and Melville, 1980), this approach, offered at the appropriate time, may help the individual to better cope with the psychotic condition. A recent example involved a man suffering from reasonably controlled manic depression with secondary severe panic disorder. He found the sense of uncontrollability during the panic particularly frightening as he feared he would lapse back into a psychotic state as a result. Attending the course allowed him greater insight into the nature of panic, allowing him to see it as a separate condition amenable to control using the skills taught on the course. Care must be taken as information on the course will look at the differences between mental illness and stress. The individual should be aware of this in advance.

Clinical judgement

As clinicians, we see the person sitting with us as an individual, not as a walking diagnosis. Recalling diagnostic issues noted in Chapter 2, caution must be applied in treatment allocation. While the course may be suitable for many people, with GAD, for example, some people with this diagnosis may not be suitable and some may not want to attend such a course. Clinical judgement is obviously important in this. It is crucial to have alternative approaches available with clinician and patient discussing treatment options fully.

THERAPY ISSUES

The flexibility of CBT

While CBTs are often impressive, they are far from offering a panacea (Chambless and Gillis, 1993). How far the reasonably impressive results are produced by the specific techniques employed and how much by non-specific factors is still open to debate (e.g. Jacobson *et al.*, 1996). However, there are three major advantages associated with CBT. One is that the theory and therapy are open to hypothesis testing. As a result CBT has developed faster than any other major therapeutic approach and continues to make inroads into areas of human distress previously not felt to respond to psychological approaches. The second advantage is that developments can be readily taught to clinicians. The third advantage, still relatively untested, may be the malleability of the approach allowing clinicians to stretch and modify research centre approaches to better meet the daily demands in the clinical setting.

A good example of these factors can be seen in the treatment of panic. We have rapidly moved from seeing medication as the main treatment for panic to a position where psychological approaches (where available) now dominate. British cognitive–behavioural researchers, in particular, have striven to develop techniques that are not only therapeutically successful but also are robust enough to move from the research centre into routine clinical treatment where time considerations are of great importance. For example, Clark *et al.* (1999) report on reducing the number of sessions required for successful treatment of (clinically representative) panic disorder with agoraphobia from between 12–15 sessions down to six. Having developed their treatment, they then offered workshops across the country allowing clinicians to quickly implement their approach in routine clinical settings. We must apply some caution to how well cognitive therapy works, however. Barlow (1997) notes that while 75% of his sample were panic free at two years follow-up, only 21% met his most stringent criteria at this stage (high endstate functioning at three months and 24 months follow-up, no panics in the last year and no further treatment).

Wells (1997) offers a detailed practice and conceptual guide to cognitive therapy of the anxiety disorders.

Clinical efficiency

To maximise efficiency, entry into the group should be open to as large a number of patients as possible. In typical outpatient settings where heterogeneity of referral type is the norm, this suggests that such an approach should be capable of helping patients with a wide range of emotional disorders at differing levels of severity. In addition to the large number of anxiety disorder sufferers reported in Chapter 2 who are unable, for one reason or another, to receive appropriate treatment, there is a need to consider other evidence also presented in earlier chapters. This evidence suggested that about half of all panic disorder sufferers have some sort of anxiety present for many years prior to meeting criteria for diagnosis (Eaton *et al.*, 1998) and that anxiety disorders often precede depression (Rohde *et al.*, 1991). Evidence from primary care settings suggested that almost half of those patients diagnosed as having common mental health problems showed a fluctuating course over an 11-year follow-up period. These patients also had a significantly higher mortality rate, from natural causes, than would be expected (Lloyd *et al.*, 1996). Early intervention with such individuals may prevent the development of serious disorders. Only services capable of handling large numbers of sufferers can hope to work, simultaneously at these different levels.

Thus flexibility must be a key constituent. The group should be easily set up and capable of running frequently in order to provide appropriate help as quickly as possible. As numbers of referrals and referral types can show significant variation across time, the approach should be capable of being run with varying numbers. Most importantly, in view of many people's lack of enthusiasm for group approaches in many cultures, it must have a good deal of face validity and appear to be within individuals' capabilities. It must run at convenient times. These issues are looked at below.

Group size

Most group approaches involve relatively small numbers—usually between six and 10. One significant problem with such groups relates to failure to attend or drop-out. While factors such as poor 'selling' may be involved, a significant problem is likely to be the reluctance on the part of often highly self-conscious individuals to disclose personal information to strangers.

Schiff and Glassman (1969) showed that psychodynamically orientated groups with fewer than six members have a greater degree of intimacy and involve more face-to-face interaction. In larger groups, less face-to-face interaction and more structured leadership emerges. In theory this is more conducive not only to didactic anxiety management but to the provision of more acceptable group work with patients who are likely to find such formats threatening due to their anxious cognitions relating to social competence, self-consciousness, etc.

Any group approach would also benefit from the non-specific effects suggested by Powell (1987) and Ormrod (1995)—the opportunity for observational learning, modelling, social reinforcement or being in a group and meeting others with similar problems—the 'all in the same boat' phenomenon. Large group work would, if anything, optimise such factors. Self-reappraisal from a belief that 'I am the only one, I am a failure' to a more appropriate set of cognitions is more likely being in a group of 30 individuals comprising both men and women from a wide age range, from different backgrounds and with different personalities whose only common denominator is that they suffer from an anxiety problem.

With over 70 groups run, my view is that size does not matter. While larger groups—50 plus—function well as didactic therapy, smaller groups of 6–10, offering a greater chance of interaction if required, also work well. Thus only the size of the room should determine the upper limit of group numbers.

Cultural factors

'Stress Control' was designed initially for a Scottish population, who are, on the whole, imbued with a Calvinistic hue that emphasises self-reliance. Scots, largely, dislike personal disclosure but like the idea of self-improvement and self-help. Thus traditional disclosure group therapy will often present problems in Scotland and other countries whose cultures incline against public self-disclosure and the display of emotion, e.g. some other parts of Britain, the Scandinavian countries and in the USA, Canadian provinces and other countries, e.g. Australia and New Zealand, heavily settled by people from these cultures. This may also apply to countries with different cultures but similar disinclination towards personal disclosure, e.g. Korea and other Asian countries. Although there may be therapeutic advantages in helping individuals discuss problems in a group, if they fail to appear in the first place not only will they miss this opportunity but also it may dissuade them from seeking any other psychological approach.

Micro-cultural factors

Personal disclosure is often strongly discouraged in areas of high social deprivation. In particular, working-class men, often having to live in macho micro-cultures, are often unwilling to admit to 'failings'. Stigma towards 'mental illness' is greatest among those of a lower educational level and social class (Hayward and Bright, 1997), while low household income and negative treatment attitudes were found to be the best predictors of attrition in panic treatment (Grilo et al., 1998). Others may feel they lack the verbal skills or social etiquette to take part in such a group. Even if they are prepared to attend such a group, there may be little face validity to such approaches as individuals may feel they have already talked about their problems to no avail.

The issue of personal disclosure

In problems as heterogeneous as anxiety and depression, failure to identify may also be a problem. In order to get them to the first session, individuals must feel convinced that the approach meets their requirements and that they have the necessary personal resources to handle the group. This has implications both for the contents and structure of the course and, as a first goal, how to persuade individuals that this is an appropriate therapy.

'Stress Control' is thus 'sold' as a purely didactic approach that not only does not require personal disclosure but also actively prohibits it. This can help control the problem of individuals dominating the proceedings and pushing their own agenda. Seating arrangements (see Chapter 8) and teaching style are designed to reinforce this. The decision to teach in this way does not simply reflect a negative decision, i.e. to avoid drop-out but a positive one. Coming to a class (not a therapy) to learn self-management skills is seen as a positive step for the majority of individuals with these anxiety conditions. There is also an implicit message from the teacher that he/she believes individuals are capable of taking personal control of their treatment. This may help them develop a sense of active 'ownership' over the therapy and help them take immediate responsibility for change.

The importance of flexibility

Therapists working in different cultures with different needs should use the framework of the approach but alter it to better meet those needs. In cultures where personal disclosure is encouraged, inhibiting this may be detrimental to outcome. Due to the amount of material to be worked on each session, a balance must be struck between the extent of discussion time and the extent of time devoted to the strategies. However, from experience, the approach is malleable enough to allow this. Recent data from Oxford, England, suggests that individuals did not want a purely didactic approach and felt better being able to discuss personal problems within the group format. Treatment outcome and degree of satisfaction at post-therapy were virtually identical to Scottish data (personal communications, Westbrook and Butler, July 1998 and February 1999).

The therapeutic relationship

Although cognitive–behavioural approaches regard the active sharing of responsibility between patient and therapist as an essential requirement of the therapeutic relation, it seems likely that, as noted in Chapter 2, in practice some patients, often from a different social class and being treated in an environment designed to reinforce traditional 'doctor–patient' relationships, adopt a more passive role that may inhibit them from actively trying out different approaches as it may be seen as going against 'doctor's orders'. The didactic set-up actively encourages students to evaluate the course contents in light of their own needs and, with encouragement, develop their own personal strategies as well as working on the most appropriate techniques taught on the course. This aids a more flexible response to the course and allows more idiosyncratic problems to be tackled by the individual, thus reinforcing self-perceptions of improved coping and control.

The balance of power

Traditional group therapy is likely to prove threatening, at least initially, to participants. The therapist is likely to be perceived to be in firm control of proceedings. In didactic group work, this balance is vitally altered. A large number of students, sitting in a phalanx in front of the teacher, may feel the balance of control is in their favour, with the set-up designed to have the teacher prove his/her worth. With the confidence that this set-up will not change, students may be able to relax and begin to feel themselves learning to control a situation that will probably have caused them much anxiety. This initial exposure to the course may, in itself, be therapeutic.

Releasing personal coping strategies

In many cases, students may already have effective, if idiosyncratic, coping strategies available to them. These strategies may be dormant due to lack of confidence or control (or, at the other extreme, excessive control) to bring them into play. By encouraging students to adopt a flexible approach to the management of their problems, they may feel encouraged to again try these approaches. This time, with a greater understanding of emotional disorders and the factors maintaining them, they may be able to more effectively and consistently employ these strategies. Any positive feedback from their implementation will lead to further confidence to explore old or new strategies while, at the same time, releasing inappropriate coping strategies.

Time-of-day factors

Running the course in the evening allows it to be sold as an 'evening class', with its positive connotations of self-help and which many people may already have experience of. This may be preferable to attending a 'group therapy' with all its negative connotations. This reduces stigma and reinforces the didactic nature of the approach. Evening sessions are easier for most individuals to attend. Running from 7 to 9 p.m. allows most people to return home from work but not too late for people to catch buses, etc. Some students may, however, be apprehensive about walking home in high-crime areas in the evening. It may be easier to arrange baby-sitters in the evening as partners etc. may be more readily available. In addition, the character of health centres and other settings is subtly different at night. There are no receptionists to get past and there is less likelihood of ongoing activity likely to fortify traditional behaviours in such settings. On the practical side, it also allows the use of large waiting rooms with comfortable seats and kitchen facilities. The absence of other patient groups, office staff, doctors etc. allows a more informal atmosphere to be built upon. Use of music etc. helps reinforce this.

Economic factors

Apart from the clinical effectiveness issues noted above, the larger the group, the more clinically efficient the approach as the teacher's time will be the same. As funding will be required to buy course materials, managers may look favourably at an approach that can be shown to be clinically efficient in this way. In private practice, larger groups should allow costs for each individual to be reduced.

Number of teachers

Much of the early work on 'Stress Control' was carried out with two teachers (JW and Mary Keenan-Ross). The advantages of two (or more) teachers relate to sharing the stress of running such groups, allowing each to develop areas of expertise within the model and, possibly, keep students' interest as speakers change during the session. Having an experienced teacher working alongside a novice teacher may be a useful training approach.

Advantages of having one teacher include a greater degree of ownership over the course that may help the teacher to maintain concentration and interest. It improves clinical efficiency, while the lack of a safety net, in the form of another teacher, should help keep a tense, creative edge on performance. Having worked in, and enjoyed, both approaches, my preference is now for single-teacher work. It also allows the teacher, using clinical experience, to depart from the script when appropriate. Improvising in this way can sometimes 'throw' a less experienced co-teacher.

Terminology

The course is called 'Stress Control', although targeted principally at the anxiety disorders. Although purists may quibble, I use the terms 'stress' and 'anxiety' interchangeably. The older definitions clearly separating anxiety and stress treatment seem to be falling out of favour. Lehrer and Woolfolk's (1993) *Principles and Practice of Stress Management* (2nd edition) contains the main techniques used in the course: progressive relaxation, Beck's cognitive therapy and Meichenbaum's Stress Inoculation Training. My preference for *Stress Control* instead of *Anxiety Control* stems from clinical experience in Scotland suggesting that the term 'anxiety' attracts the greater stigma, while 'stress management' fits better with a self-help approach. 'Stress' appears a more 'solid' term and, thus, more capable of change, whereas 'anxiety' appears to suggest something within the individual, a trait-based phenomenon less open to change.

The next chapter looks at how to set up the course.

Chapter 5

SETTING UP A COURSE

INTRODUCTION

This chapter looks at the setting up of a didactic course. It pays particular attention to the assessment interview, during which the rationale of the approach is described to the individual. The chapter divides into nine: assessment issues; the assessment interview; introducing the course; questions; the key messages; is an assessment interview necessary?; special circumstances; spouse/partner/friends; and conclusions.

ASSESSMENT ISSUES

Obtaining sufficient referrals

Courses can be widely advertised. Where the teacher works within a large organisation, e.g. the British NHS, GPs can be informed about the course and about suitable referrals. GPs can be contacted with dates and asked to refer large numbers in the month prior to the course. A dedicated teacher could seek referrals from colleagues working within the same area in the same way. A range of therapists could take turns to run such courses, with colleagues referring appropriate students. Information about forthcoming courses can be given through the local media or the Internet. From experience, once a course becomes established, students recommend the approach to their GP and friends/relatives, hence stimulating referrals.

Who should assess?

Any mental health professional who has experience of anxiety assessment and treatment should be suitable to assess. This is likely to include clinical, counselling, occupational and health psychologists, psychiatrists, social workers, psychiatric nurses, counsellors and other professionals who have additional training in anxiety, e.g. GPs and occupational therapists.

Unpublished data from my clinic suggest that attendance at the first session is more likely if the assessor and course teacher are the same individual. It is plausible that the prospect of entering a group of strangers is made more easy by knowing that at least one known face will be there. Given many people's concerns at seeing a mental health professional, a positive relationship formed at the first interview with the teacher may make attendance at the course more likely. It may also be that the ideas behind the course are explained better by those who have most knowledge of it. In practical terms, referrals to the course from various sources will allow groups to be run on a regular basis. If various therapists work together, time should be spent together looking at these issues.

THE ASSESSMENT INTERVIEW

Anxiety Disorder Interview Schedule

In a busy primary care setting, time is not available to carry out a thorough assessment using one of the structured interview formats. However, if the therapist does not have sufficient clinical experience to quickly assess anxiety, it may be useful to use the Anxiety Disorder Interview Schedule (ADIS). This semi-structured schedule was developed by David Barlow (now at Boston University) and colleagues at the Center for Stress and Anxiety Disorders, New York State University at Albany. The current version (ADIS-IV, Brown *et al.*, 1994) has been developed for use with the *Diagnostic and Statistical Manual* (4th edition)—DSM-IV (American Psychiatric Association, 1994). The assessment is thorough but time-consuming and allows the therapist to either carry out a current diagnostic interview or, in a longer version, to look at lifetime diagnoses (DiNardo *et al.*, 1994). If the therapist aims to publish, use of this tool would be of great value.

Routine clinical assessment

The ADIS is too time-consuming to be used in routine clinical practice. An experienced clinician should, in any case, be able to quickly pinpoint the salient features of the presenting problem and to formulate a diagnostic and treatment package. My current practice is to offer individuals a 40-minute assessment: 30 minutes to assess the problem and 10 minutes to discuss the course. Those with more complex presentations will be asked to attend for further individual assessment or where there is the suspicion that the individual is unable to discuss other problems, e.g. sexual abuse. Assessment revolves around a three-systems analysis (e.g. Rachman, 1978), where cognition, somatic and behavioural aspects are assessed. Reaching a DSM diagnosis is regarded as less important than obtaining a fuller dimensional view of the individual's problems. Time should also be spent looking at other factors that may exacerbate the condition, e.g. long-term unemployment, financial difficulties, poor housing, physical illness, and family difficulties such as poor marital relationships, alcohol/drug abuse in family members, etc. These factors may inhibit the degree of treatment success as they often cannot be removed.

INTRODUCING THE COURSE

In settings where such courses run routinely, many individuals will already have been told about it by previous attendees or the referring agent. Where options exist, the therapist should offer the individual information on all possible therapy options along with a clinical judgement as to what is most appropriate. If the course is seen as an appropriate approach by both, detailed information should be given about it at the assessment interview. There should be no sense of coercion and individuals should leave the session feeling that they have made a positive choice to attend rather than accepting a place simply because the therapist recommends it.

'Group therapy' versus 'evening class'

The therapist may have to overcome certain obstacles, e.g. the individual may immediately, on hearing that others will be present, assume they will have to discuss personal problems in front of them. While in some cultures this may be seen as a positive, in others it will deter many from attending because of factors noted in the previous chapter. In my own work, I avoid the term 'group therapy', preferring 'evening class', with its perceived emphasis on learning. The possible large numbers of people on the course should be described as a positive. The boxes below offer a suggested script from my large group approach.

DESCRIBING THE COURSE

'Let me make a suggestion about how you could get on top of this problem. I run an evening class for people who are under stress and who want to learn ways of controlling that stress. They will all have their own particular problems but what they will have in common are problems relaxing, worrying too much, losing self-confidence. Maybe they are avoiding doing things because of stress, maybe they will have sleeping problems and maybe they will have some depression. Some will have panic attacks. In general, they will feel that they are not in control of their life as much as they would like. As this is a very common problem, the course attracts large numbers—there will probably be anything between 30 and 50 other people on the course—all of whom have similar problems to you. No one on the course is mentally ill. Everyone is there because they want to learn how to control things a bit better.'

My own experience of 'Stress Control' in the 1980s was to spend considerable time in discussing the approach before individuals were satisfied that it was suitable. In the 1990s, there has been an accelerating trend for individuals to be immediately enthusiastic about such an approach whether or not they had heard of it or not.

HOW THE COURSE WORKS (THE JIGSAW ANALOGY)

'The course runs on Monday evenings from 7 p.m. to 9 p.m. in the Health Centre. The most important thing to remember is that it is an *evening class*, not a *group therapy*. That means we don't sit in a circle and no one talks about personal problems. Not many people around here would want to do that. It is much more practical. We use the big waiting room you have just come from. All the chairs face the front like in a classroom. I am at the front teaching you all about stress and how to tackle it.'

'Each of the six sessions is like one piece of a jigsaw. Your job is to sit back, take in what I am talking about, fit it around your own problems, go off and work at the technique I will teach you. You come back the next week, learn the next step, go off and work at it and so on until, at the end of the course, you can put all the pieces of the jigsaw together to see the full picture.'

From experience, as soon as individuals are assured that they do not have to talk on the course, they begin to look for the positive reasons for attending rather than looking for reasons for not attending. However, further information is now required before the individual can make an informed choice.

'The first session is easiest. All that happens is that I will talk about stress in some detail. We will look at how and why it affects your thoughts, body and actions. We will look at some of the myths about stress and look at what causes it and what keeps it going. This is a very important part as the more you understand stress, the better you can fight back—it's like "know your enemy".'

'Once we do this, you will learn ways to relax yourself, ways to control worry and unpleasant thoughts and how to face up to stress. Later in the course, we look at controlling panic attacks, how to sleep better and how to control depression. The main aim of the course is to turn you into your own therapist so that you feel confident going off at the end of the course, knowing that you now have the weapons to fight stress. That will serve you well in the future. It is a very straightforward approach. I think this is what you need right now. How do you feel about it?'

Individuals should be encouraged to present their own views on the course. The therapist should obviously answer any questions fully (see the questions asked by individuals, below) and deal with any other considerations that the therapist or individual feel should be voiced at this stage. These might include practical issues such as childminding provision or, with shift workers, getting time off work to attend. If the individual wishes to attend at this point, further information is given.

'The next course is x days/weeks away but I think we should start tackling these problems straight away. Here is a copy of the book that goes with the course. The book will tell you all about stress—you should see yourself in there. It will also tell you exactly what happens in each session, so there are no surprises—we strictly follow what is in the book. I want you to read this book over carefully several times. Most people who are stressed find that their concentration isn't good. So read it at your own pace. Feel free to write on it or to highlight or mark particular bits if you want to—it's yours now.

'Along with this general information, you should start to gather more information about the way stress affects you. You can do this by filling out the various forms that come with it. These will help you stand back from the stress and maybe make more sense of it. As soon as you do this, you are starting to take control back, so it is important that you think carefully about this. You should discuss your answers with those close to you and listen to what they think—their views might be helpful. Everything is in your folder—read the *"Please read this first"* handout and it will set the scene for you. Now let's talk about how you feel about this now.'

Before ending the session, some expectation, gleaned from the assessment, should be given to the individual. As, in routine clinical practice, the clinician is likely to see people with many different needs, different approaches are necessary. Some of the more common are listed below.

---

1. 'Now it seems that you have always been a stressful person—you told me you are a born worrier, is that right? Well, you can't change your nature completely, and did you notice that this course is called "Stress Control" and not "Stress Cure"? That is because you should aim to control it better rather than get rid of it. That would be asking too much of you. Even so, this problem is making your life miserable just now, so getting a better grip on it will make a great difference to you.'

2. 'Now you said that stress has never been a great problem to you until all these events in your life over the last year. Now that these events are under control, you should be aiming to get back to your old self. Your old nature is still there but it is being held down by all this stress. Use the course to push the stress away and let your old self bounce back up again.'

3. 'You have explained that there are very stressful things still going on in your life. You have to be realistic about this. No wonder you are stressed out. Anyone else in your shoes would feel the same. However, the course will help teach you ways to dampen down the stress and make it a bit easier to cope with it all.'

4. 'You have given me a good description of how stress has come and gone throughout your life and that this is one of your good spells. You should come and do the course to learn ways of preventing or, at least, controlling, future episodes of stress. You have identified the pattern yourself so you are already over the first hurdle. Come and learn ways of coping with all the others.'

5. 'We will tackle some parts of your main problem—the depression—with individual therapy but, at the same time, you will come along to the course to learn ways of controlling the anxiety side that makes things worse. The two approaches will go hand in hand. We will be hitting this problem from two angles at the same time. The course will help the individual therapy and vice versa.'

6. 'You have told me how difficult it can be for you to get through life and that from time to time everything just gets on top of you. Use "Stress Control" as a good support for you. It can help you handle things a bit better, and maybe when things get really tough it might be enough to help you stay more in control.'

Finally, information about what is expected of the individual should be given.

'The main thing to remember is that "Stress Control" has to be given top priority in your life from now on. There are no miracle cures for stress. The course will put you on the right lines by teaching you how to tackle stress. However, it is only with very hard work during and, especially, after the course that you will benefit from what you learn. If you are not prepared to do this, you should not come to the course as you will be wasting your time. I can't offer you a guarantee but I know that with hard work your chances of gaining more control are greatly increased. So finally, if there is anything that you are not sure about or anything you don't like the sound of, please let me know. OK, well I look forward to seeing you again in x days time.'

Individuals should leave the assessment session knowing exactly what the course entails, why it is suitable for them and what is expected of them. They should be given all the course materials at this point so that they can start the self-assessment and education process. Any individuals who do not want to commit themselves should be asked to read over the course material, talk it over with those close to them and contact you with a decision. Any individual who does not want to attend should now be offered alternative help.

QUESTIONS

The following are questions that are commonly asked during the assessment interview.

Question: What if I meet someone I know?
Answer: This is perfectly possible. You have a very common problem. Many of your neighbours will have similar problems. If you do meet people you know then they are here for the same reason as you. As we don't discuss personal problems on the course, you will not learn why he/she is here unless the two of you want to talk it over.

This has never, as far as I am aware, caused problems. Two sisters met on a course. Both were initially embarrassed but quickly realised that it was silly that they had been unable to discuss their problems with each other and offer support. They felt meeting at the course had had a positive effect for both of them. Working in an area where many men work(ed) in the same shipyard, frequent meetings take place. The most common reaction is one of relief, particularly where men, growing up in a very macho culture, feel reassured at seeing other 'hard' men complaining of similar problems. Unlike individual therapy in my service, the course usually comprises equal numbers of men and women, probably because men feel more comfortable in this setting.

A less happy meeting occurred where a woman realised that a woman who had had an affair with her husband was also on the course. She was distressed and told me this at the end of the first session. She had been avoiding going to a range of places in case she saw this woman who had caused her so much hurt. Immediate individual therapy was offered and accepted. However, the woman phoned me the following day to say that she wanted to stay on the course as it was exactly what she wanted and did not feel it was right to deprive herself of 'Stress Control'. She would ignore the woman but felt that, instead of running away, facing the hurt caused by her would, in the long run, help her. Both women finished the course. The first reported feeling much better not only because of the course but because she had faced this problem and felt she could move on from it. She now felt no fear, e.g. in the shopping centre in case she saw the other woman. The second woman also felt she benefited from the course although never mentioned any problems!

Question: What if I am not better at the end of the course?
Answer: 'Stress Control' is a training course, not a therapy course. This means that what you are doing over the next few weeks is learning a great deal about stress and how to tackle it. That doesn't mean you will actually be able to do it. You are learning new skills and getting rid of old habits. Both will take time. Think of learning to drive. At the end of the course, you have just passed your driving test. You still have a lot to learn. It will be some time before you feel that you are a good driver. That is what happens on the course. So don't worry if you are not better in such a short time. Work out what you feel you can reasonably achieve. Be patient.

The research data suggest that most individuals do make often substantial progress during the course (see Chapter 17). However, significant change is also likely to occur in the months following the course. The idea of the training course is central to 'Stress Control'. Hence sustained individual work following the course is crucial if long-term improvement is to be achieved. The idea of a negative expectation can also be helpful. If students believe they are doing better than the teacher expected them to do, they may gain greater confidence in working at the approach. As a result, they may develop a greater degree of personal control over their problems.

Question: What if I can't talk in front of all these people?
Answer: You will not speak in front of anyone. You are free to ask questions or make comments but I do not allow anyone to discuss personal problems. Very few would come back for the next session if they had to talk openly. So I am not going to point at anyone and ask them how they are feeling. 'Stress Control' has been designed as a practical course. We have a lot of work to get through. I want you to think a lot about how to tackle your problems and, if possible, talk to those close to you. You don't have to talk on the course in order to feel better.

Experience from over 70 such courses suggests that, for the first few sessions, no one asks questions or comments. As the course progresses, people relax, feel more in control of the process and questions and comments are made more frequently. Often questions directed towards me are picked up by other students and a discussion takes place. Individuals will pinpoint advantages or difficulties and possible solutions to difficulties. Whenever possible, I do not contribute to these discussions as I have often felt this to be a defining point on the course with 'ownership' of the course and therapy now clearly in the hands of the students and not the teacher. While the teacher's clinical skill will be helpful in reaching these points, my experience has been that they cannot be artificially produced but rather appear when the group is ready.

Question: Will the other people on the course be like me?
Answer: Stress never affects two people in the same way but you will have a lot in common. No one is mentally ill. You all have too much of a perfectly normal emotion and we are aiming to bring it down to more reasonable levels. You will find people from all backgrounds—some are old, some young; some outgoing, some shy; some tall, some short. Stress affects anyone and everyone. There is nothing special about you.

One interesting meeting concerned a middle-aged woman who approached me during the break to say that she had just been talking to the man sitting next to her, a young policeman. She expressed astonishment that a policeman could experience a problem she had previously only associated with 'middle-aged housewives, like me'. I told her that police officers frequently attended the course. The woman later told me that this single piece of information possibly did more to help her reconceptualise anxiety than anything else she learned on the course.

Question: What if I make a fool of myself?
Answer: How many times do you think you are going to make a fool of yourself and how often do you make a fool of yourself? I know it is a common fear in stress but the course is very down to earth. You will quickly find that you are in control of the situation. You just sit there—I'm the one who is more likely to make a fool of myself.

Such Socratic questioning can be useful at this stage. As would be expected from clinical experience, although anticipatory anxiety is high, actual exposure or reality testing often results in coping, not failure, particularly when individuals know, from reading the course materials and from the assessment interview, exactly what they are coming to.

Question: What if have a panic attack?
Answer: If you note a pattern of panics in busy situations, then you should look at ways of preventing the panic. Remember everyone on the course is

in the same boat. Everyone will be anxious when they first come in. They know what you are going through. Maybe sitting near the door would help for the first session. Feel free to go out and get a breath of fresh air at any time. Use some of the distraction techniques in the book. If it is any help, many people have voiced the same fear to me, yet no one has ever panicked on the course.

As with the previous question, with over 2000 individuals having gone through a 'Stress Control' course, no one has ever suffered a panic attack or, as far as I am aware, felt they made a fool of themselves. Knowing, in advance, of 'rescue factors' such as the freedom to leave the room at any time also helps in the first few sessions.

Question: What if I'm not clever enough to understand it?
Answer: Don't worry—you're clever enough. A bigger problem is concentration. You wouldn't believe how poor we are at remembering what is said to us in settings like this. I don't expect anyone to remember even half of what I say each night. That is why you have the book to remind you. You will find the actual information straightforward but some of the therapies might not make sense to you immediately. Don't worry—if you keep at it, it will soon become clear. Most people who do this course find that they have more ability and resources than they think. I think you will feel the same.

While 'Stress Control' materials and the teaching approach are easily understood (see Chapter 6), there may be a problem in socially deprived areas with literacy problems. There are plans to look at audio or video versions of the written materials to ensure that the widest possible range of anxiety sufferers can attend. An example of this is a current project investigating an audio self-help version in Punjabi for those who cannot read Urdu or English.

Question: How many???? (if running a large group)
Answer: And you thought you were the only one! It just shows you how common stress is. The only reason there aren't more people is that I couldn't fit them into the room. When you come to the course, just take a look around you at all the others. They come from all walks of life yet are complaining about the same thing. If you think you are the only one who is anxious, just remember, that is what they are all thinking about themselves.

Group size should always be seen as a positive. The smaller group allows greater involvement and concentration on personal problems; the larger group allows a reconceptualisation of the problems from 'I'm the only one' to 'I have a very common problem' (see Chapter 8).

THE KEY MESSAGES

'Stress Control' has seven key messages that students must understand and accept in order to provide a coherent framework for the course.

The causes of your stress are likely to be complex and subtle. It is likely to have been caused by more than one factor. Common interactive factors include:

- biological factors;
- childhood experience;
- life events.

It may not be possible to go beyond a general understanding of the causes in your own case. Of greater importance are the factors that keep it going.

The reason anxiety remains a problem in your life is because it has formed a vicious circle:

- Your anxious thoughts feed your anxious actions.
- Your anxious actions feed your anxious body.
- Your anxious body feeds your anxious thoughts.

This vicious circle goes round and round and round, slowly pulling more problems into it. This is the main reason your problems are unlikely to go away by themselves.

There may be other vicious circles of associated problems that feed into the main circle, so:

- depression feeds anxiety feeds depression;
- insomnia feeds anxiety feeds insomnia;
- panic feeds anxiety feeds panic.

These cannot be seen as separate problems.

You will learn not simply to break down the vicious circle involving thoughts, actions and body but replace it with a positive circle (Figure 5.1).

If we simply get rid of a problem, we leave a void which anxiety could fill at a later date. Building a positive circle where positive thoughts feed positive actions feed a positive body means that any well-being you attain feeds itself. This can leave you better equipped to deal with future, inevitable, stresses.

You will learn to break down the vicious circles involving the associated problems (if you have them) and to replace them with positive circles.

Although tackling the main vicious circle may be sufficient, tackling the other problems will speed progress and also help protect you in the future.

How your stress is feeding itself now: the vicious circle

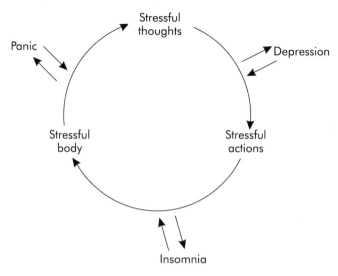

How to stay on top of stress: the positive circle

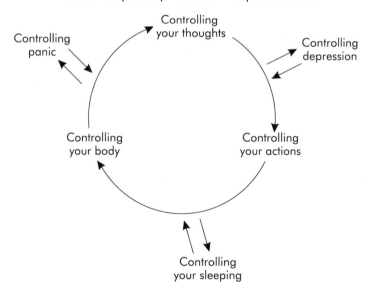

Figure 5.1. The vicious and positive circles in stress

The person in the best position to do this is you.

The teacher's role is to point you in the right direction and, with the appropriate information, you will take responsibility for change. This means that once the course is over you will have the confidence to keep controlling your stress. Realising that you have this ability will help your self-confidence grow.

Your expectations should be realistic.

Decide what kind of person you are and what circumstances you face. 'Stress Control' will not change your basic nature. If you have always been a worrier, you are likely to stay a worrier but you should aim to bring the anxiety down to a more acceptable level. Your aim is to 'control', not 'cure'.

IS AN ASSESSMENT INTERVIEW NECESSARY?

The most time-consuming aspect of running, particularly, a large course is the individual assessment interviews. Without these, courses could be set up and run quickly and easily. However, the obvious drawback in not having a qualified therapist assess would be the possibility of individuals with inappropriate problems attending. Firstly, individuals may misdiagnose their problems as due to stress, e.g. fear of going into public places could disguise a paranoid personality as agoraphobia. Secondly, their presence on a course could prove upsetting for stress sufferers who may fear that they will end up with similar problems. Thirdly, assessment allows the trained clinician to determine the best approach for individuals, e.g. someone with an eating disorder may feel that anxiety management is what they need, whereas a clinician may feel that a dedicated eating disorder treatment should be the treatment of choice. It may be that better alternatives exist that would not be open to an individual who misses the opportunity of a thorough assessment.

However, severe and enduring mental health problems make up a small minority of problems in primary care and, if family doctors are familiar with referral procedures to secondary care services, these individuals should be offered appropriate help away from 'Stress Control'. In terms of providing choice, it seems attractive to offer the chance of attending especially to individuals who may not wish to see a mental health therapist in order to get access to the course (see White, 1992). With the growing awareness of stress, individuals may be better equipped to make informed judgements about such courses. Indeed, many may be routinely offered such approaches as part of their jobs. Brown *et al.* (1998), offering large-scale workshops open to the public, attracted individuals with appropriate problems and obtained good results. Brownescombe-Heller (1994), running a walk-in clinic over many years, similarly found that all self-referrals were appropriate.

One option would be to allow the family doctor or other health professional to act as a gatekeeper with the ability to refer directly onto a course. A short training session could be offered to teach doctors who is and who is not suitable for the course and, of the former group, who would benefit from an assessment interview with a mental health worker and who could be referred directly onto the course. With the latter group, they would also be advised on how to discuss the course with the individual. Course materials would then be provided by the GP. This would reduce stigma by obviating the need to see a mental health professional while allowing GPs to better and more quickly meet the needs of the large number of suitable individuals they will be seeing. From the clinician's standpoint, such an approach would free up scarce individual assessment and therapy time for those with problems not suitable for the course. Other options could include self-assessment by computer (see White *et al.*, in press) or, bearing in mind possible insurance complications, self-referral to the course. These various options are currently under investigation.

SPECIAL CIRCUMSTANCES

Certain individuals may need special provision. Those with marked agoraphobia or social phobia in particular may feel unable to attend without some support. In these cases, several aids can be put in place, as the crucial thing is simply to have them get there in the first place. Stacking chairs are placed at the door as they enter at the back of the room. These individuals are, at the assessment interview, advised to take one of these and sit at the back, next to the door, where space will be available. Individuals may also be asked to prepare a graded exposure therapy for themselves, where they will plan to move further down into the class as the course progresses.

SPOUSES/PARTNERS/FRIENDS

Spouses, partners or friends may wish to attend the course. I have increasingly found their attendance to be valuable for a number of reasons (see previous chapter). Attending may be necessary to provide support for the student. Attendance can be helpful as it encourages involvement in the therapy. They may wish to attend on their own in order to learn more about the student's condition. They may be involved in maintaining the problems, e.g. in providing reassurance, in reinforcing avoidance. Insight into this may help reverse these behaviours. A partner may also be under stress, either independently or due to the individual's problems. This latter case often emerges after they have read the course materials (the student is encouraged to let them do so).

CONCLUSIONS

Students should leave the interview not simply having accepted a place on the course but immediately starting to prepare for it by the process of self-assessment crucial before the start of the course. This may reinforce the idea of accepting full responsibility for treatment. The next chapter looks at this preparation.

Chapter 6

DEVELOPING MATERIALS FOR THE COURSE

THE IMPORTANCE OF WRITTEN MATERIAL

Ley (1977), studying doctor–patient interaction (for medical problems) reminds us of three important factors highly relevant to mental health: (1) generally, individuals do not simply want treatment, they want to know as much as possible about their condition and expect to be told this information; (2) there is a strong positive correlation between expectations being met and expressed satisfaction with the consultation; and (3) there is a strong positive correlation between satisfaction with the consultation and compliance with treatment.

In addition, Ley discovered that much of the failure in doctor–patient communication was due to the patients' failure to understand and remember what they were told. This outcome stemmed from three interrelated facts: (1) the material presented was often too difficult to understand; (2) patients often lacked elementary technical knowledge; and (3) patients often had active misconceptions that militated against proper understanding. In terms of failures of memory, patients attending their family doctor were found to have forgotten 50% of statements made to them within less than five minutes of seeing the GP.

The implications for mental health in general and didactic group work in particular are clear. If so much information is forgotten in a GP appointment, how much is forgotten in a much longer mental health consultation with individuals who are likely to have poor concentration due to their condition? To facilitate understanding and subsequent recall, one of the more important strategies would be the use of easily understood, personally relevant written material providing both information and treatment strategies (bibliotherapy). This would allow students to learn at their own pace, particularly before the course, and to use the material to cue information presented at the sessions but subsequently forgotten. This chapter looks at this issue.

BIBLIOTHERAPY

There is good empirical evidence to support the use of self-help with a range of disorders. Gould and Clum (1993) found that problems such as panic and phobia fared particularly well. In a comparison of group therapy and biblio-therapy for panic disorder, Lidren *et al.* (1994) found both approaches to be equally effective up to six months follow-up. Similar results using the same material were reported by Gould *et al.* (1993). An important test of the robustness of self-help must relate to its ability to help the individual main-tain or enhance therapeutic gains following cessation of contact. Scogin *et al.* (1990) found self-help effective at two years follow up with depressed older adults. However, as Gould and Clum (1993) in their meta-analysis point out, there are often methodological problems that limit the generalisability of the findings from the many studies in this area. Febbraro *et al.* (1999), studying bibliotherapy with and without therapist contact in the treatment of panic, reported that the combination of therapist and self-help provided the more powerful therapeutic approach.

Psycho-education typically combines bibliotherapy and therapist contact. As noted above, often such approaches are methodologically weak and conclusions hard to draw. However Lewinsohn's 'Coping with Depression' course (Lewinsohn *et al.*, 1986) offers a useful example of the potential in this area. The course offers a highly structured 12-session (plus two booster sessions) approach for unipolar depression. It has evolved from social learn-ing theory and involves cognitive–behavioural skills and has been shown to be an effective approach (Cuijpers, 1998).

In the present context, and bearing in mind the Febbraro findings, com-bining teacher-led therapy and bibliotherapy may offer the following benefits.

Before the course

Students

- Potential students are likely to feel apprehensive about attending a group. Written material that allows students to identify with the kind of prob-lems dealt with and that offers explicit guidelines on how these problems will be tackled on the course may help empower students. This may facilitate the decision to attend. This will be particularly helpful if they believe they have the ability to stay in control in the sessions.
- Anxiety and depression are, in the general population, poorly understood problems. Some of the myths associated with them may exacerbate these problems. Written material may provide a framework for perceiving and coping with problems that is understandable, personally relevant and broad-ranging in its application (Frank and Frank, 1991). Reading the book and completing the self-assessments may help students adopt a more active, educated part in their own assessment and treatment before

the course starts. This may boost the perception that the therapy comprises a lot more than simply attending the six sessions.

- By gaining an understanding of stress in general and, through the completion of the various self-assessment forms, gaining an understanding of how stress affects them personally, students can attend the first session not as novices eager to learn from the teacher but as students already in the process of learning. The material prepares them by orientating students to appropriate models of problem definition and treatment (see Herlihy *et al.*, 1998).
- Those who are able to read up on the course beforehand but who decide not to pursue this approach can look for more personally relevant help more quickly.

Family/friends

- As noted in the previous chapter, family and friends, who may feel helpless in the face of the problem or who exacerbate the problem through their attitude or behaviour, may benefit by reading and, thus, gaining more insight, into these conditions. Thus family members and friends who may, through good intentions, sabotage progress, e.g. by counselling against exposure, may be helped to adopt a more positive facilitating role. They may be more inclined too, to attend the course and become actively involved in helping their partner or friend.
- Either due to similar environmental stressors or as a consequence of living with the student, relatives may also be under considerable stress and may benefit themselves by attending for their own self-management. Indirectly, this may aid the student if stress levels, generally, are reduced in the home.

During the course

- Given the problems of comprehension and memory noted above, it is inevitable that students will experience concentration problems during the sessions. This can be somewhat offset, e.g. by the use of short sentences, repetition, explicit categorisation, specific, detailed and concrete advice, the avoidance of jargon, exploiting primacy and recency effects and use of multimedia.
- Comprehension and information retrieval are likely to be boosted if students are hearing, from the teacher, information already read and understood and which they can read over again following the session. The teaching of techniques clearly based on this information will also aid comprehension and may improve motivation as students can more readily see the relevance of what is being asked of them.
- As the reading material has already clearly supplied the 'jigsaw' analogy, students can see each session within the wider context and, thus, see the pieces of the jigsaw slot into place.

After the course

- The continued availability of this material may be beneficial in reducing the likelihood of relapse. This is an important though neglected area in mental health (see Ost, 1989b). Anecdotal evidence suggests that some students, on having a 'bad day' where old avoidance habits begin to re-emerge, read particular sections of the course material and actively confront problems instead.
- By giving students responsibility for the management of their own treatment, the written material can begin the process of fostering students' beliefs that they can successfully execute their own coping techniques without teacher contact. This may improve self-efficacy perceptions and perhaps help reinstil a sense of control in areas of their life where they had previously felt that control to be lacking (White, 1995a).

Generally

- Patients can work at their own pace before, during and after the course. This may allow them a greater degree of personal control over their therapy.
- It is possible that written material may facilitate patients' use of their own commonsensical or idiosyncratic ways of managing problems by providing a structured way of thinking about anxiety and by giving the strong message that change is possible if only it is allowed to happen. It may generate attitude shifts that might facilitate a calmer approach to life and undercut cycles of negative thinking (White, 1993b).

'STRESS CONTROL'

The course material is taken from the 'Stresspac' materials (White, 1997a). These include a therapist manual, student self-help manual (89 pages), course diaries and self-assessment forms (see next chapter), relaxation tape and three supplements: agoraphobia, panic and depression. All this material is photocopyable. The self-help manuals can also be bulk-purchased. Other handouts, not contained in Stresspac, can be obtained from the author. The rest of this chapter looks at this material.

THERAPIST MANUAL

'Stresspac' material is designed for use in various settings: used as self-help with or without therapist contact, used for those on therapists' waiting lists, used as an adjunct to individual therapy or, this context, used as the foundation of the didactic 'Stress Control' group approach. It discusses theoretical issues associated with bibliotherapy along with advice on how the material should be used.

SELF-HELP MANUAL

General

The patient manual divides into an information section and treatment section. The agoraphobia, panic and depression supplements offer information and self-help treatment and follow the same model as found in the main book.

Reading ease

Using the Flesch reading ease formula (Flesch, 1948) and the estimations of the IQ level required for understanding (Ley, 1977), the book should be readily understood by anyone with an IQ of at least 84 (86% of the population).

Information section

Chapter 1. What is stress?
Chapter 2. Myths and facts
Chapter 3. The nature of stress
Chapter 4. The role of stress
Chapter 5. What causes stress?
Chapter 6. What keeps stress going?
Chapter 7. Seven case histories
Chapter 8. Important statements

What is stress?

This chapter introduces some of the common concepts that will be found throughout the manual and in the course. In particular, it introduces **TAB: T**houghts, **A**ctions and **B**ody (cognition, behaviour and somatics). To make more sense of emotions, a three-systems analysis is used (students will have met this concept during the assessment interview—see Chapter 5). Thus 'Stress affects your thoughts' is followed by a list of common problem areas such as:

> 'You may find yourself worrying about a lot of things you know you should not be worrying about.'
> 'You may find it very hard to stop worrying even when you want to'
> 'You may feel you are losing control of your life.'
> 'You may worry even when things are going well.'

These can help promote identification as all are very commonly found among a range of anxiety sufferers. Information on how common these problems are, the stigma still associated with them and how the manual works complete this section.

Myths and facts

Given the prevalent misinformation and misconceptions about anxiety that often, because of their frightening nature, exacerbate the stress, this section looks at some of the more common myths, e.g. 'Stress only affects inadequate people', 'Stress is a mental illness', and counters them with the facts and supporting commentary.

The nature of stress

This chapter extends the TAB concept and looks at it in detail, e.g. the 'what ifs', the characteristics of worry and its common domains, avoidance and changes in behaviour as a result and maintaining factor in stress and body reactions to stress. Each TAB system contains lists of common problems. Cartoons, spread throughout the material (e.g. Figure 6.1), help illuminate the points being made. This chapter helps provide the rationale for the treatments that will be taught on the course, e.g. worry control, exposure, relaxation.

The role of stress

This chapter explains the role of stress in order to make better sense of the signs and symptoms the student is likely to be experiencing. It is based on the fight/flight/fear/faint model best suited to panic but applicable across the anxiety spectrum. Information on how the body and mind are placed on the alert to better anticipate physical danger, and cope more effectively if it arises, is presented.

Students are asked to consider the survival value of the various bodily and mental changes to someone in a physically dangerous situation, e.g. the increased heart rate pushing blood to arms, legs and lungs to increase strength and stamina. Realising that the trigger is the same—a perception of threat—students are given a rationale for common reactions they experience when stressed. They are then asked to consider how these reactions affect an individual with anxiety. In addition, they understand the impact of these changes on the individual as this energy is not consumed, as fighting or fleeing is unlikely to be an appropriate response to a psychologically threatening situation. Thus the concept of the 'fear of fear' and the vicious circle in stress are introduced.

What causes stress?

The chapter offers a range of potentially interactive factors: biology, childhood modelling and parental style, life events and perception of these events. It suggests stress is rarely caused by just one factor, that the causes are complex and often difficult for an individual to work out. It also notes

Figure 6.1. Worry cartoon

that psychology has some way to go before definitive answers can emerge to adequately answer the question.

What keeps stress going?

The roles of such factors as loss of self-confidence, growing self-consciousness, hypervigilance, threat perceptions and loss of a sense of control are introduced. The TAB model is reintroduced within a vicious circle model where thoughts feed actions feed body feed thoughts, etc. This acts as the fuel supply keeping stress alive even in the absence of further problems in the person's life. Stress is conceptualised as a parasite that, due to the vicious circle, is feeding off the individual. Thus learning the appropriate ways of shutting off the fuel supply—by directly targeting thoughts, actions and body symptoms—can starve the stress of fuel, leaving it to weaken and, therefore, more open to control (Figure 6.2).

Figure 6.2. Fuel supply cartoon

Seven case histories

Although the course will teach a range of general coping skills, descriptions of six individuals complaining of problems suggestive of GAD (see below), PD, social phobia, agoraphobia, OCD, PTSD and depression are introduced. By avoiding a dry, academic description of these problems in favour of a 'straight from the horse's mouth' approach, readers may be more able to identify with one or more.

KATE

Kate is a 45-year-old school cleaner. She says she is a born worrier but that over the past three years she has become a 'nervous wreck'. She has no great problems in her life but she can't control her worrying and tension.

'I worry about the least wee thing—being late for appointments; what the people at work think of me; having to talk to neighbours; just everything. I can't concentrate on reading and I can't relax at all at home. I can't make even simple decisions to save myself. I never sit at peace for more than five minutes, and although I get over to sleep I wake up during the night and can't get over again. If I have to be anywhere for a certain time, I am ready hours in advance and can sit in the living room with my coat on and the keys in my pocket even although I won't be leaving for ages.

I am always looking ahead and trying to plan ways of dealing with every possible outcome and, of course, I am always waiting for the worst to happen. Even when it doesn't happen, I know I'll just be the same next time round. I don't seem to be able to learn from the past in the way any normal person would.

I'm always on edge, I bite the head off the kids all the time for no reason. I can go for days with a horrible throbbing headache that starts at the back of my neck and goes all the way to the top of my head and I just feel all tensed up most of the time.

I always feel under threat and imagine that people are putting me down even when I really know they are not. I often find myself getting into arguments with people in my mind even when there is no need to. Once this happens, I can get myself all worked up and not know how to calm myself down again. I often pick over whole conversations to see if I have said the wrong thing and worry about the impression I gave. I just feel so vulnerable—you know, not controlling things the way I should. I doubt myself all the time and I don't know how to get out of this mess. I'm just wasting my life.'

Important statements (see below)

Readers should endorse all 12 statements if they have accepted the information in the previous chapters. It is important they do so as they should be on the same 'wavelength' if the course is to be appropriate for them:

1. You do not have a unique disorder. Stress is a very common problem. You have too much of a normal emotion.
2. You should not aim to 'cure' yourself of stress but rather to control it.
3. Stress is not a mental illness.
4. You will not become mentally ill because of stress even if the stress is severe.
5. You will not die because of stress even if it is severe—no one ever has.
6. We all have the potential to develop stress but to a large extent it depends on what happens to you in life.
7. Stress can continue even in the absence of problems. Stress feeds itself because of the vicious circle involving TAB.
8. You are not weak, inadequate or abnormal. The successful treatment of stress is a lot more complex than giving yourself a good shake.
9. Tablets may help dampen the symptoms but they will not teach you how to cope with the problem in the long run.
10. Up until now, you have not known how to combat stress. 'Stress Control' will give you the tools to do this. However, it needs a lot of hard work on your part.
11. You can be taught to recognise the danger signs of stress and, thus, help prevent problems building up in the future.
12. There is no magic cure—don't be impatient. Controlling stress takes time. Believe in yourself—you can do it.

Treatment section

Each of these subsections is described in detail in later chapters. They form, along with the supplements, the core of the course material. They are:

Describing your stress
Working out the pattern
Clearing the decks
Quick control
Controlling your body
Controlling your thoughts
Controlling your actions
Controlling your future

Supplements[1]

Depression: This is a 35-page information and treatment booklet using the TAB model. It details a cognitive–behavioural approach and relies on similar skills to those detailed in the main manual.

Agoraphobia: 39 pages (as above).

Panic attacks: 31 pages (as above).

Handouts and diaries

A range of patient diaries and information handouts is included. These are detailed mainly in Chapter 7. The range of diary forms used on the course, and included in Stresspac, are detailed in the relevant chapters. In summary, these are:

Straight from the horse's mouth (1): 100 quotes from anxiety and depression sufferers describing how these conditions affect them.

Straight from the horse's mouth (2): 50 quotes from users of these materials

Describing your stress

Targeting your stress

Daily diary

Court case and relaxation diaries

CONCLUSIONS

All materials should be given to individuals several weeks before the course to enable them to begin the process of self-education and self-assessment. They should work through the manual at their own pace. Although the reading ease indicator is acceptable, owing to concentration problems caused by stress many people will be able to read only small amounts at any one time. Retention of information may also be a problem. They will be asked to read over relevant chapters between sessions to improve retention. It is crucial that individuals are allowed to keep these materials to enable long-term work to take place.

The next chapter looks at the preparation for the course using these materials.

---

[1] The Stresspac material does not contain an insomnia treatment supplement although this is taught on the course. A 'Controlling your sleep problems' handout can be obtained directly from the author.

Chapter 7

PREPARING FOR THE COURSE

THE 'STRESS CONTROL' COMPONENTS

'Stress Control' contains 15 steps:

Step 1. Learning about stress
Step 2. Describing your stress
Step 3. Targeting your stress
Step 4. Daily diary
Step 5. Setting your goals
Step 6. Clearing the decks
Step 7. Quick control
Step 8. Controlling your body
Step 9. Controlling your thoughts
Step 10. Controlling your actions
Step 11. Controlling your panic
Step 12. Controlling your sleep problems
Step 13. Controlling your depression
Step 14. Tying it all together
Step 15. Controlling your future

The first five steps relate to gathering information about the problems and come under the rubric 'Know your enemy'. Along with steps 6 and 7, these should be started in the interval between the assessment interview and the first session. All these steps should continually be revised before, during and after the course in light of experience. This chapter describes this pre-course preparation.

STEP 1: LEARNING ABOUT STRESS

Know your enemy (1)

Students should be asked to read the book several times. To cope with almost inevitable concentration problems, they should be encouraged to read the book in sections rather than at one sitting. Spouses/partners/

friends should also be asked, by the student, to read the book. The information in the first half of the book is generalised. The student, in subsequent steps, will assess how stress affects them personally. Two handouts from the 'Stresspac' material help students identify with the problem (White, 1993a):

'Straight from the horse's mouth' (1)

This handout offers 100 quotations from real-life anxiety sufferers. The student is asked to 'dip into' these quotations to get a flavour of the many ways stress can affect people. It is highly likely that the reader will identify closely with at least some of the quotations. It may also reduce the students' embarrassment about the problem and fears that their condition is odd or stupid. Some examples follow.

Common complaints

- 'I'm going to get "What if . . ." inscribed on my gravestone. "What if I'm late? . . . What if I make a fool of myself? What if they can see my hand shaking? What if I don't know anyone?" It goes on and on and I just can't stop it.'
- 'Once I get a thought in my mind, it gnaws away at me and then it sparks off other worries and it gets worse and worse until I feel I'm going out of my mind.'
- 'I never switch off, never relax. I am on the go all day long. If I try to sit in front of the TV, I will be jumping up and down doing this, doing that. I just can't sit at peace.'

Specific anxiety disorder complains

- 'I am OK as long as I don't have to think about going out. If I just grab my coat and go, I'll be fine but if I have a day to wait before I have to go anywhere, I will be in a bad way. More often than not, I would think up some excuse for not going.'
- 'I am terrified that another panic hits me. I honestly thought I was going to die when I had the last one. It came out of the blue—I couldn't breathe, my heart felt it was going to burst, I felt I was going to faint, I was covered in sweat and I felt sick. At its worst point, I felt I wouldn't survive it. It was the worst thing I have ever experienced.'
- 'If I'm in the bank, I'm terrified that I'll be asked to sign something in front of the teller or if I have to hold out my hand to get change back in a shop, I'll be shaking and everyone will notice.'

Idiosyncratic anxious complaints

- 'I saw a coffin on TV last night in a detective film and I thought "That could be me in there." What would happen to my baby if I wasn't here for her and, of course, I was in floods of tears. Stupid, isn't it?'

- 'If I'm watching an old film and can't remember the name of an actor, I get myself all worked up because the name won't come to me. I begin to worry that I might have Alzheimer's like my uncle. Maybe everyone forgets like this—I don't know. I'm too scared to ask in case they don't.'
- 'I have lost all interest in sex. I find myself deliberately going to bed after my wife is asleep to avoid this. She burst into tears the other night because she felt that I didn't want her and even was worried that there was someone else. I don't know how to explain the way I feel to her because I don't understand it myself.'

Problems associated with stress

- 'It's a chicken and egg thing—I don't know if I started to drink to reduce my stress or if my stress was caused by my drinking. In any case, I now have two problems—stress and drink—and they feed each other. I can't go into company without a couple of drinks before I leave the house. This helps me relax but, of course, I don't leave it at that. The drink seems to make my stress worse, especially the next day. I know it's not the way to cope but I don't know any other way.'
- 'I wasn't prepared for the depression that came with the stress—the loss of confidence and concentration, the crying, the bad moods. I feel really guilty about the way I have treated the children since I have felt like this. I wanted to sleep all the time and either ate everything I could or lost my appetite completely. The worst thing was the total despair that took over. I couldn't believe that a psychological problem could have such a strong effect on me. Believe me, people who tell you to pull yourself together simply don't know what they are talking about.'
- 'The way that stress affects me is that I become so full of anger. I become a horrible person when this happens. I worry about what I might do if someone says the wrong thing to me or even looks at me the wrong way. I'm ashamed to say that I have lashed out at the children for no good reason and I actually put my fist through the door as I felt that, otherwise, I would end up hitting my wife. It's not the first time that I've thrown an ornament at the wall.'

'Straight from the horse's mouth' (2)

Similar in presentation and format to the above, this form offers 50 quotations from people who have completed the 'Stress Control' course. It provides views on the course, advice on coping and helps set expectations. Examples suggest that different people take different things out of the course. Three examples give the picture.

- 'I was terrified going along to the first night. I was worried that I would meet someone I know or that I would have to speak or that I would have a panic. There seemed to be so many people but that helped and it was clear from the start that you were not to talk about your problems. I must say, I enjoyed coming along to the class. It was very straightforward.'

- 'To be honest, my stress is just as high but the difference is that I look on it in a different way. By filling out the forms and thinking of the Life Events, I realised why I was under stress—my poor sister has leukaemia, my dad looks to be on the road out and he is living with us. I have to do my job and look after my family. Put anyone in my place and I bet they would feel as bad—the stress is normal. I don't have any choice in the matter—I have to live with it.'

- 'Before "Stress Control", I saw everything in black and white. I'm better (not perfect) at balancing the good and the bad and taking whatever is positive out of any situation. So, I'm giving myself a pat on the back when I deserve it. This has helped a lot.'

STEP 2: DESCRIBING YOUR STRESS

Know your enemy (2)

'Describing your stress'

To gather information about the problem and to make it more 'concrete', the student should complete this assessment form contained in 'Stresspac'. There are 10 questions to respond to in 'Describing your stress':

1. **How would you describe your problems?**
2. **How would other people describe your problems?** Is there a difference of opinion? Why is this?
3. **How long have you been aware of it?** Do other people agree?
4. **Do you know what caused the problem(s)?** Marital problems? 'Born worrier'? A lot of changes in your life?
5. **How long have you had these problems?** Has it stayed at the same level? Has it come and gone?
6. **Do these problems run in the family?** Why do you think this is?
7. **What have you tried in the past?** Tablets? Hypnosis? Talking to friends? Relaxation tapes?
8. **What made you ask for help now?** Pressure from family? Feel you can't take any more stress?
9. **Are you taking any tablets just now?** What are they? Are they helping?
10. **Are you trying anything to help now?** Facing up to problems? Exercise? Improving social life?

Along with the other measures, 'Describing your stress' will allow the student to begin gathering information about the problem and to carry out behavioural analyses that should point the way to a personally relevant intervention. In doing so, the student is beginning the task of taking responsibility for therapy and, hopefully, realising that they have the ability to do so. By the time the course begins, they should already feel that the therapy process has begun.

STEP 3: TARGETING YOUR STRESS

Know your enemy (3)

Having described their problems, students now find out more about them by completing the 'Targeting your stress' form in the 'Stresspac' material. In this, students are to consider: What are your answers telling you? Is there a pattern emerging? Do you have a reason for the stress? Do you now know what makes it better or worse? If so, does it give you any ideas on ways of fighting the stress? It contains 12 questions:

Is there a pattern to your stress?
e.g. is it worse in the morning, at weekends, on holiday?
What things make it worse?
e.g. being in crowds, being alone, alcohol
What things make it better?
e.g. being with the family, being busy, talking to friends
What happens to your body when you are under stress?
e.g. heart racing, headaches, feel sick
What kinds of things run through your head when stressed?
e.g. feel you are making a fool of yourself, fear you will faint
How do you act when you are under stress?
e.g. avoid things, shout at others
What do other people notice when you are under stress? (ask them)
e.g. you can't sit still, look ill, withdrawn
What aspects of your life are most affected by stress?
e.g. self-confidence at work, can't relax at home
What aspects of your life are least affected by stress?
e.g. playing with the children, work
What do you think keeps it going?
e.g. unemployment, expectations too high, avoidance
Can you divide your problems into those you can do something about?
e.g. avoidance
and those you can't?
e.g. illness, unemployment
Can do:
Can't do:
What could you do to improve the situation?
e.g. How can you confront the problems you can tackle and how can you cope with the problems you can't change?

Problems you can do something about:
Problems you can't change:

STEP 4: DAILY DIARY

Know your enemy (4)

Students are asked to complete a daily diary from the 'Stresspac' materials in the evening and involving a simple stress rating. Space is provided for an explanation for the stress rating. This basic diary format was chosen in preference to more detailed diaries as clinical experience suggests that individuals often do not complete these properly. Students are encouraged to keep the diary for at least four weeks. An example is given in Figure 7.1.

STEP 5: SETTING YOUR GOALS[1]

Know your enemy (5)

This step pulls together all the information gathered in steps 1–4. Having learned more about 'the enemy', the student has to decide what goals are realistic to aim for while engaged on the course. The 'Setting your goals' form adopts, in keeping with the philosophy of the course, a dimensional rather than a categorical view of psychological distress and aims to have the student take social realities into account in developing treatment goals (Figure 7.2). The 'Setting your goals' form should be completed prior to the start of the course but regularly revisited and revised in the light of experience during and after the course. These goals could be discussed with the teacher in smaller courses (see Chapter 8).

STEP 6: CLEARING THE DECKS

Students, having learned a good deal more about their own stress and associated problems, should now use the information gleaned from self-assessment to start on the removal or control of the following.

Alcohol

Students should look for a pattern involving alcohol consumption and increased anxiety/panic. It such a pattern is found, they should decrease/avoid alcohol at least until they have better control over the anxiety. Students who believe they are alcohol dependent should seek relevant help in addition to the course.

---

[1] The 'Setting your goals' form is not contained in 'Stresspac'. It can be obtained directly from the author.

Stress Control daily diary: Week 1

At the end of each day, you should rate how stressful you have generally been by giving yourself a score between 1 and 10. Use the scale below. A score of 10 would mean your stress could not be worse. A score of 1 would mean you were not under any stress. Your score will probably be somewhere in between. You should also work out why you felt the way you did and write it in the next box. At the end of the week, note what you have learned about your stress. Look at the example below.

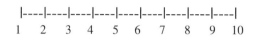

| 1 | 2 | 3 | 4 | 5 | 6 | 7 | 8 | 9 | 10 |

How stressful have you been today?   What caused you to feel like that?

Example	7	Couldn't handle work today. Felt bad since I got back home but feel a bit better now (9 p.m.)
Day 1		
Day 2		
Day 3		
Day 4		
Day 5		
Day 6		
Day 7		

What have you learned about your stress this week ?

Figure 7.1. Daily diary example

'Stress Control': Setting your goals

Now that you have gathered a lot of information about the way stress affects you, this form will help you decide what goals to set. There are three parts to this:

FIRST, decide how serious the problems noted on the next page are by rating them between 0 and 100, where 0 means it is not a problem and 100 means it could not be worse. Your scores will probably be somewhere in between. Mark the number you feel best fits (see example). Descriptions of some of these problems are given on the following page.

SECOND, on the final page, decide what goals are realistic to aim for on the course.

THIRD, during and after the course, return to this form and revise your goals in light of your experience.

Figure 7.2.

Example: Jealousy	0-----10-----20-----30-----40-----50--✕--60-----70-----80-----90-----100

Mental health factors (in general)	0-----10-----20-----30-----40-----50-----60-----70-----80-----90-----100
General anxiety	0-----10-----20-----30-----40-----50-----60-----70-----80-----90-----100
Panic attacks	0-----10-----20-----30-----40-----50-----60-----70-----80-----90-----100
Agoraphobia	0-----10-----20-----30-----40-----50-----60-----70-----80-----90-----100
Social anxiety	0-----10-----20-----30-----40-----50-----60-----70-----80-----90-----100
Obsessions/ compulsions	0-----10-----20-----30-----40-----50-----60-----70-----80-----90-----100
Post-traumatic stress	0-----10-----20-----30-----40-----50-----60-----70-----80-----90-----100
Depression	0-----10-----20-----30-----40-----50-----60-----70-----80-----90-----100
Anger	0-----10-----20-----30-----40-----50-----60-----70-----80-----90-----100
Alcohol/drugs	0-----10-----20-----30-----40-----50-----60-----70-----80-----90-----100
Sleeping problems	0-----10-----20-----30-----40-----50-----60-----70-----80-----90-----100

Social factors (in general)	0-----10-----20-----30-----40-----50-----60-----70-----80-----90-----100
Family/relationship problems	0-----10-----20-----30-----40-----50-----60-----70-----80-----90-----100
Money problems	0-----10-----20-----30-----40-----50-----60-----70-----80-----90-----100
Housing problems	0-----10-----20-----30-----40-----50-----60-----70-----80-----90-----100
Work problems	0-----10-----20-----30-----40-----50-----60-----70-----80-----90-----100
Unemployment	0-----10-----20-----30-----40-----50-----60-----70-----80-----90-----100
Neighbourhood problems	0-----10-----20-----30-----40-----50-----60-----70-----80-----90-----100

Medical problems	0-----10-----20-----30-----40-----50-----60-----70-----80-----90-----100
Other problems (describe)	0-----10-----20-----30-----40-----50-----60-----70-----80-----90-----100

Figure 7.2.

Problem descriptions

Agoraphobia   Fear of what might happen to you (e.g. having a panic attack) in busy places such as supermarket checkouts, pictures, pubs, GP waiting rooms, buses

Social anxiety   Fear of how you will cope and what others might think of you at, e.g., weddings, work nights out, breaks at work

Obsessions   Unwanted thoughts or images that persistently come into your mind. Examples include having doubts about, for example, having switched off the cooker before going to bed, fear of having knocked someone down in your car, fear of contamination or having aggressive or sexual thoughts that cause you distress

Compulsions   What you do to relieve the obsessional thoughts. These commonly include excessive washing and cleaning, counting, checking, repeating and asking for reassurance even although you know you should not have to do the acts

Post-traumatic stress   Problems that develop after being in or witnessing a traumatic situation where you believed you or someone else was under threat of death or serious injury. Rape, serious assault, car or train crashes and fires are common traumatic situations

Figure 7.2.

Setting your goals

Taking into account the answers you have just given, what are the goals you are setting yourself on the course? Make them specific and realistic (so not 'get rid of all my anxiety'). You will learn a technique called 'Problem Solving' on the course that will help you more with this:

Goals (now):

(1)

(2)

(3)

(4)

Goals (after the course):

(1)

(2)

(3)

(4)

Figure 7.2. 'Setting your goals' form

Medication

Although the decision to take medication should be discussed with a medical practitioner, some general advice can be offered. In marked contrast to 10–15 years ago, at least in Britain, few anxiety disorder individuals will be receiving repeat prescriptions for benzodiazepines. Most now are likely to be offered either beta-blockers or antidepressants—especially selective serotonin reuptake inhibitors (SSRIs). Experience suggests that around 70% of students are likely already to be using psychotropic medication when they come to the course. While 'Stress Control' teaches a drug-free treatment, it recommends individuals adopt an eclectic approach that may include psychotropic medication.

The 'miracle cure'

'Stress Control' emphasises the need to work hard to slowly break down complex problems. Students will only accept this view and respond to the demands of the course if they are disabused of the notion that quick, painless treatments exist. In accord with an eclectic approach, the use of aromatherapy or reflexology, for example, may help relieve stress in the short term. They are unlikely to have long-term benefit for individuals with severe, chronic problems as such approaches do not teach the individual how to take personal control over stress. Students would be discouraged from seeking out any of the so-called 'power therapies' such as thought field therapy, eye movement desensitisation reprocessing or emotional freedom techniques (see Rosen *et al.*, 1998).

Reassurance

If the individual is seeking it on a daily basis, this can be construed as a form of avoidance (see below). Students must accept responsibility for actions and their consequences without seeking excessive approval or reassurance. It may also irritate those who are asked to provide the reassurance, thus placing a strain on relationships with family and friends. Similarly, students should not seek medical tests etc. if their doctor does not recommend them.

Self-criticism

This will be looked at in greater detail on the course but the individual can begin to look out for a behaviour that may be largely automatic.

Avoidance

One of the most crucial factors maintaining stress is highlighted at this early stage. It will be raised in several sessions. The student is pointed to the usefulness of avoidance as a short-term strategy—i.e., avoidance is likely to lead to almost immediate anxiety reduction. However, avoidance leads to problems in the longer term and is a major factor in the maintenance of stress. Although the individual is not expected to simply stop avoiding, the marker is placed to ensure that this factor is given the prominence it deserves.

STEP 7: QUICK CONTROL

While discouraging individuals from anxiety reduction techniques such as avoidance, it can be useful to provide students with simple techniques that can help in the short term. These can be used as stop-gap measures until they learn the more involved and, ultimately, more effective cognitive–behavioural techniques on the course. In addition, by providing effective short-term techniques, motivation and expectation may be boosted by showing students that it is possible for them to control their own stress, at least to some degree, without resorting to avoidance, reassurance, alcohol, etc.

Distraction

One of the most effective short-term techniques, distraction can quickly lead to a decrease in anxiety by switching attention from the anxiety-provoking thoughts. The use of mantras, detailed describing of the student's setting and simply staying busy are recommended (see Powell and Enright, 1990, for more detailed information).

Exercise

A positive link between aerobic exercise and, at least in the short term, decreased depression and, probably, anxiety can be made (see Burbach, 1997, for a recent analysis). By joining an aerobic class or swimming club, for example, the student also gains greater social contact that may extend beyond the aerobic exercise, e.g. going for a drink together after training.

Talking

Many individuals, embarrassed by their condition, may not have told even those closest to them about their problems. 'Getting things off your chest' can be a useful start and, again, represents a change in strategy away from avoidance to confronting the problem. The assumption is that not only will a trusted person who is approached react less negatively than the student fears but will also provide positive support and empathy. Asking friends/ relatives to read the book can help in this. Care should be taken that this support does not involve excessive reassurance.

Breathing retraining

Simple controlled breathing techniques, combined with diaphragmatic breathing, can be a useful technique to promote a sense of immediate short-term control, especially in those individuals with marked autonomic symptoms. Detailed advice is offered.

CONCLUSIONS

Students who carry out these first seven steps diligently should come to the first session feeling that they have already engaged with the approach and that they have taken personal control of it. Self-efficacy beliefs may be raised by carrying out these relatively simple tasks. The individual should feel encouraged to try different strategies to help adopt a new approach to stress. This extends to approaches not included in the book; i.e., 'Stress Control' should be used flexibly by the student.

Chapter 8

RUNNING A COURSE

INTRODUCTION

This chapter looks at the infrastructure of the 'Stress Control' didactic approach. It divides into seven: selecting the venue; setting up the room; presession; group size; teaching style; teaching aids; and session format.

SELECTING THE VENUE

'Stress Control' has generally been run in large health centres where 30+ GPs are based, along with a wide range of services, e.g. physiotherapy, chiropody, psychiatry, psychology, social work, antenatal care. However, a range of venues is likely to prove suitable for these courses. The most relevant may be:

- secondary health care facilities, e.g. hospitals;
- primary health care facilities e.g. health centres, GP surgeries;
- community centres (libraries, community halls, church halls, sports centres, etc.).

Health care facilities

Advantages

- Teachers may be based there.
- Students may already be familiar with the facility and have been assessed there.
- Equipment for the group can be readily stored—projectors, screens, etc.
- Large waiting areas may have suitable comfortable seating.
- They may be readily available in the evening.

Disadvantages

- Students may more readily adopt a passive/submissive role in these settings.

- There may be security problems if no other health personnel are available, e.g. receptionists, night porters.
- Students may have to share facilities with other users.

Community centres

Advantages

- Possibly reduction of the stigma of attending a health care facility for 'psychological treatment' in favour of 'evening self-help class'.
- May help students adopt a more active, self-help strategy from the start.
- Centres may be nearer students' homes
- Students may have experience of attending other classes in the centre.

Disadvantages

- It may be more difficult to set up equipment if it cannot be stored on site.
- Students may not want others using a (multi-user) centre to see them attending a stress course.

SETTING UP THE ROOM

Seating

To immediately reinforce the image of an evening class, the students' first view of the room should meet their expectation of a class (Figure 8.1). Thus seating should be arranged in a traditional classroom manner. Students should enter, if possible, at the back of the room so that they do not have to face those who are already seated. Latecomers can also enter in a less obtrusive manner. Large comfortable chairs should be spaced well apart to allow a central aisle and two side aisles. This will give the impression of space. For those with agoraphobic/claustrophobic problems, the security of seeing an easy exit should help them to relax more quickly.

From experience, students rarely sit in the very front row. It is useful to simply place a single seat at the front of each of the two sections and place materials on it. This seems to act as a suitable 'barrier' and the second row will then be used. More seats than are required should be set up as numbers can be fluid, depending on how many relatives or friends accompany the student. It is very important for latecomers to find a seat easily to contain feelings of self-consciousness. However, if too many seats are put out, there is the possibility that the session runs with several rows of empty seats between the teacher and students as, inevitably, the seats at the back of the room are taken first. This can create an emotional as well as a physical distance between teacher and students.

The setting up of the room in this way helps to provide a 'safe' atmosphere for students. They will form a solid, cohesive group while the

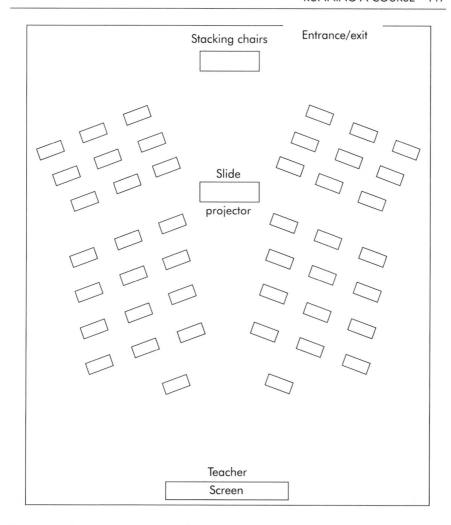

Figure 8.1. Seating arrangements (large group)

teacher is in the more exposed position. As discussed earlier, this may have important implications for initiating change.

PRE-SESSION

Facilities

Toilets should be clearly signposted. This will help individuals with irritable bowel syndrome, for example, to sit more easily in the group knowing exactly where toilets are. If possible, a tea/coffee room should be available where students can help themselves and talk to other attendees. This will help strengthen the idea of an evening class rather than a therapy.

Setting the tone

The teacher should be available, especially at the first session, to greet students as they enter. They should be encouraged to sit where they wish and there should be some personal conversation and/or encouragement. To remain sensitive to the needs of each individual, teachers should, whenever possible, read over case notes before the session to remind themselves of those who will be attending. This will help avoid a sense of an anonymous group, to help shape relevant anecdotes or to avoid anecdotes that might upset certain students.

As students would expect from an evening class, an informal atmosphere should be encouraged. Teachers should therefore use first names to introduce themselves to further dilute the doctor–patient relationship. I tend to wear more casual clothes than during daytime work. However, it is crucial that students do not see this as a leisure class but rather as the most important attempt they will have to control their problems (hence the importance of hard work both during and between sessions).

In smaller groups, it may be appropriate to ask students to introduce themselves. Depending on the group composition, more details may be given. In larger groups, students should not be asked to do this. Tea breaks, etc., serve as informal settings for students to get to know each other if they wish.

Time considerations

Sessions should start and end punctually. Most students, especially in the early sessions, do not like to sit unoccupied before the session begins. From experience, most enter the room in the five minutes before start time. Teacher punctuality will aid student punctuality. Ending sessions punctually is important as students will be more able to arrange to be picked up, arrange taxis, etc. This may be of particular importance if the course is held in high-crime areas as students do not want to stand around outside.

Distraction

Due to anxiety, most students will be quiet before the session starts. Conversations are unusual. This silence can be oppressive for students and can augment already high levels of tension. Playing music CDs or music videos can be an effective distraction at this stage. Prior to the first two sessions, this music is deliberately played loud enough to inhibit conversation, thus providing an excuse for students not to talk. As the course progresses, the music remains but is played more quietly to encourage conversation and help group cohesion. The music videos are played at the break for those who do not wish to go to the tea room.

Failure to appear and safety nets

Any students who fail to appear for a session should be sent a pro forma letter immediately inviting them to attend the next session or to get in touch if they are unable to attend. From experience, this is particularly valuable following the first session.

If a student fails to appear for two consecutive sessions, I write to ask them to get in touch to make an individual therapy appointment and write to the referring GP to inform them of their patient's failure to appear. The GP is asked to remind the patient to contact me to make an appointment if they have not done so.

Communicating with the referring agent

A detailed letter is sent to the GP following the assessment interview. At the end of the course, a pro forma letter is sent to the GP stating that the individual has attended. In large groups, the teacher cannot expect to know how each individual has fared but the use of questionnaire data can be used to give some indication of progress. GPs are told that students are now expected to work hard at the approach and that they are free to attend any future course as required (see Chapter 16). If GPs feel the individual has not improved, they are asked, if appropriate, to refer back for individual therapy.

GROUP SIZE

This approach is designed to be used flexibly, i.e. in a range of settings, with a range of problems. Group size should also be viewed flexibly. Most of the early research on this approach was on groups of around 25 students (e.g. White *et al.*, 1992). Groups as small as eight have been successfully run by the author. The current trend, due to large numbers of appropriate referrals and the growing desire for spouses/partners to attend, is for groups of 40–60. Different sizes have different advantages and disadvantages.

The small group (up to 10)

Advantages

- Therapists are able to personalise the course more as they should recall most students' individual needs. While the ban on personal disclosure should, if appropriate, remain (as the student will have been promised), there is the chance to use relevant anecdotes and/or the chance to alter the teaching format to best fit individual needs.
- Depending on the mix, small groups may cohere more quickly and strongly.

- Students may feel more able to ask for specific advice.
- Where relatively few appropriate referrals are received, it allows the course to run frequently.

Disadvantages

- Individuals may feel more pressurised, for example, to ask questions.
- The relative smallness of the group may reinforce a more traditional therapist/patient relationship, with the student adopting a more passive/submissive role.
- It may reinforce a stigma that their problems are uncommon.
- It is more open to the influence of one student who may attempt to dominate the group.

The medium group (10–25)

Advantages

- These are much as with the small group, although weaker.
- Safety in numbers will allow the student more ease, with the student less likely to fear becoming the centre of attention.
- The 'balance of power' will move more to favour the students; i.e., the onus will be on the teacher to 'perform' rather than the student.

Disadvantages

- These are similar to the small group, although weaker.

The large group (25+)

Advantages

- The balance of power is now firmly on the students' side, with a phalanx of students able to sit back and watch the teacher perform.
- Individuals are less able to adversely influence the group.
- It reinforces a view of how common these problems are.
- It is economically efficient.

Disadvantages

- There is little room for personalising the course.
- Students will be deterred from seeking personalised help (this is probably an advantage).
- There may be practical difficulties getting a large group together or finding appropriate venues to run the group in.

Maximum size

As a dedicated self-help, non-disclosure group involving a didactic approach, there appears no reason for placing a limit on numbers attending. As a personal preference, I favour the larger groups. Current plans are to test a variation where a city-wide course is held, offering hundreds of students the opportunity to attend using a city-centre theatre.

TEACHING STYLE

Teaching style should be influenced by the skills and preferences of the individual teacher. I favour an informal style with the use of first names. Some may prefer a more formal approach. However, it is crucial that, whatever the nature of the teaching style, teachers should see themselves as the medium of change rather than the catalyst. Thus the teacher does not provide therapy through the group but facilitates the process whereby students provide their own therapy through the group. This allows the student to more easily attribute improvement to their own growing personal skills.

Students should, by reading the course materials, come to the course with the belief that responsibility for change lies in their hands. If they do achieve change, they should feel that they, and not the teacher, were responsible for that change. This will lessen dependence on the teacher and may be important for further improvement following the end of the sessions.

Depending on personal style, humour can be used to great advantage and may help encourage students to use humour as an antidote to anxiety. It should, from experience, be avoided in the first few sessions as the generally high anxiety level does not allow students to respond well to this approach.

There is also a place for a certain theatricality in presentation. The teacher is talking for long periods without much/any student participation. While following a relatively strict programme, regarding the students as an audience can help the teacher transmit the information more easily. Students should not be seen as being an undifferentiated audience. Teachers should work to promote a strong alliance with students—a factor found to be strongly associated with favourable outcome in the NIMH trial of treatments for depression (Krupnick *et al.*, 1996). Basic social skills such as establishing eye contact with as many individuals as possible during the session can help retain their attention and help them perceive that they are obtaining personal help. Scrutinising students' behaviour may also help teachers determine whether they are getting the information across successfully.

The use of metaphor, anecdote and vignette is valuable. Metaphors can help develop new ways of construing the world and help communicate the concepts used on the course. As Meichenbaum (1985) noted, people readily identify with vignettes and we remember anecdotes more readily if they elicit affect. Thus the anecdote acts as a retrieval cue for relevant material. Similarly metaphors are readily remembered, e.g. a ship surrounded by icebergs to represent an individual surrounded by problems with no apparent escape route. A volcano can be used to represent the lack of, in the students' eyes, external signs of stress/panic while great emotional upheaval is going on inside until, eventually, it erupts. Finally, personal anecdotes about stress can help break down barriers with the students. Teachers should be careful not to rely on 'easy' anecdotes of clear-cut problems, e.g. panic attacks. These should be balanced with stories that emphasise the 'messier' problems with no clear aetiology, no clear pattern, etc., to emphasise that these are also common. This acts as reassurance to the many students who do not have such clear-cut problems.

It is also useful to point to the many deficiencies of current theory and therapy, e.g. accept that we do not fully understand why many people develop significant problems. What causes anxiety, in particular, still seems a vague area. There is a perception among some clinicians (myself included) that some theorists try too hard to fit individuals to theories, while many clinicians would like to see the reverse pertain. If students do not see themselves in what the teacher is saying, they will switch off, drop out or remain lukewarm about working at the approaches (see Castonguay *et al.*, 1996).

The emphasis should be on positive encouragement but with a clear acceptance that progress can be slow and that particular techniques may not work for everyone. As previously noted, the analogy of learning to drive a car may be useful:

> The first time you sit behind the wheel, you will be unable to move the car. As you practise, you will slowly master the various skills but will probably make only fitful progress, with much stalling. There will be a lack of coordinated action as you will have to pay great attention to each function as you use it. Only at a much later date, when you have practised a great deal, will you coordinate and complete the various functions involved in driving smoothly almost automatically. You will be able to accelerate without first looking to find the right pedal, while checking your mirror, selecting the appropriate gear, etc. Controlling stress is the same—you are learning a difficult skill. Don't expect it to come easily.

Students should be encouraged to critically examine the techniques taught on the course. If they do not feel certain ones are appropriate for their problem, they should look at other options that they feel might better fit their needs. The choice of these options may be idiosyncratic but a 'horses for courses' approach possibly best fits the treatment of anxiety disorders, with different people benefiting from different approaches. More importantly, this strategy encourages the individual to take control in a way *they* think is appropriate while not seeing this as going against the teacher. The teacher should actively reinforce such student experimentation. It seems perfectly reasonable to suggest that perhaps different people can attain the same goal of anxiety control by different routes.

TEACHING AIDS

To simplify the transmission of difficult and extensive material to a student group whose concentration levels are likely to be poor, teaching aids are essential.

Slides

A total of 140 slides accompanies the 'Stress Control' course.[1] These help break the course into more manageable bits for both student and teacher. By acting as retrieval cues, they help the teacher to follow more easily the structure of the course. Although overheads could be used, the number involved makes the use of slides easier and, using slide-making software, attractive to the viewer. They can also be used as a computer presentation. This latter option allows greatest flexibility. Some examples follow.

JOHN, 34 YEARS OLD, PRINTER

'I worry about everything. I can't put my finger on why I worry—I just do. I'm a nervous wreck. I can't cope with things that everyone can cope with. My self-confidence is nil. I feel that I have lost control of my life and I don't know how to get it back.'

VIGILANCE IMPROVES

- Focus on the source of danger.
- Stop ongoing activity.

Side effects:

- Feeling keyed up or on edge, easily startled, sleep problems, poor concentration, mind going blank, irritation.

THE COURT CASE

Step 1
- Write down your thoughts

Step 2
- Look for evidence for.

Step 3
- Look for evidence against.

Step 4
- The summing up and verdict.

---

[1] Examples of slides used in 'Stress Control' are used throughout this book.

CONTROLLING PANIC ATTACKS

- What is a panic?
- Controlling your breathing.
- Controlling your thoughts.
- Controlling your actions.
- Reducing the risks.

Video

Video can allow the transmission of useful information in a new modality, thus improving concentration. The 'Stress Control' course uses several videos on anxiety, panic and depression. Current work is looking at using volunteer anxiety sufferers talking, in local dialect, about their problems and perception of the course.

SESSION FORMAT

A typical two-hour session divides into eight phases:

1. **Review** of previous session and homework assignment
2. **Introduction** to the session
3. **Education**
4. **Treatment** strategy based on education
5. **Break**
6. **Workshop**—opportunity to practise the treatment strategy
7. **Review** of the session
8. **Homework assignment**

From experience, two sections of around 50 minutes and divided by a break appear to work well. It allows the two segments to be used differently; i.e., the first part provides information about the problem and the way to treat it, while the second part provides time to practise using the strategy.

Review of previous session and homework assignment (5 minutes)

The first few minutes will be spent revising the previous session and the homework assignment. Although personal discussion about homework tasks is not encouraged, students will be asked if they need anything clarified or if any problems were met. Time may be spent offering suggestions, correcting misconceptions, etc. As when the homework assignment was set, expectations should be made explicit.

Students will be updated on how to continue with this homework, i.e., told they should consider, for example, moving from 'Deep' to 'Rapid' Relaxation if they feel ready. Although students are encouraged to keep their written diaries, questionnaires, etc., they can hand them in for comment if they wish. These are reviewed and the diaries returned with comments at the next session.

Introduction to the session (5 minutes)

A few minutes will be spent on summarising the session topic. This will be placed within the context of what has already been taught in preceding sessions using the jigsaw analogy (see Chapter 5).

> 'Tonight we will look at thoughts—how stress affects them and how they affect stress. Remember the vicious circle we looked at in session 1 when we saw how stressed thoughts feed stress in our bodies, how this feeds stress in our actions and how this, in turn, feeds stressful thoughts. We know this is why stress goes on and on and on. Last week, you learned the first major technique to destroy this vicious circle by using relaxation to control signs of stress in your body. Tonight you will learn the second major treatment: controlling thoughts. Remember the aim is not just to destroy the vicious circle of thoughts, actions and body. We also aim to replace it with a positive circle where thoughts, actions and body are working to build confidence and strength.'

Education (20 minutes)

The main part of the session before the break comprises a didactic lecture on the session topic—controlling thoughts, controlling actions, etc. A description of the problem using 'real' examples, a theoretical account of why the topic is important and how it fits in with the previous session topics will be discussed. Students are encouraged to ask questions or to request further information, etc.

The information offered should be based on that in the course book and augmented with anecdotes, etc. Interesting aspects of the topic, although not directly related to the treatment, may be added to increase interest in the talk, e.g. the role of pre-attentive bias in anxiety (Bradley *et al.*, 1995).

Treatment strategy (20 minutes)

This should appear as a separate lecture and a moment of rest may be offered before starting. Students should already be able almost to create the appropriate therapy based on what they have just heard. It is crucial that students have an immediate intellectual understanding of why using this strategy will:

1. specifically tackle the problems looked at during the education lecture; and
2. generally fit in with the other techniques they have learned on the course (the jigsaw analogy).

Break (15–20 minutes)

The break should be seen as an integral part of the treatment. If possible, tea/coffee should be available elsewhere in the building. Students should be given the option of remaining in the group room, going outside to smoke or going to the tea room. The opportunity to chat, especially if the teacher is responsible for making the tea/coffee, helps to further break down the barrier between teacher and students. Informal feedback about the session can often be useful for the teacher. Most students, in the early sessions, remain too tense to converse well. For this reason, early sessions involve a shorter break due to students' social anxiety. Generally, by session 3, students begin to relax, become a great deal more talkative and split into subgroups—often defined by sex.

Impressions are that students tend to talk constructively about the course rather than swapping symptoms. It is also in this setting that the first signs of students' strengths become apparent; for example, some use humour about how they react to anxiety. Some show skill in group cohesion, while others may offer advice on improving treatment outcome. My impression is that, often, these are not newly learned skills but are newly released older skills kept dormant, until now, by the emotional problems. By releasing them, individuals start to regain a sense of control using their own, often idiosyncratic methods. It seems possible that the 'Stress Control' approach helps free these strategies more effectively than more traditional approaches that de-emphasise active experimentation with personal strategies whether or not they fit in with the therapeutic orientation.

Some individuals, in adjunctive individual therapy, may be asked to practise different exposure tasks; for example, someone with social phobia may be asked to initiate a conversation and immediately discuss the behavioural experiment with the teacher for a few minutes during the break.

Workshop (30 minutes)

Immediately following the break, and an attendance sheet being passed round,[2] the workshop offers students a chance to practise the treatment

---

[2] Students should tick their name from a list rather than write it, in case of social anxiety concerns about writing in front of others.

strategy they will be given as their homework assignment. This will be carried out by each individual rather than, for example, in small groups, although this could be an option if there is more than one teacher. The teacher may carry out *in vivo* relaxation, students may practise challenging anxious thoughts, or may construct a problem-solving list. Students are encouraged to develop personally relevant interventions.

Review (5 minutes)

A short presentation will review the critical aspects of the session. Problems will be clarified or further advice offered. The aim is to ensure that students have understood how the therapy works and how it fits in with the teaching.

Homework assignment (10 minutes)

Students are given the appropriate diary or handout (diaries from previous sessions will also be available). Appropriate expectations are set—how much time should be spent on these tasks and how much/little progress is expected. In general, relatively negative expectations are given to ensure that:

- students can fairly easily achieve the expected level;
- any students surpassing this level may feel they are doing better than expected, thus boosting their self-efficacy perceptions and reinforcing their motivation to carry out the homework tasks.

Students are also encouraged to return home and, either that night or the following day, read over the current session information in their books to aid recall of the session.

Part 3 looks in detail at the specific content of each session.

Part 3

The Stress Management Course

Chapter 9

LEARNING ABOUT STRESS

SESSION 1: INTRODUCTION AND INFORMATION

How your stress is feeding itself now: the vicious circle

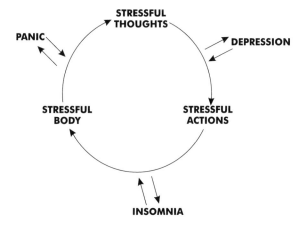

How to stay on top of stress: the positive circle

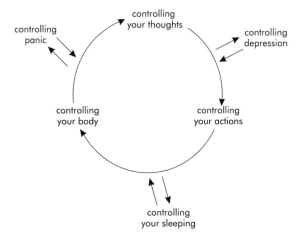

COURSE OUTLINE

Chapter 7 described the 15 steps involved in 'Stress Control'. The first seven should have been started prior to the first session. The first step—'Learning about stress'—is tackled when the course booklet is read and is revisited in the first session, which is exclusively devoted to information provision. The remaining steps are:

Step 8. Controlling your body (session 2)
Step 9. Controlling your thoughts (session 3)
Step 10. Controlling your actions (session 4)
Step 11. Controlling your panic (session 5)
Step 12. Controlling your insomnia (session 5)
Step 13. Controlling your depression (session 6)
Step 14. Tying it all together (session 6)
Step 15. Controlling your future (session 6)

Teachers should use their judgement in deciding how much information should be presented in each session. I often run the information provision (session 1) into session 2 and the 'Controlling your thoughts' material (session 3) into session 4. As mentioned previously, the number of sessions and number of topics presented can be increased or decreased depending on student and teacher needs. The degree of student participation will also depend on many factors and teachers must use their judgement about this. My experience, in working in Scotland, is to strictly keep to the rule of no discussion of personal problems under any circumstances. Later in the course, students, although not discussing personal problems, may be happy to discuss concepts, present modifications to techniques, etc.

STEP 1 REVISITED: LEARNING ABOUT STRESS

Session format

 1. **Introduction and practical information**
 2. **How the course works**
 3. **Case histories**
 4. **Myths and facts**
 5. **Thoughts, actions, body**
 6. **Break**
 7. **The role of stress**
 8. **Different types of stress**
 9. **What causes stress?**
10. **What keeps stress going?**
11. **Important statements**
12. **Homework assignment**

Goals

This session aims to provide the framework for the treatment to come. By offering easily understood, personally relevant information, students can begin to understand their problems more readily, thus making them more 'concrete' and open to change. The session should reinforce the knowledge gained from the book. The maxim taught to students, that the principal goal of the course is to 'turn you into your own therapist', should now be understood and grasped.

Key concepts

The session aims to have students readily accept the 'Important statements' (see Chapter 6).

Rationale

Students should feel empowered by the information initially in the book and then in the session. They should understand the importance of learning more about stress and learning, through the assessment tools, about the way it affects them. The treatment, tailored to the students' needs by that individual, should flow from what they have learned. Thus the self-help techniques should not be passively accepted and used but actively manipulated to meet these specific needs. Students should also be encouraged to seek their own coping strategies outside the course and to work out which treatments on the course are relevant and irrelevant to their needs and ignore the latter. The principal goal of the course—'turning you into your own therapist'—will only be met if students adopt this rationale.

Students tend to be highly anxious before and during the initial stages of this session. Presentation style in this session is best kept relatively formal—humour, for example, does not work well when people are so tense. There should be little or no attempt to interact with the group early on in the session, for example by asking if there are any questions, as they are unlikely to respond. Assuming that students' concentration is at its lowest, any significant pieces of information are best given at the start or end of each of the 11 sections to benefit from a primacy/recency effect or should be repeated. Sections should be clearly differentiated to break up the provision of so much information. If appropriate, lighting in the room is dimmed to allow greater anonymity among students, while increasing the quality of the slide presentation. It also further emphasises the evening class format and diminishes any idea of a traditional group therapy. An important first goal is to help students relax by allowing them to feel that they can handle the situation. Thus information should be kept as straightforward as possible to enable immediate understanding. Once students see that they can handle the situation, passive coping behaviours can begin to be replaced by active coping behaviours.

THE SESSION

(1) Introduction and practical information

- The teacher should introduce him/herself and indicate, if felt appropriate, that first names should be used.
- The teacher should acknowledge the tension ('I know how tense you will be feeling just now—everyone feels like this at this stage') and congratulate them for making it to the session in the face of the apprehension about attending.
- A restatement of the rule against discussing personal problems should, if appropriate, be made.
- Any practical information—location of the toilets, smoking rules, length of the session, etc.—should be made now.
- Suggesting that any student who feels too warm, for example, should feel free to leave the room at any point will help students to remain in the knowledge that an easy escape route is available.
- Use the group size to advantage—'So you thought you were the only one. Look around you. You come from all backgrounds. There is nothing special about being stressed.'
- Emphasise that attendance at all the sessions is important and that hard work between sessions is crucial.

(2) How the course works

Begin with a statement of intent—how the course works, the role of the teacher, the role of the student, expectations, etc. Then quickly describe each session to allow students to see how comprehensive the approach is. A suggested format would be as follows.

Now recall that this course is called 'Stress Control', not 'Stress Cure'—we are aiming to get a better grip on stress, not cure it. My job is to give you all the relevant information and put you on the right lines. It is your job to fit this information around your own problems and to go off and work hard at what you have learned. Then come back next week, learn the next step and so on until, by the end of the course, you will be able to put all the bits of the jigsaw together. Then you will be able to see the full picture and become your own therapist. That is when the real work begins. You should have some idea of the progress it is reasonable to expect—that will depend on many factors, e.g. what problems you have in your life, your basic nature. However, once you have your goal in view, you must give 'Stress Control' top priority in your life over the next few months so that you can reach your goal. Before we get started on the information in this session, let's just look at what we will be doing over the next few weeks.

(3) Six case histories

Six diverse 'straight from the horse's mouth' quotes are looked at in slide presentation. Each emphasises a different aspect of the problem: two on worry, social anxiety, agoraphobic avoidance, panic attacks and a mixed anxiety/depression presentation. Students are asked to look for commonalities, with the expectation that they will identify with at least one. It is important that the quotes used suggest that the people come from a range of backgrounds—different jobs, ages, social class, etc. The use of local dialect in the quotes helps identification.

JENNY, 54 YEARS OLD, CIVIL SERVANT

'I'm always scared. Even if there is nothing going wrong just now, I worry about what might go wrong in the future. In fact I worry about worrying.'

Although students are not expected to discuss personal problems, there will be subtle behaviours—head nods, non-verbal utterances, etc—indicating identification with the quotes. Students can, in this way, get some indication that others are suffering in similar ways to them.

(4) Myths and facts

Many students gather information about stress from folklore, the (often sensationalist) media, and from the family. Terms such as 'nervous breakdown' can be used to describe a range of disorders. Common misconceptions about stress and its effects are widespread. This section discusses the more common myths and compares them with the facts.

MYTH Stress is a mental illness.

FACT Stress is described as a common emotion and the student simply has too much of it. Mental illnesses, on the other hand, are to be seen as quite separate disorders. An example of someone believing that the TV newsreader is sending special messages to them or believing that voices inside their heads are discussing the individual are suggested as signs of a mental illness. The probable lack of insight into these problems is contrasted with the student's knowledge that they are getting worries, etc. out of proportion, that they realise these thoughts, fears, etc. are unrealistic but cannot stop them.

MYTH Although stress is not a mental illness, it will lead to mental illness. You can't stand that pressure for any length of time without developing serious problems.

FACT Stress will not lead to mental illness but can get worse and affect more and more aspects of the student's life.

MYTH Stress directly causes heart attacks, cancer and other serious illnesses.

FACT This is more difficult to answer and care should be taken not to provide a blanket denial. It should be stated that stress can *indirectly* cause such illnesses through increased alcohol consumption, smoking, etc. Although chronic stress is likely to negatively affect physical health, the problem is that in stating this students are simply likely to become more stressed. While it is reasonable to assume that psychological experience does affect the activity of the immune and cardiovascular systems, there are significant methodological problems in the definition and measurement of these concepts, between the effects of acute and chronic stressors, etc. (see Evans *et al.*, 1997, for an interesting discussion on stress and the immune system).

MYTH You need medication to control stress.

FACT The majority of students are likely to be taking medication at the start of the course. Students should not be dissuaded from taking appropriate medication during or after the course. Antidepressants may be useful to help 'lift' the individual enough to give them greater energy and motivation to practise the psychological approaches. There is little room for the clinician to be too precious about any particular approach. Again the idea of flexibility is useful—students should decide what their own needs are and, in the case of medication, discuss them fully with a medical practitioner. Ultimately, the course would aim to have students take control of their lives without being dependent on medication but, realistically, some students are likely to benefit from long-term or occasional use of antidepressants, for example. Anxiety management courses such as 'Stress Control' may be the most important part of any combination treatment (see Lydiard *et al.*, 1996, for a review of this area).

MYTH Stress only affects inadequate people.

FACT Stress affects everyone and anyone. Students are encouraged, at some point, to look around the room to see how many people there are, how normal they look and that they represent all types.

MYTH You are born with stress. It's in the blood so you can't change.

FACT By this stage, students should have completed the 'Targeting your stress' and 'Daily diary' forms. They should have identified patterns—times when the stress is high and times when it is low. From the 'Describing your stress' form, even 'born worriers' should have identified factors involved in making stress come and go. This points to a more complex relationship between the student and stress than simply 'It's my nerves.' The concept of *'state-dependent memory'* is introduced. This suggests that the individual's current emotion determines, to some extent, what memories are more readily available to them; i.e., anyone currently depressed will have better access to memories involving a depressed state. This may result in memory bias—recalling only blanket depression instead of a more mixed range of past emotions. Students are encouraged to ask parents, siblings, etc. to see how well their memories match.

---

(5) Thoughts, actions and body: the TAB model

In order to make more sense of stress, dividing it into cognitions, somatics and behaviour (thoughts, actions and body) will help make the problem more concrete to the student. By creating the vicious circle containing these systems, it will also make a three-systems treatment more coherent.

Thoughts

The concept of worry is looked at in detail. The nature and effect of anticipatory anxiety (the *'what ifs'*) on behaviour and somatics and the role of vigilance in detecting stress-provoking thoughts are explained. Lists of anxiety-related thoughts are shown on slides to help identification.

Actions

These are divided into two: avoidance actions and the effect on behaviour, e.g. speaking too quickly. The damaging effects of avoidance are highlighted. Lists of both are offered.

Body

The most obvious of the systems, the body symptoms, are divided into muscular/motor system and autonomic symptoms.

At this point, examples of the vicious circle can be sought. Imagine a man at a meeting at work who lacks the confidence to speak—he fidgets, he is sweating, he thinks everyone can see how badly he is coping, he won't maintain eye contact, he fidgets more, he sweats more . . . By understanding these relationships, students should see why treating each system should weaken the others.

(6) Break

See Chapter 8.

(7) The role of stress

While the ability to recognise the symptoms of stress will prove reassuring, understanding their role should help decrease the fear of fear so prominent in anxiety. By using a fight/flight/faint/freeze model best suited to panic but relevant to many anxiety problems, students can learn why they are reacting in the way they are. Using examples involving realistic danger, e.g. being confronted by an aggressive group of youths, students can see the survival value of such mind and body changes, e.g. the ability to focus on the danger, the ability to anticipate where the danger is most likely to come from and how to cope with it, to have greater physical power—in this example, to run or fight. The crucial role of the *perception* of threat is studied, with psychological threat triggering the same reaction as physical threat. The same physical and mental changes can now be seen to work against the individual. The role of the autonomic nervous system in helping create these changes can be examined and a rationale for treatments designed to desensitise the 'hair trigger' currently activating the fight/flight process can be made.

(8) Different types of stress

This section briefly looks at some of the more common anxiety disorders— general anxiety, phobia, panic, OCD, PTSD and depression—looking at the unique attributes but also emphasising the commonalities. The role of stress in other areas, e.g. anger or alcohol abuse, can also be discussed.

(9) What causes stress?

This section looks at biological predispositions, the role of childhood factors, life events and, in particular, the interpretation of these events. My approach suggests to students that we are far from wholly understanding the causes and that some students will not identify with the models I present. From experience, around 20% do not. It is important not to try to force these models onto students but to accept the limitations of our current knowledge.

It seems clear that biological predisposition varies from individual to individual but that practically anyone, under the right conditions, can develop clinical anxiety. Childhood factors that may be important relate to a developing sense of uncontrollability and unpredictability. These may result from life events such as frequent changes of house and school, illness and family break-ups. Certain parenting styles may also be important, e.g. placing inconsistent boundaries, being overly critical, overprotective, and intervening too readily to make sure the child succeeds, instead of allowing the child to learn to stand on his/her own feet. Certain beliefs transmitted to the child—it is dangerous to think certain things, it is dangerous to be ill with common ailments, etc.— may also increase vulnerability anxiety (see Barlow, 1998; Chorpita and Barlow, 1998). These may act as an Achilles heel in adult life.

Seeing life events in the context of these vulnerability factors can help explain the nature of the interpretations students make about the events and, hence, helps explain their reaction to them. It is important for students to understand that the effects of life events vary from individual to individual; e.g. Kessler *et al.* (1987) showed that financial strain was the main mediating variable in the relationship of unemployment to mental health in a blue-collar sample. Important factors in middle-class unemployment— reduced self-esteem, a sense of purposelessness and a lack of fulfilment— were not important themes in working-class unemployment. As this section is often carried over into the second session, a life events form is given as homework in Session 1 and discussed in Session 2.

(10) What keeps stress going?

The vicious circle involving thoughts, actions and body continues to strengthen the stress even in the absence of current problems. Students readily identify with a slide looking at the effects of this vicious circle.

(11) Important statements

By the end of the information part of the course, the hope is that students accept these 12 statements (see 'Key concepts'). Discussion can look at disagreements, misunderstandings, etc.

(12) Homework assignment

The life event form allows a gentle introduction to homework. This helps reinforce the need for students to work outside the course. By the end of session 2, students will be expected to work daily on homework.

THE EFFECTS OF STRESS

Self-esteem and self-confidence drop.

You become more and more self-conscious.

You feel threat from all sides.

You question your ability to cope with things you coped with in the past. You may avoid them as a result.

Worry becomes second nature to you.

Your body reacts so easily to even minor stress or for no apparent reason at all.

You may feel your back is to the wall, that problems keep hitting you and that you have no way to fight back.

You may feel that stress brings out the worst in you—you become more small-minded, petty, irritable.

You may feel that stress changes your personality.

CONCLUSIONS

With only information provision on the agenda, this session should be kept as simple as possible. This allows the student to settle to the course, to ensure that students do not feel the course is too difficult, that it is relevant to their needs and that they will be motivated to attend the remaining sessions. While students should be discouraged from remaining behind to ask for personal help, they may wish to talk to the teacher, for example, to clarify something in the session. Although there should be provision to do this during the session, many will lack the social confidence to do it in front of others, so it is reasonable to allow for some individual time. Care should be taken not to provide this to the same individuals each week. Students should leave the session on the same wavelength as the teacher and with the 'road map' showing the route from the vicious circle to the final destination of the positive circle firmly in their minds.

Chapter 10

TREATING SOMATIC ANXIETY

SESSION 2: STEP 8—CONTROLLING YOUR BODY

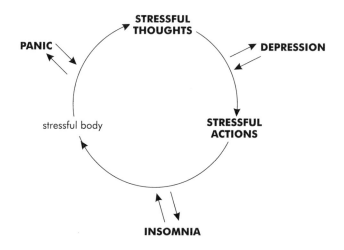

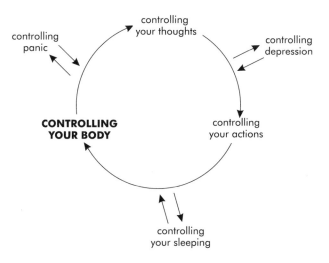

STEP 8: CONTROLLING YOUR BODY

Session format[1]

1. **Review and introduction**
2. **Education**—the role of the body in stress
3. **Therapy**—breathing retraining, aerobic exercise, progressive relaxation
4. **Break**
5. **Workshop**—progressive relaxation/breathing retraining
6. **Review**
7. **Homework**—relaxation tapes and diaries

Goals

This session aims to educate students about the effects of anxiety on the body and, thus, to provide a rationale for the use of progressive relaxation and, from the pre-course work, breathing retraining and aerobic exercise. As these techniques are among the easiest to understand and are typically seen as being highly relevant and appropriate, they are carried out first to help students quickly develop a sense of control.

Key concepts

Using the vicious circle, it can be explained that controlling body symptoms can help control thoughts and actions (and vice versa). Thus the power of the vicious circle will be diminished as an important component is brought under control. The main concepts in this session are as follows:

- The body can react strongly to stress with a wide range of symptoms.
- Symptoms can best be understood by dividing them into autonomic and motor symptoms.
- Symptoms can change over time.
- Symptoms can mimic those involved in feared physical conditions.
- Controlling symptoms can weaken the vicious circle of stress.
- Progressive relaxation can become the first main weapon that can be wielded to fight back against the stress.

Rationale

Using the information from the 'Role of stress' in the previous session, students are aware that the perception of threat leads to autonomic and motor system change, and that the resulting symptoms may be perceived as

---

[1] This format is retained during most of the therapy sessions.

unpleasant and/or dangerous. In turn, actions change in order to decrease physical symptoms; for example, individuals will leave a threatening situation, try to avoid exertion, or engage in ritualised behaviour. While not ascribing a primary role to any of the three systems, it should be clear that successfully intervening at the body symptom level could help prevent or slow down the resulting build-up of safety behaviours. Muscular relaxation may be particularly useful to those with GAD as they may be particularly prone to motor tension associated with autonomic inflexibility (Hoehn-Saric et al., 1989). However, combining these with breathing exercises may also be beneficial to those individuals with panic and agoraphobia for example, who present with autonomic arousal (Brown and Barlow, 1995).

THE SESSION

(1) Introduction and review of previous session

As some students may be attending for the first time and because many present at the first session will have been too anxious to concentrate on opening remarks, the session begins with a summary of the key points of the information session, along with a restatement of basic principles of the course (see previous chapter). The session topic will then be introduced along with an overview of the contents of the session.

(2) Education

Students tend to be well acquainted with the somatic presentation of anxiety. Most will have originally consulted their GP with a physical complaint that they may or may not have realised was due to anxiety. Most will also have tried some relaxation technique (Butler et al., 1987). The slide presenting body symptoms will be shown to point out again the large number of ways in which anxiety can affect the body. It is important to point out that many other somatic symptoms of stress exist and that space limits what can be shown. Students are asked, as a homework assignment, to consider which autonomic and motor system symptoms they commonly experience.

Experiments

To demonstrate the link between stress and body reactions, students may be asked to consider what would happen if they stood on what they believed to be a snake while walking through a field of long grass. They will readily describe the somatic symptoms. The next step would look at the effect of a stressful thought on body reactions, e.g. walking into a room full of strangers.

To understand why some are so sensitive to somatic symptoms, it is explained that we all have a 'third ear' and, in some, it has extremely acute hearing. While their first two ears listen to the world outside, the third ear listens to what is happening inside and scans for slight changes in normal body functions. On detecting change (that happens naturally, e.g. after eating, walking upstairs, feeling angry), the individual focuses on that part of the body. This results in the symptom being augmented. As an example of this, students may be asked to close their eyes and to concentrate on their hearts. Many will be able to report that their heart rate increases. Asked to explain why this should happen, most will see the link between the 'third ear' and the resultant change. This provides a less threatening rationale for somatic change and a rationale for the treatments on the course.

The role of habit

It is explained that many people have now got so used, for example, to their shoulders being tense that they see this as their normal state. The body has developed the *habit* of being tense. They may also realise that they have no ability to stop the development of symptoms; for example, the pain felt in the back of the neck will inevitably develop into a tension headache, thus further increasing their sense of lack of control.

(3) Therapy

Progressive muscular relaxation (PMR)

Although there is little evidence suggesting that PMR is a useful technique when used in isolation, combining it with the other techniques in 'Stress Control' can make it part of a powerful fusion. Although there are many well-produced tapes commercially available, there are advantages for teachers recording their own tapes as these provide greater continuity between the course and homework. The version used on the course is based on protocols of Bernstein and Borkovec (1973). There are three stages:

- 'Deep Relaxation';
- 'Rapid Relaxation';
- 'Putting it into Action'.

This progression helps students gain greater control in shorter periods and, finally, lose any dependency on the tape as they learn to 'slot the tape into their minds'. This built-in obsolescence counteracts the possibility of passivity and inevitable boredom. The message is that students can learn to identify stress entering their body at a much earlier stage and take action against it immediately. Thus the aim is to prevent rather than cure.

(4) Break (15 minutes)

This should last longer than in the first session to encourage socialising.

(5) Workshop

In vivo presentation

A 15-minute abbreviated 'deep relaxation' is given in the session to give an insight into what the relaxation tape contains. A negative expectation is deliberately given, i.e. no one will relax—'*It isn't the best place to do this but it will give you an idea of what is on your relaxation tape.*' Lights are dimmed and relaxation and breathing control combined.

Invariably, several people will report relaxing. As the others have met the negative expectations, i.e. have not relaxed, it allows them to think that relaxation may well work for them with practice. At this point, relaxation tapes are given for home use.

Relaxation-induced anxiety (RIA)

Heide and Borkovec (1984) reported that 30% of a generally anxious population experienced increased tension during a progressive relaxation session. The figures were significantly higher for individuals who undertook a session of meditation. Adler *et al.* (1987) reported on relaxation-induced panic (RIP). Although interesting theoretical insights are offered by both of these research groups, I have never found either RIA or RIP to be as common as these papers suggest. However, it is best to point out, in advance, that some people may find themselves becoming more tense when they try to relax. Suggesting that students should persevere has always avoided any significant problems with relaxation.

Relaxation instructions

Students must have appropriate expectations about relaxation tapes. In particular, they must realise that it takes time to work and that they should not be put off by initial inability to relax or concentrate. The following instructions can be helpful.

(a) Learning deep relaxation

Deep relaxation is the form of relaxation most favoured by experts in stress control. I have put it on tape to make learning it as straightforward as possible. You will need a cassette player or a personal hi-fi. If you have any serious physical problems, e.g. a back injury, that makes you unsure about carrying out these exercises, ask your doctor. If you find that your muscles hurt the following day, you may be tightening too much. Ease off next time.

WHAT IS IT?

PMR teaches you how to relax your body and mind. You first become aware of the way stress affects your body (*'I didn't realise that my shoulders were up at my ears all day'*). Having become aware of this, you then use the tape to get rid of it. The plan is that you use the tape to prevent stress building up in the first place—as soon as stress begins to creep into the body, an early warning signal will be picked up by your mind telling you to nip it in the bud. In other words, prevention is better (and easier) than cure.

WHAT DO YOU DO?

Relaxation is a skill to be learned. Like all skills, you won't pick it up overnight. You should expect that it will take a few weeks to even start to feel relaxed when you play the tape. Bear in mind you are learning something you have lost the knack of or even haven't had in the first place. So be patient.

SHOULD YOU SIT OR LIE DOWN?

Suit yourself. The best places may be the bed or the sofa. You may prefer the floor. If you have a comfy chair (recliners are very good), you could use this.

WHERE SHOULD YOU PLAY THE TAPE?

Play it in a room where you can get some peace and quiet and where you can be comfortable. Many people find the bedroom a good place; others prefer the living room—suit yourself. You could try out different rooms to see which is best for you. *Don't* play the tape while driving your car, for obvious reasons.

WHEN SHOULD YOU PLAY YOUR TAPE?

Every day. Don't miss playing the tape for any reason. You have to give the tape top priority if you are serious about controlling your stress. Decide what time of day suits you best and then stick to this time.

WHAT WILL HAPPEN WHEN YOU PLAY THE TAPE?

You will hear my voice. I will help you relax your breathing to a steady pace and lead you into a series of exercises designed to slow down your body and mind. You will tense and relax various muscles. The idea is that you become aware of the difference between tension and relaxation in your muscles.

Once you have gone through these exercises, you will move onto relaxing your mind. Don't worry if you find this bit more difficult. After I stop talking on the 'Deep relaxation' tape, you may want to stay where you are, continue to relax and enjoy the feeling.

Please note that this is not a hypnotic tape, so don't worry about going into a trance. You will be in complete control.

(b) Learning rapid relaxation

Rapid relaxation allows you to fine-tune your new skills. The idea is the same as that behind deep relaxation except that now, because you are a good deal more skilful, you can relax more quickly. You again concentrate on your breathing and relaxing your muscles. This time, however, you relax whole groups of muscles at the same time. The same rules apply—play the 'rapid relaxation' tape at the same time each day—and as before, don't expect to pick it up at once. So don't be put off when it doesn't work first time.

If you want to play both your 'deep relaxation' and 'rapid relaxation' tapes each day then go ahead—you can't get enough relaxation. The whole aim of deep and rapid relaxation is, of course, to teach you a way of controlling your own stress. Don't think you have to play your tape forever—you will probably become bored with it after a while in any case. So your final job is:

(c) Putting it into action

Imagine a soldier entering enemy territory. He expects to be attacked at any moment and carries a weapon so that he can fight back. As he is alert to any danger, he has a better chance of hearing the enemy and will be in a better position to avoid them in the first place or, if necessary, fight them off.

The *soldier* is you; the *enemy* is stress; the *weapon* is the skill of relaxation; *enemy territory* is anywhere you feel under stress. Because of your new skill, you can go into these places armed with a weapon that you did not have before. So instead of being at the mercy of the situation, you now have a way of controlling it. As you will be more alert to stress building up, you can nip it in the bud before it gets the chance to get a grip on you.

So carry out relaxation *before* you get into enemy territory and keep doing it *during* your time there by carrying out the exercises which no one will notice—controlling breathing, relaxing your shoulders, etc. Therefore, you should:

Prepare yourself by working out what situations cause you stress. Use relaxation before you have to face up to them.

Control the situation by staying in command in the face of stress.

Stay in control by keeping in mind that you now have a way of fighting back when stress threatens you.

TEN TIPS TO HELP YOU RELAX

1. Get as comfortable as possible before starting. Take off your shoes and wear loose clothes. Make sure the room is warm. If you can, take the phone off the hook and make sure no one in the house interrupts you.
2. At first, you should play the tape when you are feeling fairly calm as you will be able to concentrate better. This will let you pick it up more quickly.
3. When you go to play the tape, you may think of all the other things you should be doing instead. This is a common problem in stress. Do not allow yourself to be distracted. You must allow yourself time to relax.
4. As with learning any skill, it will take time and patience. So practise at the same time each day, every day.
5. Don't worry about how well or badly you are doing. Most people find that their concentration wanders during the first few weeks. This is normal. As you get used to the tape, your concentration will improve.
6. Steady and regular breathing is very useful in helping you to relax. Practise slowing down your breathing to about 10–12 breaths per minute at various times of the day (use the seconds hand on your watch). This will help you become aware of changes in your breathing and let you do something about it at the earliest point.
7. Deep relaxation, especially when you become good at it, can leave you feeling nicely drowsy. Some people fall asleep. If this happens to you, don't worry but bear in mind that you are learning a skill. So you will get more out of it if you can stay awake. If you are doing something that requires your full attention after playing the tape, e.g. driving, make sure that you give yourself time to feel fully alert before setting off.

8. You may find that when you are tensing your muscles you hold your breath. Don't worry, most people do this at the start. You will soon get the hang of breathing normally while you go through the tape.
9. Keep a diary of your progress. This will help you see how well you are getting on and will help your motivation. A relaxation diary will be given to you. Complete this every time you play the tape (Figure 10.1).
10. Continue playing your 'Deep relaxation' tape until you can relax well. At this point, you can either continue playing 'Deep relaxation' or switch to 'Rapid relaxation'.

Aerobic exercise
It is worthwhile again emphasising the value of aerobic exercise. Apart from the inherent benefits, the idea of actively developing any new strategy to tackle stress is likely to be of benefit.

(6) Review

Five minutes should be spent reviewing the major topics covered. Answer any questions students may have.

(7) Homework assignment

Students should write down the common motor and autonomic symptoms they experience. Relaxation diary forms are handed out (Figure 10.1). Students can submit these forms at the start of the next session if they wish. However, I encourage them to stockpile these forms so that, week on week, they can see the progression from inability to relax to developing competence. Diary forms are available each week on the course.

CONCLUSIONS

Starting with the more straightforward of the anxiety management techniques allows students to leave feeling they can cope with this approach, thus helping decrease anticipatory anxiety concerning handling the other techniques. As relaxation typically has a high degree of face validity, students may increasingly feel the course is appropriate for their needs.

'Stress Control': Relaxation diary

Before you play your tape, rate how stressful you feel using the 1–10 scale below. A score of 10 would mean your stress could not be worse. A score of 1 would mean you were not under any stress. Your score will probably be somewhere in between. When the tape ends, rate your stress again using the same scale. You should also make some notes about how you got on listening to the tape. Look at the example below.

$$|---|---|---|---|---|---|---|---|---|$$
$$1 \quad 2 \quad 3 \quad 4 \quad 5 \quad 6 \quad 7 \quad 8 \quad 9 \quad 10$$

	Time and place	Stress level before playing tape	Stress level after playing tape	Comments
Example	7 p.m., in the bedroom.	7	5	Lost my concentration for a bit but got it back before the end. Getting the breathing sorted out now and I felt a bit better by the time the tape ended. I'll try relaxing like this at work tomorrow.
Day 1				
Day 2				
Day 3				
Day 4				
Day 5				
Day 6				
Day 7				

Figure 10.1. Relaxation diary

Chapter 11

TREATING COGNITIVE ANXIETY

SESSION 3: STEP 9—CONTROLLING YOUR THOUGHTS

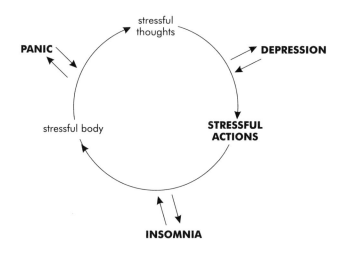

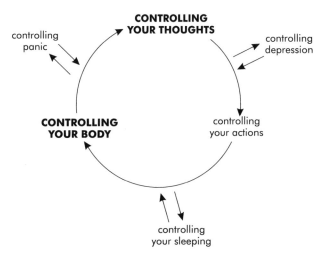

STEP 9: CONTROLLING YOUR THOUGHTS

Session format

1. **Review and introduction**
2. **Education**—the role of thoughts in stress
3. **Therapy**—cognitive therapy
4. **Break**
5. **Workshop**—cognitive therapy: **Challenging thoughts (1)**—the Court Case; **Challenging thoughts (2)**—Short cuts; **Challenging thoughts (3)**—Breaking stress up
6. **Homework**—Court Case diaries

Goals

This session aims to educate patients about the effects of anxiety on thinking and the effects of thinking on anxiety. In so doing, it will provide a rationale for the use of cognitive challenges. The cognitive approach described here has evolved over the years and always towards a much more simplified version of the basic Beckian model. Even so, these 'Court Case' challenges are difficult to learn and participants need to have appropriate expectations about the difficulty of the session. The concept, however, has to be straight-forward in order to be picked up quickly by the individual. If so, they are more likely to persevere with the techniques. 'Short cuts' and 'Breaking stress up' will be taught later in the session (or, possibly, depending on students' reaction, held over to session 4). This format does not allow detailed cognitive interventions such as modification of schemas although this could easily be inserted if extra sessions were available. I have generally avoided focusing on core schemas because of the limitations inherent in a didactic group approach. Recent evidence also may suggest that such approaches do not significantly add to therapeutic strength. Jacobson *et al.* (1996) found that dysfunctional attributional style in major depression was altered equally successfully by a core schema-focused intervention, a cognitive intervention that concentrated solely on modifying automatic thoughts and a behavioural intervention with no cognitive elements (see also Gortner *et al.*, 1998; Jacobson and Gortner, 2000).

Three related techniques are taught:

1. The Court Case;
2. Short Cuts;
3. Breaking stress up.

Key concepts

The vicious circle, used in the previous session, now expands to include thoughts. Vignettes and anecdotes are useful in getting over these concepts. The key concepts are as follows:

- Cognition feeds anxiety and anxiety, in turn, feeds cognition.
- You are likely to worry about the same things everyone else worries about but at a much more distressing level.
- Unlike others, you will not be able to stop worrying even though you want to.
- By increasing vigilance, individuals continually find evidence to back up their fears.
- Anxiety places 'blinkers' on the individual's eyes, blinding them to alternative explanations.
- 'Controlling your thoughts' aims to pull back the blinkers in order to see the full picture.
- This is not easy and takes time and effort.

Rationale

THE ICEBERG ANALOGY

Think of a ship sailing through Arctic waters. The ship's radar scans the seas for icebergs. When an iceberg is detected, the captain steers a course into safe waters. The radar rarely sees danger where none exists. The captain has faith in his radar, feels in control of his ship and experiences little anxiety.

We all have a 'radar' that scans for danger. The problem is that, once stress gets a grip of you, your radar is much too sensitive and you can no longer trust it. It detects danger when no real danger exists. You are seeing 'icebergs' everywhere. As a direct result, because you see so many icebergs, you cannot see any safe water to steer towards. Putting up these blinkers effectively blinds you, leaving you feeling powerless to escape danger.

THE ICEBERG IN REAL LIFE

You have a fear of making a fool of yourself while talking to people at a wedding. It is late at night. You see one man yawn:

Step 1. Your radar detects the yawn. You think *'He thinks I am boring.'* Even although no one else has yawned, your radar now zooms into this threat (or iceberg). As a result the threat seems to get bigger and become more 'real'. As you are zooming into the threat, you are now blinkered and unable to see that everyone else appears happy to talk to you (clear water). So you move to:

Step 2. You *generalise*. You next say to yourself *'They all think I'm boring. I want out of here.'* You are now forced to move to:

Step 3. *'I am boring. I'm always going to mess things up. Why can't I be like everyone else?'* You have *generalised* again; i.e., you are not just boring at weddings but everywhere. This time the generalisation is about yourself.

THE BLINKERS ANALOGY

Stress is seen as forcing blinkers onto your eyes, allowing you to see only the facts consistent with your anxiety. You are blinded to all the information that is not consistent with the anxious interpretation, e.g. maybe the man was tired, no one else yawned, you yawned. Once the blinkers are on, your imagination is set free with the *'what ifs'*. What if I make a fool of myself? What if these headaches are not caused by stress? What if I lose my job? And so on. The aim of this session is to force back the blinkers and let you see the full picture. This allows you to challenge thoughts more effectively and get your imagination under better control.

THE SESSION

(1) Review of previous session

The session begins with a quick review of the previous homework task, i.e. playing the relaxation tape on a daily basis. Common problems relate to students reporting they have not had the time. This should be addressed immediately. Relaxation-induced anxiety should be looked at. Anyone reporting marked anxiety should be counselled at the break. Those reporting mild anxiety should be asked to persevere on the understanding that the anxiety should disappear with practice. Expectations should again be that students will not relax in the coming week as they are still learning the technique. They should stick to deep relaxation for at least the next week. Anyone wishing individual feedback on their relaxation diaries should be encouraged to submit them. Additional copies of the diary should be available at the end of the session.

Introduction to the session

The session begins with a short summary of the session. As the cognitive work is likely to be the most difficult for most students, I tend to use negative expectation at this point. Thus students should expect not to pick this up immediately—indeed, they may end the session quite confused. It is important to highlight how important challenging thoughts is in controlling stress and why this strategy will be revisited later in the course.

(2) Education

By way of introduction, two contrasting responses to the same life event—the break-up of a relationship—are discussed:

> 'This is awful, I never wanted this to happen but things were going from bad to worse. Now is the time to end it. I'm very fragile and tense now. I know the next year is going to be rough but I will have to cope with it as best I can and I know I will get through this.'

> 'This is awful, I never wanted this to happen. It's all my fault. I just want to run away from all of this. I'll never marry again—it would just happen again. My life is always going to be a mess. I always screw things up. I'm so unhappy. I don't know what to do.'

If felt appropriate, a short group discussion can take place around the theme of which of the two will cope better and why. The concept of thinking influencing anxiety and depression will be clear, thus easing students into the session. Time should be spent on the iceberg and blinker analogies along with information from the key concepts involved in this session.

The role of habit

As in the previous session, it can be explained that one of the factors maintaining stress is the habit of not challenging thoughts. Ask the students how anyone would feel if they thought like the second person in the above example. Try to imagine thinking like this day after day after day—is it possible to be relaxed, content, self-confident? Why not? So would it be worthwhile to challenge these thoughts in case they are not accurate?

Experiments

As the therapy involves students in actively challenging instead of ignoring thoughts, there should be a demonstration of why ignoring thoughts does not work. Ask students suddenly not to think of a pink camel, repeat the instruction sternly—do *not* think of a pink camel. The laughter from the students, when they think of or imagine the pink camel, will clearly make the point to them.

(3) Therapy: challenge 1—The Court Case

This is the approach I have found most useful in quickly teaching simple cognitive approaches in group settings. Most people can visualise a court scene and, by asking the individual to play different roles in the court, it allows them to stand back and better interpret the available information. It is based on Scottish law (although the defence is presented first in this approach).

The scenario

Your thoughts are on trial charged with causing stress by deception. You must play all the roles in this court case. Your roles are:

Defence lawyer (Evidence for)

You must initially defend these thoughts by producing as much evidence as possible showing that these thoughts are accurate and true.

Prosecution lawyer (Evidence against)

You must attack these thoughts and produce as much evidence as possible showing that they are inaccurate and false.

Judge (Summing up)

You must sum up fairly by presenting the key points made by both prosecution and defence.

Jury (Verdict)

You must carefully weigh up all the evidence and come up with a verdict. You should note that few 'real' trials are black and white. Most involve a balanced decision (shades of grey)—'On the one hand . . . but on the other . . .' Your verdict will probably be similar.

If individuals understand that their thinking can make anxiety worse, then it should be equally clear that challenging their thinking can make their anxiety lessen. Thus, the aim is to let people stand back and better evaluate information, to stop them jumping to conclusions by having them challenge thoughts and by offering them a weapon that allows them to fight back against what are probably seen as uncontrollable thoughts or worries. The blinkers analogy can be usefully used at this stage. The workshop offers examples of court cases for anxiety. The same approach is used for depression in the final session.

(4) The break (15–20 minutes)

(5) Workshop

Challenging your thoughts (1)—The Court Case

COURT CASE 1

The scene. Robert is worrying about his wife. She has been irritable and distant for some days.

Step 1. Anxious thoughts

Why is Jenny acting like this? What have I done? What if she is becoming fed up with me? What if there is someone else? I'll go to pieces if she leaves me.

Step 2. Evidence for (defence lawyer)

She isn't usually like this. We have had several arguments recently and she was very angry. If she still wanted to be with me, she would be happy. She is very good looking and she meets all these high-flyers at work. Maybe she realises she made a mistake marrying me.

Step 3. Evidence against (prosecution lawyer)

All I know is that Jenny is irritable and distant. Why have I jumped to the conclusion that it is my fault? Are there any other possible reasons for her behaviour? She has been working hard recently and her father is back in hospital. Maybe she is unwell. There may be any number of other explanations for her behaviour.

Step 4. Summing up and verdict (judge and jury)

On the one hand, she is acting out of character. On the other, she has been like this in the past. It lasts only a few days. We are normally happy together—am I making too much of her recent behaviour? Stop jumping to conclusions. I have not even asked her what is wrong with her. There could be any number of things. I am being too self-centred in thinking that Jenny can't have a fit of the blues or whatever unless I'm to blame. What is wrong with being like this for a few days—I feel like this from time to time and it doesn't mean anything, so why can't Jenny? Instead of worrying, I should find out more by asking Jenny what is wrong. Even if there is a problem in our relationship, I do not have to jump to the worst outcome. By finding out if anything is wrong, I may be able to find out if there is anything I can do to help.

COURT CASE 2

The scene. Brian's fears centre on driving. He is worried that he might lose control and has a vivid image of causing a multiple crash. He now avoids driving on busy, fast roads but is increasingly tense on any road.

Step 1. Anxious thoughts

'What if I feel the stress coming on when I am driving at rush hour? I might lose control of the car and I'll end up causing a disaster.'

Step 2. Evidence for

'Every time I go on this road, I feel under stress. I feel that I'm not concentrating enough. I'm very edgy until I get off the road.'

Step 3. Evidence against

'It has never happened in the past even though I have been very stressed in the car. If I did feel the stress getting too high then I could take a turning off the main road. If it was very bad, I could pull into the side of the road.'

Step 4. Summing up and verdict

'It is probably quite normal to feel stressed for the first few minutes on the road. I now know that this stress is made worse by the way I am thinking about it. Maybe if I get a better grip on my thoughts, the stress won't be able to build up to the same degree.'

The court case should not be seen as an instant antidote to stressful thoughts. The mechanisms allow for the possibility that the thoughts are accurate and the emotional response justified. In some cases, it leaves open the possibility that the thoughts are true but places them within a context that allows the individual to see that they are simply one of many possible interpretations. This allows evaluation of probability to be calculated, thus usually taking some of the sting out of the initial unchallenged thoughts.

It can be useful to end the session at this stage as there is the danger of providing too much information in the one session (the other techniques are described below). This allows students to concentrate on the one technique in the coming week. Court Case diaries should be made available (Figure 11.1).

'Stress Control': Court case diary

Stressful thought(s)	Evidence for	Evidence against	Conclusions
Example *(printer asked to do skilled job)* I'll make a mess of this job. I'm not up to this. They all think I'm useless.	I'm so tense I'm bound to screw it up. I can't concentrate when I'm like this. This is too hard for me.	The boss asked me to do it — he must have confidence in me. I've done similar jobs many times before. I always think I'll screw it up yet I always manage in the end.	I'm making too much of this. Concentrate on the job. Divide it into stages and take them one at a time. I won't feel overwhelmed if I do it this way.

Figure 11.1. Court case diary

Challenging your thoughts (2)—Short cuts

Although the formal structure of the court case is important as a first approach, the artificiality has many clear drawbacks. Thus, individuals should be encouraged, in their own time, to attempt some short cuts. These, essentially, compress the court case into one challenge. As with the court case, they are not designed to get rid of the anxiety but to get it more in proportion. The challenges therefore put a ceiling on how bad things can be.

The three main challenges are:

1. What's the worst thing that can happen?
2. What are the chances . . .?
3. Am I right to think that?

WHAT'S THE WORST THING THAT CAN HAPPEN?

Anxious thought

'What if I blush in front of my work-mates? I would want to curl up and die.'

Short cut

'What is the worst thing that could happen? I've blushed in front of them before. I was very self-conscious but nothing else happened. So if it happens again, will it be the end of the world? Will they disown me? Would I disown someone else if it happened to them? So, at worst, I will be embarrassed. I don't like it but it isn't going to kill me. Keep it in proportion.'

WHAT ARE THE CHANCES?

Anxious thought

'If I don't get out of here, I'm going to faint.'

Short cut

'What are the chances of my fainting? I always think that I am going to faint yet I never have since I was pregnant. On the few occasions when I haven't been able to get out, I have felt very faint but then the feeling passed and I was OK. So I must stay where I am and brave it out. This is as bad as it will get but if I stay the anxiety will die down and I will have controlled it myself.'

AM I RIGHT TO THINK THAT . . .?

Anxious thought

'Everyone is looking at me. They can all see that I can't cope with this.'

Short cut

'Am I right to think that everyone is looking at me? Look around—everyone is getting on with their own business. They are not interested in me. This anxiety makes me way too sensitive. I know I hide my anxiety well. I probably look OK and, in any case, even though I am very tense just now I am still coping.'

Challenging your thoughts (3)—Breaking stress up

Based on coping self-statements used in Stress Inoculation Training (Meichenbaum, 1985), this section attempts to have individuals think ahead to prevent the build-up of anxiety. In other words, the emphasis is on prevention rather than cure. My approach uses three of the four stages used by Meichenbaum:

- preparing to face stress (*before*);
- coping with stress (*during*);
- reviewing (*after*).

Meichenbaum notes that the role of this guided self-dialogue is to help individuals:

1. assess the demands of a situation and plan for future stressors;
2. control negative self-defeating, stress-engendering thoughts, images and feelings;
3. acknowledge, use and relabel the arousal experienced;
4. cope with intense dysfunctional emotions that might be experienced;
5. 'psych' themselves up to confront stressful situations; and
6. reflect on their performance and reinforce themselves for having attempted to cope (Meichenbaum, 1985, p. 70).

These self-statements should not be used as, in Meichenbaum's words, a 'psychological litany' that tends towards rote repetition. Individuals should be encouraged to develop their own personally relevant self-statements and to modify them in light of experience. Similarly, negative self-statements should be looked upon as cues for the production of positive self-statements.

I have found this approach particularly useful when combined with the behavioural concept of exposure, i.e. allowing the individual to actively prepare, both cognitively and behaviourally, to face stress-inducing situations.

(6) Review

Individuals should see their attempts at the Court Case as a way of melting or at least shrinking the icebergs to allow a better view of the clear waters into which they can now sail. Students should be given the expectation that the court case will be difficult to do at first in order to help them persevere until, with sustained practice, progress is made.

(7) Homework assignments

- Court Case diaries to be completed (Short cuts and Breaking stress up should be attempted at the students own pace).
- Relaxation diaries to be completed.

CONCLUSIONS

These straightforward cognitive challenges can be used on a daily basis for a range of anxious thoughts. Students, once they become competent, will believe they now have some way of controlling thoughts previously believed to be outside their control. This will reduce anxiety, which in turn will reduce cognitive misinterpretations. Along with relaxation skills, the vicious circle is weakening and being replaced with a positive circle, reinforcing individuals' beliefs that they can control their anxiety by using these new coping strategies.

Chapter 12

TREATING BEHAVIOURAL ANXIETY

SESSION 4: STEP 10—CONTROLLING YOUR ACTIONS

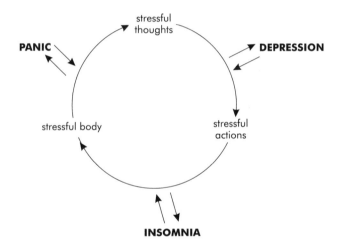

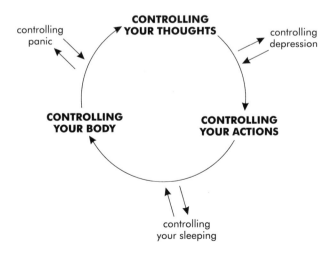

STEP 10: CONTROLLING YOUR ACTIONS

Session format

1. **Review and introduction**
2. **Education**—the role of actions in stress
3. **Therapy**—exposure and other behavioural techniques
4. **Break**
5. **Workshop**—challenging your actions—exposure, coping strategies and problem solving
6. **Review**
7. **Homework assignment**—exposure, finding hidden problems

Goals

After spending 20–30 minutes on 'controlling your thoughts' (see previous chapter), this session aims to educate patients about the effects of anxiety on behaviour and the effects of behaviour on anxiety. The session aims to provide a rationale for the use of exposure and other behavioural techniques within a cognitive-behavioural framework. Individuals are also helped to look for hidden problems. It also attempts to integrate the behavioural, cognitive and somatic approaches learned so far. Thus the exposure techniques are seen not simply within an habituation model but are seen as a continuation of the cognitive model taught in the previous session. This model emphasises the letting go of safety behaviours to test the dangerousness of feared situations.

Four techniques are taught:

1. finding hidden problems;
2. exposure;
3. coping strategies;
4. problem solving.

Key concepts

The vicious circle used in the previous session now expands to include actions. Vignettes and anecdotes are useful in getting over these concepts. The main ones are as follows:

- Now that individuals have learned a lot about stress and how it affects them, they should check that their focus on treatment goals is accurate.
- Behaviour is affected by anxiety and then feeds anxiety.
- Avoidance works well in the short term but adds to problems in the long term.
- Exposure to stressful situations or activities adds to stress in the short term but reduces stress in the long term. This is also helped by reducing safety-seeking behaviours (see Salkovskis, 1991).

- Problem solving and other stress reduction strategies can add to the growing sense of control.
- This is not easy and takes time and effort.

THE SESSION

(1) Review of previous sessions

Relaxation. Most students should be able to sit through the deep relaxation without too much difficulty. Some may be able to relax. This relaxation may be short lived and may disappear as soon as the tape ends. Students should be advised to stay with the deep relaxation but to move onto quick relaxation if they feel ready.

Controlling thoughts. Students should still expect to find challenging thoughts difficult to do. They should continue to try to stand back from situations and work out what they are thinking, how these thoughts affect their stress level and, if possible, try to alter these thoughts either by using the Court Case or the Short cuts. Whenever possible, they should be planning ahead to an anticipated stressful event using the Meichenbaum techniques (Breaking stress up) learned earlier in the session.

The emphasis for both controlling thoughts and body remains on the need to practise and any feelings of improvement are to be welcomed but not thought likely at this early stage.

(2) Education

Rationale and treatments

Hidden problems. If students have carefully completed diary forms and have begun to develop a formulation of their own problems, session 4 is an appropriate time to look for hidden problems. These are problems that will exacerbate overt problems and, if left untackled, may lead to continued problems or relapse. Anecdotes are again used. If appropriate, these can be used for a class discussion. The first is simple, the second more subtle.

ANECDOTE 1

An elderly woman presented for help with anxiety. This anxiety seemed to be worse at weekends. It became apparent that her husband drank heavily at the weekend, would often return late at night and be verbally, and often physically, abusive towards her. This greatly stressed her. Should she simply attend for anxiety management or is there a hidden problem that needs to be addressed?

ANECDOTE 2

Susan presented with a one-year history of agoraphobia. Before this, she had been outgoing, socially skilled and enjoyed her job working in a bar at the weekends. Owing to the fears of leaving her home, she had to give up her job. Her partner, Alan, had to take over most of the responsibilities in the household as Susan felt she could no longer cope. *What treatment would work?*

Let us add more information. Susan's father had died, unexpectedly, the previous year. Susan was on holiday at the time. She organised everything and felt she had to be strong for her mother and younger brothers in the weeks following the death. She was very close to her father. She seemed unable to talk about him and had been unable to visit the grave. When visiting her mother, she was unable to sit in 'his' chair. *Does this information change our approach to treatment?*

Alan had a long-standing problem with low self-confidence. He believed, in his heart of hearts, that Susan had married 'beneath her' and that one day she would realise this and leave him. *What effect does this piece of information have?*

The idea is to engage the students in analysing this problem and generating treatment ideas. My experience is that quite profound thinking often arises and a cooperative approach often develops. This may lead students to feel that they are now able to act as 'therapists'—a halfway stage to their believing they can act as their own therapist—a key goal in the course. Students often state that, while they do not wish to talk about personal problems, they relish this opportunity to work on these scenarios.

In the first scenario, they immediately perceive that anxiety management, at least alone, is not the answer to the woman's problems. Discussion often looks at options—or the lack of them—in many people's lives and how they could best cope in less than perfect circumstances.

Commonly, in the second scenario, the group quickly perceive that there could be some secondary gain for Alan in having his partner grow more dependent on him. The problems with mourning for her father will also be noted. In terms of treatment, the idea of multiple problems requiring intervention will hopefully slide into their own formulations and be seen as common rather than overwhelming.

It is important to point out that by no means everyone has hidden problems and, for those who do, they may be quite simple to find. Hidden problems could lie with relationships within the family, with friends or at work; they could relate to financial, sexual, alcohol, drug or gambling problems; they could reflect behaviours involving stubbornness, immaturity or excessive dependency. These may be problems students have or they may be affected by these problems in others. The aim is to tackle these problems if possible.

Discussion with relatives and friends may be a useful activity. The aim is for students to develop, if necessary, a more complex self-help treatment based on this additional knowledge.

(3) Therapy: exposure

Rationale

In order to explain the role of avoidance and the necessity for exposure, the following can be helpful:

> 'Many of you may have felt, when I discussed the idea of this course to you, that it was just what you needed. As the course got nearer and nearer, your thinking probably started to change—you began to worry about meeting someone you know, you were afraid you might have to talk openly about your problems, you worried that you might have drawn unwanted attention to yourself. Still, you made it to the course and now those fears have probably died. You feel you have achieved something simply by facing up to the fears and overcoming them. You have *exposed* yourself to your fears and won.
>
> Imagine a woman who wanted to come to the first session. She may have left the house but as she got nearer to the health centre her anxiety rose and rose. As she tried to enter the building, she felt panicky and turned back.
>
> How would she feel? Probably a mixture of disappointment, self-criticism and maybe relief? Avoidance works—it reduces anxiety very quickly.
>
> Think of that woman now—is she getting better? *No.*
>
> Is she more or less likely to make it to another course? *Less.*
>
> Is her self-confidence rising or falling? *Falling.*
>
> Why? *Because she avoided.* She didn't allow herself to discover if she could have coped or not—she did not 'reality test'.
>
> Compare her experiences with your own.
>
> Now think about the things you do to avoid something unpleasant happening. Do you rehearse what you are going to say to someone in case you appear stupid in front of them? Do you hold your hand over your face to hide your blushing? Do you avoid running for the bus in case your heart races? Well, it may be that these *safety behaviours* are also important in keeping stress alive because you never get the chance to test the reality of your fears. So, I want you not only to face up to the places or things that cause you stress but also to drop your safety behaviours to see what happens. So you are running an experiment as well as just facing up.

(4) Break (15 minutes)

(5) Workshop

(a) Exposure

Students should be offered the 'Facing up' form (Figure 12.1) and asked to create a list or hierarchy of avoidance behaviours. This can be carried out in the session or as a homework assignment. A plan of action should be compiled and acted on.

(b) Coping strategies

This section focuses on easily understood, commonsensical stress management strategies. These will differ according to the needs of the students on the course. A section in 'Stresspac' on '25 ways to cope' is designed for routine outpatient anxiety and mixed anxiety/depression disorder sufferers. Here are six examples.

MUSTS AND SHOULDS

'I must see my mother today', *'I should offer to be treasurer for the football team.'* Work out what is reasonable for you to achieve and be happy with this—*'If I get through all the things I want to at home, I'll visit my mother. If not, I'll see her later in the week', 'I don't get a chance to relax as it is, so it's crazy to take on more pressure—someone else can take a turn.'*

ONE THING AT A TIME

Think of someone at work cradling a phone between his shoulder and his ear. With one hand, he is writing a letter and, with the other, searching through some papers. At the same time, he is trying to grab a quick snack. This is overloading the system. If you are making a phone call, make only the call and nothing else. The message is, don't keep too many balls in the air at the one time.

EXERCISE

If you are lying in front of the TV all day and night, you are not helping your stress. Think about becoming more active. Aerobic exercise may be best. Taking up something new can often give you a challenge. Meeting this challenge can help your self-confidence. It will give you a feeling that you are doing something worthwhile.

'Stress Control': Facing up form

Situations/activities you are avoiding because of stress	Facing up: Plan of action What safety behaviours are you dropping? What do you think will happen? What happened?	

Figure 12.1. 'Facing up' form

DON'T ACCEPT OTHER PEOPLE'S TARGETS

If you feel that people expect too much of you, don't try to satisfy these expectations. Have a quiet word and reach agreement. If agreement can't be reached, say 'NO'.

CAFFEINE

Caffeine is a stimulant (like nicotine). It can increase bodily stress. Caffeine is contained in a range of products: tea, coffee, fizzy soft drinks (especially diet-free versions), some headache tablets and pain killers. Everyone has their own limit but, as a *very* rough guide, 12 cups of tea, 10 cups of instant coffee or six cups of fresh coffee a day may be enough to produce symptoms. If you get symptoms from caffeine, cut back slowly to avoid withdrawal effects. Switch gradually to decaffeinated coffee, caffeine-free fizzy drinks or pure fruit juice instead.

BUILD UP SUPPORTS

Having a range of supports—friends, interests, hobbies, etc.—can help if you are having problems in one area of your life as you can fall back on the others for a while. The moral is, don't put all your eggs in the one basket.

(c) Problem solving

Jarvis *et al.* (1995) list six stages in problem solving:

1. defining *exactly* what the problem is;
2. brainstorming options to deal with the problem;
3. choosing the best option(s);
4. generating a detailed action plan;
5. putting the plan into action;
6. evaluating the results (Jarvis *et al.*, 1995, p. 66).

Using this framework, students are asked to identify problems not yet tackled and which, if left untouched, may hamper outcome. A problem-solving form (Figure 12.2) based on Jarvis *et al.* is provided.

Six steps to successful problem solving

---

(1) Define *exactly* what the problem is

Make sure the problem is concrete and, if necessary, broken down into several smaller problems

My problem is:

---

(2) Brainstorm options to deal with the problem

Look for every possible solution no matter how unlikely

Figure 12.2.

(3) Choosing the best option(s) by examining the pros and cons of each potential solution

Possible solution	Pros	Cons
(1)		
(2)		
(3)		
(4)		

Best option is:

Figure 12.2.

(4) Generate a detailed action plan

Plan the 'when, where, how, and with whom' of your solution

My plan is:

How?

When?

Where?

With whom?

(5) Put the plan into action

Mentally rehearse the plan and then do it

(6) Evaluate the results to see how well it worked

If it didn't work, go back to stage 3 and look for another plan

Figure 12.2. Problem-solving form

(6) Review

Students have learned a lot in this session. They should be asked to spend time looking at each area in the coming week, work out which areas need to be worked on, and develop plans for doing so. They should be mindful of integrating the skills learned in previous sessions with the 'Controlling your actions' skills.

(7) Homework

- 'Facing up' form.
- Problem-solving form.
- Time should be spent looking for hidden problems. The most appropriate coping strategies should be selected.
- Court case diaries should still be available.
- Relaxation forms should still be available.

CONCLUSIONS

These straightforward behavioural techniques will, along with the cognitive and relaxation skills, continue to weaken the vicious circle. At the same time, the positive circle is strengthening individuals' beliefs that they can control their anxiety by using these new coping strategies.

At this stage in the course, students should have accepted responsibility for analysing their own needs and developing appropriate interventions. Thus, for example, the exposure treatment should be entirely self-generated. This should communicate further the belief that the individual is capable of handling this responsibility.

Chapter 13

TREATING PANIC ATTACKS

SESSION 5: STEP 11—CONTROLLING YOUR PANIC

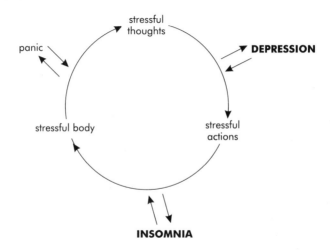

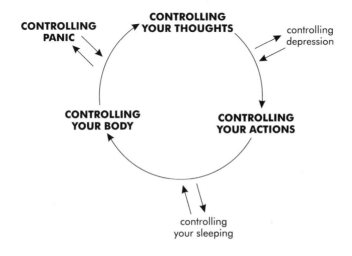

STEP 11: CONTROLLING YOUR PANIC

Session format

1. **Review and introduction**
2. **Education**—the nature of panic
3. **Therapy**—CBT
4. **Workshop**—breathing retraining, court case, exposure, reducing the risks
5. **Break**
6. **Review**
7. **Homework assignment**—panic diary, cognitive–behavioural interventions

('Controlling your sleep' is dealt with in the final 30 minutes of this session—see next chapter.)

Goals

This session aims to educate students about the nature of panic, how to assess panic and how to control it. A cognitive–behavioural approach uses techniques already learned on the course. As some students will never have experienced panic, it is important to emphasise that this session also offers further insight into treating stress and thus is relevant to all.

A three-systems (TAB) approach is used:

- controlling your body—the role of breathing;
- controlling your thoughts—the Court Case;
- controlling your actions—exposure;
- reducing the risks;
- emergency help.

Key concepts

Now that the TAB vicious circle is being tackled, we must tackle other vicious circles that also feed anxiety:

- Panic, a state of terror and uncontrollability, leads to apprehension about having another panic.
- This leads to a rise in generalised anxiety.
- It is likely to involve avoidance as a tool to avoid further panic. This reinforces the problem.
- Learning ways to control or, even better, prevent panic will lead to a greater sense of personal control enabling the individual to face up to situations and behaviours thought likely to trigger panic.
- This will result in shutting off another fuel supply for the stress.

Rationale

Panic can be seen as the purist form of fight/flight/faint/freeze. Some people may be biologically more sensitised to panic but it is a common problem, with possibly over 30% of the population experiencing at least one panic attack each year (Norton *et al.*, 1985). As many panic disorder sufferers will experience generalised anxiety, the main techniques taught on the course will be of value. However, learning specific anti-panic techniques will help speed up progress.

THE SESSION

Unlike other sessions, the teaching of the therapy and the workshop are not separated as a range of techniques is taught. The break is fitted in whenever seems appropriate.

(1) Review of previous sessions

Relaxation. Those wishing to progress from deep to rapid relaxation should be encouraged to do so.

Controlling thoughts. Information on Court Case progress should be sought. Most students will probably continue to find the 'court case' and other cognitive techniques difficult. They should be told this is to be expected and to persevere with these approaches.

Controlling actions. Hidden problems should have been looked for. Those finding them should have looked at ways of controlling them, while those who did not should move on. Particular importance should be placed on exposure and problem-solving techniques for both psychological and social problems.

Bearing in mind the emphasis on the course to 'be your own therapist', students should be strongly encouraged to move at their own pace and not to set rigid timetables for these techniques.

Introduction to the session

Students will see the flexibility of the techniques taught in this session as they have, in one guise or another, appeared before. The detailed work on breathing will add another dimension to the array of techniques they are accumulating.

(2) Education

> 'I'm terrified another panic hits me. I honestly thought I was going to die when I had that last one. It came out of the blue—I couldn't breathe, my heart felt it was going to burst, I felt I was going to faint. I was covered in sweat and I felt sick. At its worst point, I felt I wouldn't survive it. It was the worst feeling I have ever experienced.'

Use of this slide can help those who have experienced panic to identify with the session's content. Discussion can centre on the consequences of the panic—how that individual would be affected by it and how it could feed the vicious circle of stress. At this point, panic should be discussed within the context of TAB.

The TAB approach

THOUGHTS

Panics are likely to involve a sudden rush of intense fear and a feeling that you are losing control. You are likely to feel that something awful is about to happen to you even though you may not be able to say exactly what. Common fears include a fear of dying, fainting, going mad, making a fool of yourself or losing control in some way.

ACTIONS

The fear of panic may make you avoid going to certain places where you think you are more likely to panic, e.g. busy shops, social nights, being alone at home. You may avoid doing certain things for the same reason, e.g. exerting yourself.

BODY

A panic attack involves very strong physical symptoms—heart racing, breathlessness, dizziness, nausea, shaking, sweating, etc. These symptoms may be similar to those involved in stress but much more intense. It is not unusual to find heart rate almost doubling in a matter of minutes. That is frightening, especially if you do not know why it has happened.

Slides detailing specific TAB symptoms can be used at this point. Emphasis should be placed on the surge in sympathetic nervous system activity along with the general acute bodily sensitivity noted in those prone to frequent panics. Panic attacks can best be divided into *predictable*—e.g. 'If I go to the supermarket, alone, at a busy time, I will probably panic'—*unpredictable*—the 'out-of-the-blue-panic'—and *nocturnal panic*—often occurring between the second and third hours of (slow-wave) sleep. The latter can be tied in with relaxation-induced anxiety (RAI) (discussed in session 2), where the body relaxes and these personally relevant stimuli are misinterpreted by the sleeping individual as a sign of losing control. This point helps cement the course as connections are made across the various sections.

The TAB vicious circle in panic

THE ROLE OF THOUGHTS

TAB feeds itself. As the panic may seem to come out of the blue and because it hits you with such strength, you may think, for example:

'This can't be stress. I'm so dizzy and confused. I can't seem to see straight. I'm losing control. I'm having a stroke.'

THE ROLE OF ACTIONS

You will be very aware of the changes in your actions caused by panic and this will feed back into your thoughts:

'I can't stop shaking. Everyone is looking at me. They all know I am out of control.'

If you are avoiding going places or doing things for fear of provoking a panic, you are aware that you are restricting your life out of fear. This will affect your self-confidence. You will not discover whether you could have dealt with the situation or not as you have failed to test the reality of your fears.

THE ROLE OF THE BODY

If you are prone to panic, you are likely to be very aware of the way it affects your body. (You will generally be very sensitive to even small natural changes in your body.) This isn't surprising given the very unpleasant reaction your body has to panic. So your thoughts tend to relate to body problems, for example:

'I'm so dizzy. I'm going to pass out.'

'My stomach is heaving. I'm going to throw up.'

The TAB vicious circle model, used in stress, can now be shown to feed panic sensations.

The panic diary (Figure 13.1)

Those students who are experiencing panic are encouraged to complete the diary over several weeks to learn more about the nature of their panic attacks.

(3 and 4) Treatment and workshop

(a) Controlling your body: the role of hyperventilation

Although the suggestion that hyperventilation is an important symptom-producing mechanism in panic has been challenged (e.g. Garssen *et al.*, 1996), controlled breathing as a coping technique has been shown to be a useful component in panic control treatments (e.g. Brown and Barlow, 1995). In my experience, the vast majority of students with heterogeneous anxiety disorders can answer positively to questions on hyperventilation. Thus the usefulness in controlling breathing will be seen as a personally relevant strategy by practically all. Breathing retraining can be started prior to the course if the quick control techniques contained in 'Stresspac' are used. Placing breathing control exercises on the relaxation tape can, along with advice on diaphragmatic breathing, reinforce the importance of this technique. A suggested rationale is as follows.

RATIONALE AND ANALOGY

When we breathe in, we breathe in oxygen. This is taken into the lungs and bloodstream and it feeds the cells in our body to keep us alive. Once it is used, it is converted into carbon dioxide—a waste product. This is taken back through the bloodstream, into the lungs and is breathed out. There should always be a balance between the oxygen going in and the carbon dioxide going out. This balance will stay the same whether you are running for a bus or sitting in front of the TV.

Now think of a car—the faster the car goes, the more fuel is used. If the car goes slower, it burns less fuel. Your breathing works in a similar way with oxygen acting as your fuel. If you need more stamina and muscle strength—for example, if you are playing football, running for a bus or digging the garden—then your breathing will automatically speed up and you will take in more oxygen. As you will be burning up oxygen more quickly, you will continue to breathe quicker and deeper to replace the oxygen you have used. When, a few hours later, you are sitting at home in front of the TV, your breathing will be much slower as you are not using up as much energy.

'Stress Control' Panic diary

(1) Where and when did you have the panic?					
(2) Was there a reason for the panic?					
(3) What body symptoms did you have?					
(4) At the worst point, what were your thoughts?					
(5) What did you do?					
(6) What can you do next time to help control or prevent panic?					

Figure 13.1. Panic Diary

Hyperventilation

Hyper (too much) *ventilation* (breathing) results when you are breathing too quickly for your needs. One of the problems in stress is that the threats you are worrying about are not those that you can physically fight or run away from. Yet the fight/flight process we spoke about in session 1 prepares you for physical exertion. So you are left filled with energy in the shape of oxygen that you cannot quickly burn up. It is like producing enough oxygen to let you play a hard game of football when all you are doing is sitting in front of the TV.

As you are not burning up the extra oxygen straight away, it remains in the body longer before eventually being converted to carbon dioxide. Of course, because you have to breathe out after you breathe in, you are losing too much carbon dioxide. At that point, you have lost the all-important balance. The body is, in fact, sensitised not to the amount of extra oxygen but to the loss of carbon dioxide. This causes changes in the blood and lungs. These changes are short lived and are not dangerous. The changes directly cause the following symptoms to appear:

- There is a slight drop in the amount of blood going to the brain. This may leave you with a dizzy feeling, a sense of unreality, or feeling confused. You may have a choking feeling, feel breathless or have visual disturbance.
- There is also a drop in blood reaching some parts of the body. This can produce a rapid heart rate, numbness, tingling in the hands and feet, tight muscles and cold, clammy hands.
- Yawning and/or sighing.
- Feeling flushed, hot and sweaty.
- Chest tightness or pains.
- Exhaustion.

Note that the symptoms I have just listed are *directly* caused by hyperventilation and are very similar to the symptoms people describe when they have a panic attack. So if you are hyperventilating, controlling it will help in controlling panic attacks. Don't forget:

Hyperventilation is not dangerous.

If you hyperventilate quickly and powerfully, these symptoms may come on in seconds (e.g. if you get a sudden shock). However, you are more likely to do so in a much slower, subtle way over a period of minutes or hours. In this case, the body compensates somewhat and you may not get many of these symptoms. However, you may go into panic without any warning when your carbon dioxide level drops below a certain level. This could happen even if you yawn (you lose a lot of carbon dioxide when you breathe out during a yawn). It's like the straw that breaks the camel's back. These symptoms can be very unpleasant and are likely to cause stressful thoughts (think of the TAB vicious circle). As you won't be aware of these very slow changes, it helps explain why panics can seem to come out of the blue. It also means that if you control your breathing, you make it less likely that you will panic. However, a critical point must be made—hyperventilation only produces the *symptoms*. The *panic* is produced by the way you interpret the symptoms. Hence, we need to look again at controlling your thoughts.

(b) Controlling your thoughts

Using the Clark, D.M. *et al.* (1994) model, which emphasises that it is the misinterpretation of normal bodily sensations that may trigger the panic, it should be clear that reappraisal techniques combined with breathing are the appropriate treatment. Using Court Case or the Short cuts taught in session 3 can now be directly applied to the control of panic.

Examples can be discussed, e.g. using a vignette of someone who experiences breathlessness, chest pains, and tingling in their fingers. Interpretations of these symptoms can be looked for and likely responses to these interpretations assessed. The students should quickly understand why a cognitive intervention is important and should be able to apply the skills already learned. An example of a short-cut approach is given below.

WHAT IS THE WORST THING THAT CAN HAPPEN?

. . . if I have another panic?

The worst thing that can happen is that I'll be full of fear, I'll feel that I can't breathe, I'll be drenched in sweat and I'll feel very dizzy. I will end up in tears and feel miserable. That is bad news but it won't be the end of the world. And that is *if* it happened. I now know of ways to prevent it or, at least, keep it under better control. I know that I can't come to harm so I'll keep thinking how to control things.

(c) Controlling your actions

Much of the advice in this section will relate to avoidance and ways of facing up more effectively to situations. As many students are likely to have some agoraphobic or social phobia symptoms, information on exposure techniques fits in well at this stage. However, it is also important to look at more subtle forms of avoidance, e.g. suppressing anger or avoiding sex as a way of keeping your body calm. Reasons for exposure therapy being applied in these areas should be offered.

(d) Reducing the risks

Based on Clark, D.M. *et al.* (1994), advice should be offered on risk factors such as rapid postural change, low (normal) blood sugar, alcohol, illness, caffeine, premenstrual phase and tiredness. This last factor flags up the relevance of controlling sleep problems (dealt with later in the session) and, again, suggests the importance of completing the jigsaw comprised of these interrelated sessions. The other major risk factor—high anxiety levels—will further reinforce the need to work at the general anxiety management techniques previously taught.

(e) Emergency help

Although prevention rather than cure has been the main approach used in this session, advice on coping in a panic is useful in terms of reducing somewhat the sense of uncontrollability. The expectation is given that panics cannot easily be stopped, so the student should aim to cope with it more effectively rather than aim to 'cure' it.

Experiments

Occasionally, I will ask students to voluntarily hyperventilate in order to reproduce the symptoms they may associate with panic. Using a checklist of symptoms and asking them to consider similarities and differences to a panic can help them see whether the proposed model fits their experience. Instruction in using a paper bag can be helpful. No pressure should be placed on students to carry this out.[1] This experiment, apart from its specific benefits, seems to work well as a non-specific. Students are tense before the test but often positively animated after, seeking out each other's views on the test while disclosing their own. Humour tends to come to the forefront at this stage. It seems to bond the students more than any other approach.

(5) Break

(6) Review

(7) Homework assignment

Those currently experiencing panic should use the panic diary forms. All students should be asked to practise breathing control. Along with the rest of the students, they should continue to practise the other techniques using the Court Case, relaxation, facing up, and problem-solving forms.

---

[1] Students who suffer from heart disease, high blood pressure, epilepsy, respiratory disease, a metabolic disorder, diabetes, kidney disease or those who are pregnant should not do the hyperventilation provocation test.

CONCLUSIONS

These straightforward cognitive–behavioural techniques will be helpful in increasing the individual's repertoire of coping strategies. They may increase the student's sense of becoming quite sophisticated therapists in their own right as they continue to learn more about their difficulties through the various assessment devices they are completing along with the range of treatments now at their disposal. As in all the sessions, emphasis will be placed on the individual being responsible for selecting the most appropriate techniques to match the information arising from their self-assessment.

Chapter 14

TREATING INSOMNIA

SESSION 5 (CONTINUED): STEP 12—CONTROLLING YOUR SLEEP PROBLEMS

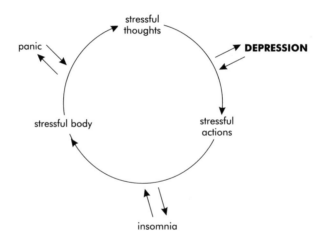

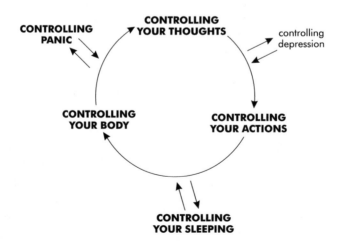

STEP 12: CONTROLLING YOUR SLEEP PROBLEMS

Session format

1. **Education**—the nature of insomnia
2. **Assessment**—'sleep diaries'
3. **Treatment:**
   (a) Sleep hygiene
   (b) Progressive relaxation
   (c) Cognitive therapy
   (d) Stimulus control
4. **Review**
5. **Homework assignment**

Goals

This part of session 5 aims to educate patients about the nature of insomnia, how to assess it and how to control it. The treatment approach uses stimulus control techniques (Bootzin and Nicassio, 1978) along with sleep hygiene advice and the cognitive and relaxation approaches previously learned on the course.

Key concepts and rationale

Poor sleeping fails to recharge the individual's batteries. Thus, during the next day, the individual is less able to fight the effects of stress. Stress then feeds the sleep problems the following night and a vicious circle has developed. Over a period of weeks or months, the individual's ability to cope slowly declines. Learning how to improve the quality and quantity of sleep will leave the individual in a better state to fight daytime stress. Fighting daytime stress will help the individual overcome sleep problems. A positive circle has replaced the vicious circle.

THE SESSION

(1) Education

The provision of information about sleep—the function of sleep, the various stages, expectations of sleep and the various forms of sleep disorder—starts this section. In terms of treatment, poor sleeping is placed within a vicious circle containing anxiety and depression. Daytime anxiety may lead to initial insomnia when, less able to use distraction, unwanted thoughts and stresses flood into the individuals' mind and prevent sleep. Frustration, anger and a sense of lack of control will further inflame the problem.

A range of techniques is described, two of them relying on procedures already taught (to increase the sense of students learning *general* coping skills and to bond different parts of the course together). Students are invited to choose which treatments best meet their needs.

(2) Assessing insomnia

Diary forms relating to sleep assessment are available for those who require them. It is suggested that individuals complete them for at least three weeks before devising a tailored treatment (Figure 14.1). These diaries are best started following the individual assessment, thus allowing the student to fully assess the problem before this session. This will allow the student to immediately put the new therapy skills into practice.

(3) Treatment

(a) Sleep hygiene

Information on topics such as exercise, the bed, the bedroom, smoking, alcohol, milky drinks, eating, etc. are offered.

(b) Relaxation therapy

As participants will probably be proficient in progressive relaxation skills by now, this is offered as one approach to aiding sleep.

(c) Cognitive approaches

If worry and anxiety are involved in insomnia problems, students are encouraged to tackle these concerns using the cognitive challenges taught in session 3.

(d) Stimulus control ('retraining your sleeping')

Students are taught the 'environmental' rationale behind this approach, i.e. understanding the stimulus–response connections. In this context, time is spent understanding the stimuli that are discriminative of sleep-incompatible behaviours.

RETRAINING YOUR SLEEPING

Sleeping problems are often affected by bad associations. If, for example, you are a good sleeper, you probably associate your bed-room with pleasant, positive things—the place where, when you are

'Stress Control': Sleep diary

	When did you put the light out to go to sleep last night?	How long did it take you to fall asleep?	How often did you wake during the night?	How long did it take to get to sleep each time?	What time did you wake this morning?	What time did you get out of bed?	How would you describe your sleep last night?
Example	10.45	85 minutes	Twice	(1) 25 minutes (2) 60 minutes	7.15 a.m.	8 a.m.	Usual — was restless and getting angry with myself. Didn't feel rested at all when I woke. Couldn't stop worrying about work when I went to bed.
Night 1							
Night 2							
Night 3							
Night 4							
Night 5							
Night 6							
Night 7							

Figure 14.1. Sleep diary

tired, you fall asleep without any great trouble, where you enjoy your sleep, where you feel rested, etc. If you have insomnia, you may associate your bedroom with unpleasant, negative thoughts—it is the place where you lie awake for a long time, where you toss and turn, feel frustrated, angry, stressful, etc. These associations may affect your ability to sleep whenever you are there. So your ability to sleep is hindered by having developed the *habit* of sleeping poorly.

You may also attempt to get to sleep by watching TV in your bedroom, reading for long periods, etc. Although doing these things seems like common sense, they do not help in the long run. As these are not related with actually sleeping, i.e. you can't be asleep if you are reading, doing these things may, in fact, make sleeping *less* likely. Again, you have the wrong associations.

This approach looks at a way of retraining the associations you have in your bedroom. In a nutshell, it tries to get rid of bad habits and replace them with good habits. This approach should be followed to the letter. There are six stages involved, as explained in the following boxes.

---

(1) DON'T GO TO BED UNTIL YOU FEEL SLEEPY

Once you start to get the signs of tiredness—yawning, eyes getting heavier, concentration lapses, etc.—go to bed. Don't go to bed just because you feel bored, because everyone else is going to bed or because it is 'bedtime'. Stay up until you feel tired *no matter how long this takes.*

---

(2) YOUR BEDROOM IS ONLY FOR SLEEPING

To change the associations you have with your bedroom, anything you do which isn't sleeping is now banned. So you shouldn't read, watch TV, listen to the radio, write letters, phone friends, think about problems, etc. Sex is the sole exception—sex may help relax you and make sleep easier afterwards.

As soon as you get into bed, put the light out and try to sleep. Although you may know many good sleepers who read in bed or watch TV, it is important that you do these things outside the bedroom at least until you get on top of the problems.

(3) IF YOU DON'T FALL ASLEEP IN 20 MINUTES, GET UP

Remember you are trying to change the associations you have with the room. If you continue to lie awake for a long time, your bad associations will just get worse. So after 20 minutes, go back to the living room. Quietly relax. Don't eat or drink. You must stay in the living room until you feel tired again, no matter how long this takes. When you feel this way, go back to bed and try to sleep straight away.

Initially, expect to be up many times each night. It is hard to get out of a warm bed but it is crucial that you do this.

(4) IF IT DOESN'T WORK, REPEAT

Go through the same procedure each time you return to bed. So you have 20 minutes each time to fall asleep. If you don't—it's back to the living room. Keep repeating this all through the night.

(5) GET UP AT THE SAME TIME EACH MORNING

Decide in advance what time you are getting up each morning. It should not be later than 8.30 a.m. So set the alarm and as soon as it goes off, get up and go out the bedroom.

Even if you feel that you have hardly slept a wink, you must follow this to the letter. You should also try to do this seven days a week, i.e. no sleeping late at the weekend until you get this problem sorted out.

(6) DON'T TRY TO CATCH UP ON SLEEP

You may be tempted to sleep during the day to catch up on lost sleep or you may simply enjoy a sleep after a meal, for example. We go back to the retraining of your associations—bed is the place to sleep and night is the time to do it. Save your sleepiness for bedtime.

It might help if you work out in advance when you are most tempted to sleep and work out something else to do at this time—go out for a walk, phone a friend, etc.

(4) Review

(5) Homework assignment

For those experiencing sleep problems, sleep diaries should be available. Other homework assignments are as noted at the end of the previous chapter.

Chapter 15

TREATING DEPRESSION

SESSION 6: STEP 13—CONTROLLING YOUR DEPRESSION

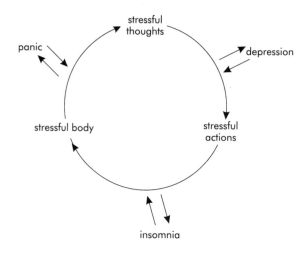

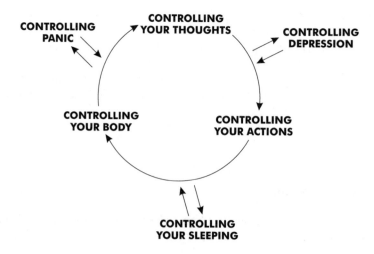

STEP 13: CONTROLLING YOUR DEPRESSION

Session format

1. **Review and introduction**
2. **Education**—the nature of depression
3. **Therapy**—CBT
4. **Workshop**—Court Case, activity scheduling, aerobic exercise
5. **Review**
6. **Homework assignment**
7. **Break**

(Step 14—'Tying it together'—and Step 15—'Controlling your future'—are looked at after the break.)

Goals

'Controlling your depression' takes places in the first half of this final session. It aims to educate students about the nature of depression, how to assess depression and how to control it. The treatment approach uses techniques already learned on the course, e.g. the Court Case, along with behavioural approaches such as activity scheduling. Therefore it can be taught more quickly as a result. Advice on aerobic exercise and antidepressant medication is also offered.

Key concepts and rationale

Now that the TAB vicious circle has been tackled, we must continue to tackle the other vicious circles that also feed anxiety:

- Owing to the high levels of comorbidity between anxiety and depression, most individuals attending the course are likely to identify with depression either at a clinical or subclinical level.
- Although successful treatment of the anxiety is likely to improve depression (Brown *et al.*, 1998), shutting off another 'fuel supply' is likely to further weaken the anxiety.
- Based on Zinbarg and Barlow's (1996) work on negative affectivity, anxiety and depression can be seen as two sides of the same problem. Thus hitting that general higher-order factor in a pincer movement is likely to be seen as an appropriate and personally relevant approach.

THE SESSION

(1) Review of previous sessions

Relaxation. Those wishing to progress from rapid relaxation to the final stage of 'Putting it into action' should be encouraged to do so.

Controlling thoughts. As previous session.

Controlling actions. Importance should continue to be placed on exposure and problem-solving techniques for both psychological and social problems.

Controlling panic. Those prone to panic should continue with panic diaries to gather more information. 'Reducing the risk' techniques and breathing retraining should be used.

Controlling insomnia. Students should be completing sleep diaries or working on some/all of the techniques taught in session 5.

Introduction

As depression is commonly found with anxiety, learning ways of controlling both will have a positive effect on the other. The session will reinforce the flexibility of skills already learned and introduce some new ones. Students should, at this juncture, begin to select the techniques they find most useful and concentrate on them. This further reinforces the sense of individuals taking responsibility for, and controlling, their own treatment.

(2) Education

> 'I do get a lot of stress but I think the depression is worse. I just feel so sad all the time. I cry for hours. I am so irritable, I have no motivation and I'm tired all the time. Nothing feels good any more. The blackness that comes over me really frightens me. I must admit I go to bed at night not caring whether I wake up in the morning.'

Use of this slide can help identify the nature of depression and allow students to identify with the session. Students can assess the likely effect on mood if sufferers talk to themselves in this way day after day. Depression can now be looked at in the context of TAB.

The TAB vicious circle in depression

Rather than simply looking at lists of symptoms, the meaning and impact of symptoms are looked at in greater detail.

THE ROLE OF THOUGHTS

Whereas anxiety makes you look forward with apprehension—the 'what ifs'—depression may make you look backwards—the *'if onlys'*: *'if only* I had got that job', *'If only* my girlfriend hadn't ended the relationship', *'If only* my mother hadn't died', etc. Symptoms similar to those looked at in anxiety, e.g. poor concentration, loss of self-confidence, can be contrasted with 'purer' depressive symptoms, e.g. guilt, self-hatred, brooding.

THE ROLE OF ACTIONS

Symptoms such as increased use of alcohol can be used in a vicious circle explanation. Thus, alcohol can increase the possibility of anxiety or panic the following day. Poorer performance at work due to depression can lead to a lowering of self-esteem. Frequent crying—often appearing out of the blue—can lead to self-consciousness and a sense of uncontrollability. Irritable or aggressive behaviour can lead to a strain on relationships, leading to a lowering of social support, reinforcing depression, etc.

THE ROLE OF THE BODY

Appetite changes and related weight changes will alter thoughts and behaviours. Poor sleeping will lower energy levels. Lack of energy will affect motivation and reinforce withdrawal and avoidance of constructive activities.

The vicious circle invoked for anxiety is again looked at in the context of depression where thoughts lead to behavioural change, e.g. social withdrawal, irritable behaviour, that leads to body changes—poor sleeping, feeling worn out—that leads to a strengthening of depressed thoughts, etc. The effect of this on the anxiety vicious circle and the reciprocal effect should also be outlined.

(3) Therapy

(a) Assessment: 'targeting your depression'

Students are asked, with the help of relatives or friends, to complete the questions contained in the 'Targeting your stress' form but this time for depression—for example, how depression affects thoughts, actions and body; what other people notice when they are depressed; what aspects of their lives are most affected. Students are encouraged to tailor the treatments they learn to best fit the answers they obtain from the assessment.

(b) Controlling your thoughts: the Court Case

Stemming from the education section, the court case should appear to be an obvious intervention.

(c) Controlling your actions: activity scheduling

As a behavioural technique, this should be readily seen as providing a structured intervention aimed at increasing activity and a sense of self-worth.

(d) Controlling your body: aerobic exercise

The case for aerobic exercise has already been made in the pre-course work. Antidepressant medication is also discussed at this stage.

(4) Workshop

(a) Controlling your thoughts: the Court Case

Participants are asked to use the same techniques learned previously in the course. At this stage on the course, most are able to use the Court Case to at least some effect; thus motivation to apply the technique is likely to be high. In any case, as students will not restrict the Court Case to anxiety difficulties, they will, in all likelihood, already be challenging depressive thinking in this way.

Court Case example for depression

STEP 1: WRITE DOWN YOUR THOUGHTS

'I just can't go on like this. I have no pleasure, everything is a struggle. There is no point in life any more. I've messed things up for everyone. I'm useless. The family would be better off without me.'

STEP 2: EVIDENCE FOR

'I know I shouldn't think like this but it is just so hard to do anything about it. I know my husband is sick to death of me and I'm always screaming at my wee girl for no reason.'

STEP 3: EVIDENCE AGAINST

'Let's start by accepting the harsh realities. It's true I have very little pleasure these days and, yes, everything is a struggle, but I've felt like this before and things did get better. So where do I go from here? Life does have meaning. I love my family and they love me (although why, I don't know). I'm not useless—I put myself down all the time—others don't. How do I know that they are wrong? Maybe they see things straighter than I do just now. How can I say my wee girl would be better off without me. She needs me and I need her.'

STEP 4: SUMMING UP

'It's hard to break out of this way of thinking even though I know it isn't the real me saying these things. I know I'm not the easiest person to live with just now but things can change—hang in there. I was never the most confident person in the world but I have coped in the past so I can cope again.'

(b) Controlling your actions: the activity diary (Figure 15.1)

As a way of proving a structure to the student's day and to reverse the social withdrawal, activity scheduling is taught, with students given the responsibility for choosing daily targets.

Depression and anxiety often make you stop doing things because of a lack of energy, lack of enthusiasm, fear, etc. You may now feel that you are not doing anything useful. You may feel overwhelmed at the prospect of doing things that, in the past, would have been easy to do. This may now be a big part of the problem.

As a first step, you should keep an activity diary to see what you *are* doing. If you are doing more than you thought, you should feel better. If you are not doing much, you can use it to note the daily goals you have set yourself. The aim of planning activities is to help you feel you are part of the world again and not standing on the sidelines. It will show you that you are fighting back.

Look at doing straightforward things like phoning a friend, taking a walk in the park, going to the shops. In the first instance, you only need to *do it*. You don't need to enjoy it or do it well. That can come later. So if your goal is to clean the living room window, it doesn't have to be perfectly cleaned. If you have cleaned it then you have done what you set out to do. So a pat on the back is in order.

KEEP YOUR GOALS SPECIFIC.

'Weed the rose garden for half an hour' rather than 'Do some gardening'; 'Dust the hall' rather than 'Do some housework'.

KEEP YOUR GOALS REALISTIC.

Don't aim to 'be back at work next week' if you have been off for six months. 'Fix the plug on the lamp' rather than 'Decorate the house.' Walk before you run.

DON'T WORRY IF YOUR PLANS GET KNOCKED OUT.

If someone asks you to go to the football, for example, when you had planned to weed the rose garden, go to the football—do the weeding the next day.

DON'T BE PUT OFF ON A BAD DAY.

When you feel bad, really go for your goals. If you fail, don't despair— stand back, see where you went wrong. Did you bite off more than you could chew? Did you handle things wrongly? Learn from your mistakes. If you succeed on a bad day, you have taken a big step forward.

TRY NOT TO WORRY ABOUT WHERE THE ENERGY WILL COME FROM.

Not doing things will tire you a lot more than doing them.

ASK OTHERS TO HELP DECIDE ON GOALS.

Apart from useful advice, your family and friends will feel involved in your treatment and will be there to pat your back when you succeed.

READ OVER YOUR DIARY EVERY NIGHT.

How did you get on today? What did you learn? What will you do tomorrow?

'Stress Control': Activity diary

Date	What did you do?	Cope (1–10)	Enjoy (1–10)
Example Monday	Put the TV off. Got my coat on and took the dog for a long walk in the park. Brooded a bit on my problems but it was good to get out of the house for a while.	7	4
Day 1			
Day 2			
Day 3			
Day 4			
Day 5			
Day 6			
Day 7			

Figure 15.1. Activity diary

(c) Controlling your body

Aerobic exercise. With encouraging evidence suggesting that aerobic (and perhaps non-aerobic exercise) can be useful in the treatment of depression (Burbach, 1997), students are encouraged to begin some form of exercising. Sports centres offering a thorough physical assessment are a good place to start. The social benefits of attending a fitness class or playing team games, for example, are highlighted although solitary activities such as running and brisk walking are also encouraged.

Antidepressants. Information is offered about these drugs as misinformation is common. Many students are likely to be using these drugs although often not using them properly, e.g. not taking the medication on a good day or at the weekend when they want to take alcohol. Students are encouraged to discuss this option with their GP.

(5) Review

(6) Homework assignment

Relaxation, Court Case, panic diaries and sleep diaries should be available, along with activity diaries.

(7) Break

The remainder of the course—'Tying it all together' and Controlling your future'—are taught after the break (see next chapter).

CONCLUSIONS

These straightforward cognitive–behavioural techniques will be helpful in increasing the individual's repertoire of coping strategies. As with the treatment of panic, the individual is increasingly developing a sense of their problems on a broad canvas while learning a range of techniques that can be applied across of range of problems.

Chapter 16

COMPLETING THE JIGSAW

SESSION 6 (CONTINUED): STEP 14—TYING IT ALL
TOGETHER *AND*
STEP 15—CONTROLLING YOUR FUTURE

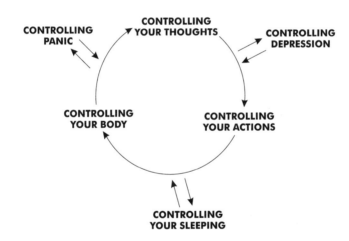

Controlling your future

STEPS 14 AND 15: TYING IT ALL TOGETHER *AND* CONTROLLING YOUR FUTURE

Goals

Participants should feel that they now have the ability to continue assessing and treating their own problems without necessarily having further contact with a therapist.

Key concepts and rationale

'Stress Control' large-group didactic therapy has been described as a training course, not a therapy. The difference being that, following a training course, the expectation is that although individuals may have learned new skills, they will only master those skills in the forthcoming weeks and months. Thus participants' expectations must be that, to use the analogy of learning to drive a car, they have successfully completed the lessons and passed the test of basic skills. They must now gain experience and refine those skills before they can become competent drivers. The essential message at this stage is that the student must work hard and has the capability to do so. They are expected to continually assess progress (see 'After the course ends' form).

However, the teacher should not give the message that everyone can make great changes in their lives. As pointed out previously, many students return home to significant psychological and social problems. Thus it is imperative that appropriate expectations, generated at the start of the course, are again referred to at this stage.

Tying it all together

Time should be taken to review the main ideas in the information section along with the main treatments. Students should realise how much they have learned, how much they now know about stress and how it affects them compared to before they sought help. It should be highlighted that students, although knowledgeable in all the techniques taught, will not yet be proficient in them. Students should note that the techniques they have learned can be applied in different areas, e.g. challenging thoughts in anxiety, depression, panic and sleeping problems. This helps to simplify the course for students and emphasises the wide-ranging applicability of the skills that they have been learning.

While emphasising that the skills students have been taught are all empirically tested, they should not believe that they are the only way to tackle stress. Our knowledge of treatment outcome does not allow that degree of confidence. Students should be encouraged to stand back from problems and develop their own, perhaps highly idiosyncratic, strategies for handling difficult situations as long as they involve, one way or another, facing up to and challenging these problems. If students feel that the use of these techniques allows them to regain control in an area of their lives where that control was previously missing, the outcome is likely to be therapeutic.

Controlling the future: information for students

'Now that you are near the end of this course, you are at a crossroads. One road leads to greater control over your stress. The other leads back to square one. Don't put the information you have learned into a corner and forget about it. You now know a good deal more about stress and how to control it. Simply knowing this won't change anything. You now have to work hard at putting what you have learned into action. If you do this, you are heading down the first road. If you don't, you are going back down the second road. The advice on the next pages, along with the "After the course ends" form (Figure 16.1), will help you go down the right road.'

Keep your expectations realistic. Don't expect progress to be easy or smooth. Setbacks are very common. You should aim to slowly increase the number of good days you have and decrease the number of bad days.

Try to predict when a setback is more likely. After an argument at home, at work, being on holiday, etc. Then plan to stop it happening.

Don't panic if you have a setback. Accept what is going on. Stand back and work out why you are having the setback. Then work out what you can do about it.

Don't see a setback as putting you back to square one. If you have taken five steps forward and a setback puts you back one step, you are still four steps up on the deal.

Let other people help you. Express your feelings to them and get things off your chest. Listen to their advice, be comforted by their concern and get back to fighting the stress again.

Learn to pat yourself on the back. If you have just done something you couldn't/wouldn't do in the past, you deserve some praise—give yourself some straight away.

Face up to problems that lie in the future. Don't just worry about the problems—work out how you are going to deal with them in advance. Make sure you use the TAB techniques you have learned.

Return to the course in the future if you feel you would benefit from it. You are in control of your treatment. You will be doing a range of things to make things better. If you want 'Stress Control' to be one of those things, don't hesitate to return.

'Stress Control': After the course ends

Now that the course has ended, the hard work must begin. It is like passing your driving test—you know what to do but you have to practise hard before you will become a good driver. So don't expect miracles. You must now put all you have learned into practice. Over the next few weeks and months, you should monitor your progress using this form.

End of the first week:

End of the first month:

Figure 16.1.

End of the second month:

End of the third month:

Keep up the hard work you have been doing on the course. Don't be put off by set-backs and . . . **Good luck!**

Figure 16.1. 'After the course ends' form

Homework assignment

Students should now take full control of homework. All diary forms should be available, with students taking as many copies that they require. They may, at this stage, be selective in the forms they wish to have. They should be encouraged in this as it suggests they are tailoring a therapy to meet their personal requirements.

Future use of the course

The course aims to provide a flexible approach to meet the heterogeneous needs in primary care. While the majority of students will not require to repeat the course, this option should be available for the following reasons:

1. Some students, owing to concentration problems, may not have understood or retained some of the information given on the course. They may wish to return to all or some of the sessions of the next course.
2. Students who missed one or more sessions may wish to attend the next course for those sessions.
3. Students who have coped well may still wish to use the course in the future for 'booster' sessions.
4. Students who may hit problems in the future should be welcomed to repeat courses at any time if they feel they are not coping well alone.
5. For many students, a symptom reduction approach may not best fit their needs. Some students, owing to psychological and/or social circumstances, will be left with significant anxiety and depression problems that may come and go to some extent across the years. Attending future courses may help them cope, at least on a palliative level, more effectively. They should be warmly encouraged to do so and should not feel that this represents failure.

However, in order not to reinforce dependency, it is suggested that students, with the exception of those in (1) and (2) above, should work on 'becoming their own therapist' for several months before deciding whether they would benefit from using the course again. Easy access to the course should be available so that students do not have to jump through the usual hoops to be seen; i.e., they should not regard themselves as future 'patients' but remain as students who may wish to revise their skills. Teachers should make it plain that we are continually learning more and more about the nature and treatment of these problems and that, in some areas, models are likely to change quite significantly for the better. The course will continually develop to reflect these advances in our knowledge. Students may wish to attend at any stage in the future to take advantage of these developments.

Some students may decide that 'Stress Control' has not benefited them. It may be that their problems are not open to change or perhaps they should be encouraged to try different approaches, e.g. individual therapy, or therapy with a different theoretical orientation. Care should be taken, if the student has worked hard on the course, to prevent such students seeing themselves as failures.

CONCLUSIONS

Students should now feel that the potential for control is now in their hands. As noted above, the degree of control it is realistic to expect should be clear to the individual and goals set accordingly. A good teacher, although hopefully respected by the students, should merely be seen as the medium of change rather than the catalyst. This will help students feel less inhibited about fully accepting the role as their own therapists that they must continue to adopt as they leave the course.

Part 4

Evaluation and Future Developments

Chapter 17

RESEARCH EVIDENCE

EVALUATION

Research samples

'Stress Control' has always been evaluated using clinically representative individuals, i.e. students with high levels of comorbidity and demoralisation. They have always been taken from routine referrals from GPs. All students have been treated at their local health centre within the NHS. Thus they are not the highly motivated, self-starting individuals who too often comprise research samples. Although decreasing internal validity, using lenient exclusion criteria allows a greater degree of confidence in generalising from the research data to routine clinical work.

One major limitation with the available research is that it has been carried out with the author as sole therapist or co-therapist. However, there is now some recent research carried out in another NHS setting with other therapists. This will be discussed below.

The 1986 pilot study

White and Keenan (1990) reported on the first 'Stress Control' course. Of 38 students assessed, 34 were offered a place on the course. Four dropped out. Results at six months follow-up showed significant change on the few measures used: General Health Questionnaire (Goldberg and Williams, 1988) and the Dysfunctional Attitude Scale (Weissman and Beck, 1978). Despite all the methodological limitations inherent in uncontrolled pilot studies, the interesting result centred on the continuing significant improvement between post-therapy and follow-up. This suggested that our attempt to have students use 'Stress Control' as a training course and, thereby, take responsibility for further change in the absence of therapist contact seemed to be successful.

CONTROLLED EVIDENCE: THE 1987 STUDY

White et al. (1992) reported on 109 (DSM-III-R) GAD students, assessed using the ADIS-R (DiNardo et al., 1985), allocated to either the standard cognitive–behavioural course (CBT), a purely cognitive version (CT), a purely behavioural version (BT), a placebo version—'Subconscious Re-training' (SCR) (White, 1993b)—and a waiting list control. Unlike the active therapy conditions, SCR asked students to adopt a purely passive role—simply listening to tapes supposedly with subliminal anti-anxiety messages embedded in music. A theoretical background explained why this would be effective. All versions had a dedicated booklet and students across conditions all rated their course highly in terms of how well they described stress, how well they described their own problems, how well they felt the therapy would work and how sensible the approach was.

Results at post-therapy

Drop-outs across conditions were low: between 0% (SCR) and 16% (CBT). Using a range of measures, all conditions showed significant improvement compared to the waiting list. No differences existed between any of the treatment conditions.

Results at six months follow-up

Postal return rates were high: between 81% (CBT) and 90% (SCR). No students were referred for help (or contacted for help) during this follow-up period. Again, with one exception, no differences existed between the therapy groups although the active treatment conditions, in general, continued to improve significantly from post-therapy levels while SCR maintained progress. Comparing GP consultations in the six months before therapy and the six months post-therapy, significant reductions (around 50%) were found across conditions. Similarly, benzodiazepine prescribing, at that point by far the most common medication prescribed by GPs, reduced by around 60% over the same period although this was not a focus of any course.

The results suggested that cognitive–behavioural techniques were flexible enough to be transcribed into large-group didactic settings. The general lack of differential responding, especially taking into account the surprising SCR results, suggested that non-specific factors were of great importance. With similar outcome achieved using theoretically and therapeutically distinctive approaches (easily distinguished by independent raters using audio tapes of sessions), a study looking at the process of change was carried out on the same sample.

Process of change at six months follow-up

Measures looking at daily and weekly ratings (e.g. Four Systems Anxiety Questionnaire, Koksal and Power, 1990; Coping Responses Questionnaire,

Billings and Moos, 1981) were used to try to determine if the various treatment conditions reached the same goal by the same or different routes. Some interesting results emerged (White *et al.*, 1995). No evidence was found to suggest that the cognitive approach triggered initial change in cognitive systems or behavioural therapy in behavioural systems. The placebo condition—SCR—showed impressive change immediately then slowed somewhat as the other conditions caught up. The purely behavioural condition showed uniform progress throughout, with evidence of an acceleration of change from session 4 onwards. The purely cognitive approach and the CBT approach showed significant deterioration immediately following session 3 before rallying significantly from session 4 onwards. This suggested to us that the introduction of the cognitive material in session 3 was perhaps too difficult and negatively affected students' perceptions of their ability to control problems. We had noted from routine courses at this time (the late 1980s) that drop-out was more common after session 3. The course was then modified/simplified to include the 'Court Case' approach currently recommended.

LONGER-TERM FOLLOW-UP

Two years follow-up

Most research studies stop at six months follow-up. A few look at data at two years, e.g. Barlow *et al.* (1992) and Butler *et al.* (1991). In the case of 'Stress Control', where the aim is to 'turn the student into his/her own therapist', assessing longer-term outcome is crucial, particularly as a major goal of the course is to prevent relapse.

Students were again contacted by post and asked to return selected measures. Reasonable returns were obtained (between 58% for BT and 70% for SCR). No differences emerged comparing responders to non-responders. Only 11% of these students had had specialist mental health treatment since post-therapy. This compares reasonably to Butler *et al.* (1991), where 11% of the cognitive therapy group and 37% of the behaviour therapy group also required extensive additional treatment during a two-year follow-up period. Generally the results show a maintenance of progress shown at the six-month follow-up period for all treatment conditions. Ratings of positive expectation (i.e., how well they felt the therapy had worked) remained high. Again, no evidence of between-group differences emerged (White, 1998a).

Eight years follow-up

Students were again contacted and asked to return measures by post. Return rates were high: CT 67%, BT 67%, CBT 50% and SCR 80%. No differences emerged comparing responders to non-responders. Mean A-State, A-Trait and Beck Depression Inventory (BDI) results show maintenance of improvement from six-month data across conditions. Highly significant differences within groups from pre-therapy to this follow-up point emerged but no significant differences between conditions. Across conditions, 92% said they continued to read the booklet or practise the techniques learned on their course, 52% had consulted their GP at some point about anxiety and 50% had, at some point, been given psychotropic medication—21% were taking medication at the eight-year assessment point. Only 11% of these responders had been referred back for further specialist help (all to clinical psychologists). Asked how strongly they would recommend 'Stress Control' to a friend who was anxious, an 89% recommendation across conditions emerged. Although subject to demand pressures, these results suggest that 'Stress Control' is capable of creating long-term change in a condition often conceptualised as an Axis II personality disorder (Sanderson and Wetzler, 1991). The attempt to turn individuals into their own therapists appeared to be successful (White, 1995b).

Clinical significance

Statistically significant results may hide important clinically relevant findings. So, using the least arbitrary definition of clinical significance suggested by Jacobson and Truax (1991) *where 'the level of functioning subsequent to therapy places that client closer to the mean of the normal population than it does to the level of the dysfunctional population'* (p. 13), evidence for clinically significant change is available at various times following therapy (Table 17.1). Students had to meet criteria on both the BDI and A-Trait scales. SCR data should be very cautiously assessed in light of low numbers.

Table 17.1.   Students meeting criteria for clinically significant change on both BDI and A-Trait at six months, two years and eight years follow-up

	6 months	2 years	8 years
Cognitive therapy	66	66	65
Behaviour therapy	65	70	75
CBT	53	60	77
Placebo (SCR)	66	83	63

Conclusions from the 1987 study

The evidence appears clear that, tested on clinically representative students with a principal diagnosis of GAD, 'Stress Control' is a viable approach. That no significant differences were found between the treatment conditions suggests the importance of non-specific factors. We suggested that teaching individuals a range of coping strategies while, at the same time, placing the onus of responsibility on the students for the self-management of their treatment may help foster students' beliefs that they can successfully execute these coping techniques. This may reinstil a sense of self-control in areas of their life in which they felt control to be lacking. Thus potentially, the actual techniques may not be crucial as long as students believed them to be relevant to their needs and easy enough for them to master and implement. Perhaps this emphasises the importance of 'selling' any technique in therapy. SCR results may suggest a paradoxical intention/affect modification or a simple relaxation/distraction effect.

As a result of these findings and clinical experience of running many such groups, the treatment format was substantially altered. Principally, the amount of general information in the booklet and individual-specific information in the form of self-assessment before the course was significantly increased. The basic cognitive–behavioural focus was retained but the cognitive components were simplified. A greater emphasis was placed on social factors and, to broaden the relevance to other disorders, a greater emphasis on the model of the trait diathesis of negative affectivity.

RECENT RESEARCH

Student diagnostic characteristics

Recent work has looked at the effects of comorbidity on treatment outcome. Using ADIS-IV/DSM-IV diagnoses, a range of anxiety disorder students has been included in treatment outcome studies using 'Stress Control' as the sole intervention.

GAD students

An ongoing current study of 71 GAD students shows that 36 (51%) met criteria for an Axis II personality disorder (GAD/PD). Although some had cluster B diagnoses (usually borderline or histrionic), these disorders were much more likely to be in the cluster C group and were evenly spread across these conditions. Over 80% were assigned more than one Axis II diagnosis. All of these students also met criteria for at least one additional Axis I disorder, with almost 70% having major depression or dysthymia as secondary diagnoses. Of those GAD students who do not have a secondary personality disorder, 88% met criteria for at least one additional Axis I disorder. These disorders were much more likely to be social and specific phobias.

Comparing those GADs with and without an Axis II disorder, there was no difference in treatment outcome at post-therapy on a range of measures. However, process measures showed a distinctly different pattern of change especially on approach and avoidance coping responses where GAD/PD students showed no change on both these measures, whereas GADs without personality disorder showed significant change in the expected directions.

At six months follow-up, GAD/PDs maintained progress, unlike GADs, who enhanced post-therapy gains. There seems to be evidence, however, that GAD/PDs started to use approach coping strategies and decrease avoidance coping strategies during the follow-up period. This work is ongoing and hopefully the implications of these findings will become clearer (White, 1997b).

Other diagnostic groups

Students with DSM-III-R Panic Disorder without Agoraphobia (PD) were compared to GADs in a 'Stress Control' course. Eighty per cent of PD students had at least one additional diagnosis. On main measures, both groups showed significant change to post-therapy and then a non-significant trend to further improvement during the six-month follow-up period. No differences existed between the two. In terms of panic attacks, at post-therapy 90% of the PD sample were panic free in the previous week. At six months, 70% were completely panic free in the month before assessment (White, 1997c). The results suggest that 'Stress Control' is a reasonably effective treatment for PD students.

A continuing study gathering data on 24 PD with agoraphobia students suggests that results on main measures are similar to GAD and PD students. More specific measures of agoraphobia also show promise. Similarly, 17 social phobia students appear, generally, to have benefited from using 'Stress Control' as their sole therapy, although no specific measures of social anxiety were used in this continuing audit project. Single-case studies on three PTSD students involved in violent assault and one following a road traffic accident showed significant improvement. These students did not wish individual therapy, although this was recommended. Data from PTSD students who received adjunctive individual therapy show that they appear to have benefited from the course, with all stating that the course was a significant factor in their improvement. Data are currently being collected on both mixed anxiety/depression students. More detailed research is planned in all these areas.

Students perceptions of the therapy

Component analysis

Analysing components from the White et al. (1992) study, White (1995c) asked students to rate what factors they felt to have been most beneficial. Overwhelmingly, students reported the provision of information techniques ('hearing the psychologists talk about Stress Control', and 'the booklet') to be more important than the specific therapy components. Initial identification with the book seemed particularly helpful; i.e., many students commented that they had recognised themselves in the descriptions, that they were not alone and this had led them to feel that the course would be relevant. Of interest is the finding that ratings of positive expectation about treatment outcome significantly rise following reading the book (White, unpublished data).

Although open to demand pressures, these findings again offer weight to the importance of the provision of easily understood, personally relevant information. Since this study, new information handouts—'Straight from the horse's mouth (1 and 2)'—have similarly been highly rated by 'Stress Control' students (White, 1993a).

True therapy?

A clinical psychology colleague, influenced by Frank's (1986) discussion of therapeutic components shared by all psychotherapies, investigated whether 'Stress Control' could be regarded as 'true therapy' as it did not appear to involve factors posited by Frank to be central to all psychotherapies, namely the act of confiding or confessing to a sympathetic other; the discussion of painful material in a confidential setting; the importance of raised emotions in effecting change; a plausible rationale for explaining symptoms; a ritual involving active participation of both student and therapist; and a sense of atonement and absolution. 'Stress Control' clearly fails to meet several of these criteria and in particular the first two. Twenty-one heterogeneous DSM-IV anxiety disorder students took part. Evidence suggested that they found the course helpful and sufficient. Asked to rank specific factors, all rated 'learning ways of coping' highly, followed by 'being given information'. Commonly found non-specific factors such as 'knowing I am not the only one with problems', 'finding hope' and 'understanding why I am having problems' were also highly rated.

In terms of the Frank criteria, surprisingly over half reported having 'talked about painful subjects' and 'talked about things for the first time' even though there was no provision for this on the course. In terms of confiding, over half believed they had been helped by someone listening. This may have emanated from the individual assessment appointment. It may be that this feeling was generated from the belief that the course leaders and author of the book understood the problems as the person readily identified with the material. Absolution may have been influenced by the sense that the therapists and other participants created a relaxed and friendly atmosphere. This may lead to a sense of acceptance from the therapist and others. It does not readily appear that emotional processing is a central part of the course. Yet many noted that attending the first few sessions was an emotionally daunting experience as they had to sit with a large number of strangers in a strange environment. Finally, with a strong ritual involved in the course and strong rationale, 'Stress Control' meets these criteria. Gray and White (1998) concluded that 'Stress Control', judged by the Frank criteria, did appear to be a 'true' therapy.

Effect on pre-attentive bias

According to cognitive models of anxiety, processing biases for threat information may contribute to the development and maintenance of clinical anxiety states. Several researchers, e.g. Mathews and McLeod (1986), have suggested that anxiety is primarily characterised by a bias for threat information that operates in preconscious processes, i.e. before information has entered awareness. We have found evidence supporting this theory with GAD students without a concurrent depressive condition (Bradley *et al.*, 1995). In a further study, 11 GAD students were tested before a 'Stress Control' course and again at post-therapy and 20 months follow-up. Pre-attentive biases found at pre-therapy disappeared at post-therapy and significantly reduced at follow-up. One interpretation of these results is that 'Stress Control' successfully modified the cognitive mechanisms that underlie the production of anxious thoughts and worries in clinical anxiety (Mogg *et al.*, 1995).

COMPARISON WITH OTHER TREATMENT OUTCOME STUDIES

Clinical effectiveness

Borkovec and Whisman (1996) reviewed the 11 controlled GAD outcome studies that employed semi-structured diagnostic interviews. 'Stress Control' compares well with all the studies on methodological grounds and on treatment outcome. Figure 17.1 compares 'Stress Control' (White *et al.*, 1992) with recent major individual therapy research trials—Barlow *et al.* (1992); Borkovec and Costello (1993); Butler *et al.* (1991) and Durham *et al.* (1994). It displays mean change scores on A-Trait pre-therapy to six months follow-up using the most successful treatment in each trial.[1] The results suggest that 'Stress Control' performs well in relation to these studies (although students in all still remain anxious following treatment).

However, a recent analysis of recovery defined using the A-Trait measure (Fisher and Durham, 1999) suggests the 1987 'Stress Control' study has a poorer showing compared to the main individual outcome studies. Preliminary analysis of the first 48 students involved in the current GAD trial comparing those with and without personality disorder suggests that those without the Axis II diagnosis achieve similar rates of recovery to those in the individual therapy studies, although those with a personality disorder show a poorer outcome. Although tentative, this may suggest that the significant changes made to the course following the 1987 trial have resulted in an improved treatment.

Clinical efficiency

Figure 17.2 displays clinical efficiency by assessing the amount of therapist time needed to treat each student (excluding assessment time). The 'Stress

---

[1] Barlow *et al.* (1992) post-therapy only.

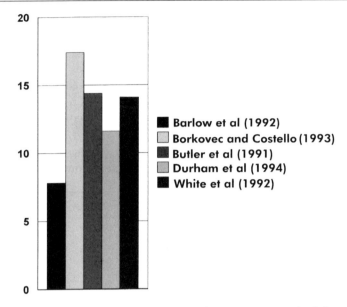

Figure 17.1. Mean change on STAI A-Trait (pre-therapy to six months follow-up)

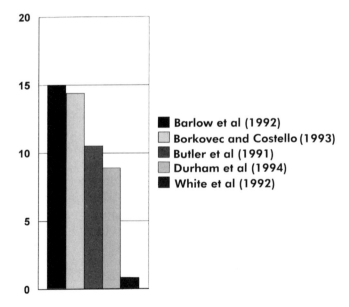

Figure 17.2. Therapist hours per patient

Control' figure is calculated by dividing 12 hours' therapy by 24 students (average size group in that trial) and multiplying by two (as two therapists were employed in these earlier trials). The results clearly indicate that 'Stress Control' is as clinically effective and significantly more efficient than these other studies.

Using the therapist efficiency score suggested by Scott *et al.* (1995),[2] where higher scores represent greater clinical efficiency, Table 17.2 demonstrates the superiority of group therapy on this important clinical measure.

The White *et al.* (1992) study involved two therapists running groups of around 25. 'Stress Control' has become increasingly efficient, with one therapist now running groups of typically 40 students. This reduces the (individual) assessment time to 40 minutes and (group) treatment time to 18 minutes per person.

Table 17.2.   Clinical efficiency scores (higher score represents greater efficiency)

Study	Efficiency score
Barlow *et al.* (1992)	0.95
Borkovec and Costello (1993)	2.2
Butler *et al.* (1991)	1.71
Durham *et al.* (1994)	2.36
White *et al.* (1992)	23.7

'STRESS CONTROL' RUN BY OTHER TEACHERS

Comparison to individual therapy

In a recent study in Oxford, Gillian Butler and David Westbrook jointly ran a 'Stress Control' group with 19 heterogeneous anxiety disorder students (7 panic with agoraphobia, 3 panic without agoraphobia, 4 social phobia, 3 specific phobia and 2 GAD). Eight had at least one comorbid Axis I disorder. The sample was compared to routine Oxford NHS patients treated in individual CBT for an anxiety disorder (Figure 17.3). Oxford patients appear less severe in terms of pre-therapy Beck Anxiety Inventory (BAI) (Beck and Steer, 1990) and BDI (Beck and Steer, 1987). Although not randomly assigned, both individual therapy and 'Stress Control' patients in Oxford show reasonable and similar change at the end of therapy. Results showed very similar scores in client satisfaction (both high).

Due to the group format, 'Stress Control' in Oxford was notably more clinically efficient: 2.8 hours per student compared to 11 hours per (similar) patient treated in individual therapy (Westwood and Butler, personal communication, June 1998). However, six months follow-up appears to be showing relapse instead of the usual pattern of maintenance or enhancement of post-therapy gains (Westwood and Butler, personal communication, February, 1999). It is not clear why this has emerged. There was a major difference between the Scottish and Oxford samples as students in the latter group

---

[2] Mean percentage change on the STAI A-Trait divided by the amount of therapy time needed to achieve the change per patient.

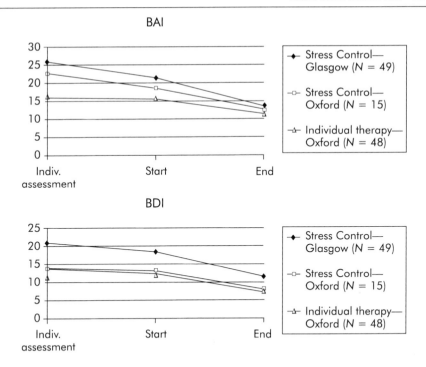

Figure 17.3. Comparison between Glasgow and Oxford 'Stress Control' and Oxford individual therapy on BAI and BDI at individual assessment, start and end of treatment

were much keener to disclose personal details in the group. Following the didactic model, Butler and Westbrook initially tried to stop this, but following discussion allowed rather than encouraged it. Given the outcome scores, it suggests that 'Stress Control' may be flexible enough to allow personal disclosure to be a part of the course with populations who regard this as an important part of their therapy.

DEVELOPMENTS

One of the key goals of 'Stress Control' was to develop a flexible and clinically robust approach designed to achieve the best compromise between clinical effectiveness and clinical efficiency. There is now reasonable empirical evidence suggesting this has been achieved. Recent work, based on experience of this approach, has looked at using this material in different formats and media. A summary of this work is now given.

'Stresspac'

'Stresspac' is a self-help version of the course that can be used by individuals without any therapist contact or while they sit on a waiting list. It can also be used adjunctively with individual therapy, thus releasing scarce therapeutic time to work on focal problems.

There is now good controlled evidence for its effectiveness with patients who initially used it while awaiting therapy. Even though patients in the two other conditions were given similar tailored individual therapy, those who also received 'Stresspac' showed significantly greater gains at the end of the waiting time (40% did not then require to go onto individual therapy), at the end of treatment, at six months and three years follow-up (White, 1995a, 1998c). 'Stresspac' (White, 1997a) now contains most of the materials for use in 'Stress Control'.

A revised version designed to be used by GPs, nurses and other primary care workers is currently being developed.

CD-ROM version

Twenty-six heterogeneous anxiety disorder patients with high levels of co-morbidity took part in a three-session computerised version of 'Stresspac'. Working at their own pace and taking control of what treatment options they looked at, statistically significant change was found in the sample as a whole and clinically significant change found in 50% of the sample. High ratings of 'user-friendliness' and personal relevance were found. A controlled trial is currently under way (White *et al.*, in press).

'STRESS CONTROL'

Depression

Given the reasonable results with anxiety disorders, there may be scope for developing the approach now to cover depression. Although the current version offers one session on depression containing similar techniques used with anxiety, it may be useful to devise a dedicated version, especially given the relatively poor responses to individual therapy (Shea *et al.*, 1992) and the problems discussed in Chapter 2 regarding missed diagnosis or misdiagnosis in primary care settings. This approach is currently being developed.

'Satellite' therapy

While mental health research has, on the whole, developed increasingly specific approaches to specific problems (e.g. Wells, 1997), the 'Stress Control' experience has been to look for the commonalities between conditions. Reflecting on the Zinbarg and Barlow (1996) contribution, there may be a place for a 'halfway house' approach. Current plans are to devise a series of satellite therapies around the main 'Stress Control' course. Thus, in addition to attending the course, students would have the opportunity to attend one or two group sessions devoted to more specific problems often related to anxiety, i.e. anger, jealousy, alcohol and drug problems. The format of these sessions would be similar to those on the course. Students would be free to attend as many or as few as they wished. There may also be scope for stripping the course down to the basic techniques and including panic, insomnia and depression as satellite options.

CONCLUSIONS AND SUMMARY

This book has attempted to provide, very much from the perspective of a clinician/scientific practitioner, a review of current practice and research. It has looked critically at the many weaknesses in routine practice and research centre work but has tried to draw on the many strengths inherent in both areas. The 'Stress Control' approach appears to be a robust, pragmatic approach to both improving effectiveness and efficiency in routine clinical practice. Where the active ingredients lie is still a matter of speculation (I suspect they may differ from individual to individual). It is hoped that, on reading this book, others may be prompted to further develop psycho-educational approaches and help answer the many outstanding questions.

REFERENCES

Addis, M.E. and Jacobson, N.S. (1996). Reasons for depression and the process and outcome of cognitive–behavioral psychotherapies. *Journal of Consulting and Clinical Psychology*, **64**, 1417–1424.

Adler, C.M., Craske, M.G. and Barlow, D.H. (1987). Relaxation-induced panic (RIP): when resting isn't peaceful. *Integrative Psychiatry*, **5**, 94–112.

Akiskal, H.S. (1998). Toward a definition of generalized anxiety disorder as an anxious temperament type. *Acta Psychiatrica Scandinavica*, **98** (Suppl. 393), 66–73.

Albee, G.W. (1990). The futility of psychotherapy. *Journal of Mind and Behavior*, **11**, 369–384.

Allan, C.A. (1995). Alcohol problems and anxiety disorders: a critical review. *Alcohol and Alcoholism*, **30**, 145–151.

Alloy, L.B., Kelly, K.A., Mineka, S. and Clements, C.M. (1990). Comorbidity of anxiety and depressive disorders: a helplessness–hopelessness perspective. In J.D. Maser and C.R. Cloniger (Eds), *Comorbidity of Mood and Anxiety Disorders* (pp. 499–543). Washington, DC: American Psychiatric Press.

American Psychiatric Association (1952). *Mental Disorders: Diagnostic and Statistical Manual*. Washington, DC: APA.

American Psychiatric Association (1968). *Diagnostic and Statistical Manual of Mental Disorders* (2nd edn). Washington, DC: APA.

American Psychiatric Association (1980). *Diagnostic and Statistical Manual of Mental Disorders* (3rd edn). Washington, DC: APA.

American Psychiatric Association (1987). *Diagnostic and Statistical Manual of Mental Disorders* (3rd edn, revised). Washington, DC: APA.

American Psychiatric Association (1994). *Diagnostic and Statistical Manual of Mental Disorders* (4th edn). Washington, DC: APA.

American Psychological Association Monitor (1998). APA helps prompt suit against *California MCOs*, **29** (November), 1.

American Psychological Association Monitor (1999). In the trenches: bolts of pain, rays of hope, *APA Monitor*, **30** (February), 1.

Anderson, K. and White, J. (1996). Evaluation of an opt-in system in primary care psychology. *Clinical Psychology Forum*, **93**, 28–30.

Andrade, L., Eaton, W.W. and Chilcoat, H. (1994). Lifetime comorbidity of panic attacks and major depression in a population-based study. *British Journal of Psychiatry*, **165**, 363–369.

Andrews, G. (1996a). Talk that works: the rise of cognitive behaviour therapy. *British Medical Journal*, **313**, 1501–1502.

Andrews, G. (1996b). Comorbidity in neurotic disorders: the similarities are more important than the differences. In R. Rapee (Ed.), *Current Controversies in the Anxiety Disorders*. New York: Guilford Press.

Angst, J., Vollrath, M., Merikangas, K.R. and Ernst, C. (1990). Comorbidity of anxiety and depression in the Zurich cohort study of young adults. In J.D. Maser and C.R. Cloniger (Eds), *Comorbidity of Mood and Anxiety Disorders* (pp. 123–137). Washington, DC: American Psychiatric Press.

Aseltine, R.H., Kessler, R.C. (1993). Marital disruption and depression in a community sample. *Journal of Health and Social Behavior*, **34**, 237–251.

Ashurst, P.M. and Ward, D.F. (1983). *An Evaluation of Counselling in General Practice: Final Report of the Leverhulme Counselling Project*. London: Mental Health Foundation.

Barkham, M., Rees, A., Shapiro, D.A. *et al.* (1996). Outcomes of time-limited psychotherapy in applied settings: replicating the second Sheffield psychotherapy project. *Journal of Consulting and Clinical Psychology*, **5**, 1079–1085.

Barlow, D.H. (1991). The nature of anxiety: anxiety, depression, and emotional disorders. In R.M. Rapee and D.H. Barlow (Eds), *Chronic Anxiety, Generalized Anxiety Disorder and Mixed Anxiety Depression* (pp. 1–28). New York: Guilford Press.

Barlow, D.H. (1997). Cognitive–behavioural therapy for panic disorder: current status. *Journal of Clinical Psychiatry*, **58** (Suppl. 2), 32–37.

Barlow, D.H. (1998). The nature and origins of panic and anxiety: new developments. Invited address. Annual Convention of the Association for Advancement of Behavior Therapy, Washington, DC.

Barlow, D.H. and DiNardo, P.A. (1991). The diagnosis of Generalized Anxiety Disorder: development, current status and future directions. In R.M. Rapee and D.H. Barlow (Eds), *Chronic Anxiety: Generalized Anxiety Disorder and Mixed Anxiety–Depression* (pp. 95–118). New York: Guilford Press.

Barlow, D.H. and Lehman, C.L. (1996). Advances in the psychosocial treatment of anxiety disorders. *Archives of General Psychiatry*, **53**, 727–735.

Barlow, D.H. and Wincze, J. (1998). DSM-IV and beyond: what is generalized anxiety disorder? *Acta Psychiatrica Scandinavica*, **98** (Suppl. 393), 23–29.

Barlow, D.H., Hayes, S.C. and Nelson, R.O. (1984). *The Scientist–Practitioner*. New York: Pergamon.

Barlow, D.H., Rapee, R.M. and Brown, T.A. (1992). Behavioral treatment of Generalized Anxiety Disorder. *Behavior Therapy*, **23**, 551–570.

Barlow, D.H., Lerner, J.A. and Lawton Esler, J. (1996). Behavioral health care in primary care settings: recognition and treatment of anxiety disorders. In R.J. Resnick and R.H. Rozensky (Eds), *Health Psychology Through the Life Span: Practice and Research Opportunities* (pp. 133–148). Washington, DC: American Psychological Association.

Beck, A.T. (1981). *Cognitive Therapy in Depression*. Chichester: Wiley.

Beck, A.T. and Steer, R.A. (1987). *Beck Depression Inventory Manual*. San Antonio, TX: Psychological Corporation.

Beck, A.T. and Steer, R.A. (1990). *Beck Anxiety Inventory Manual*. San Antonio, TX: Psychological Corporation.

Beck, A.T., Emery, G. and Greenberg, R.L. (1985). *Anxiety Disorders and Phobias: A Cognitive Perspective*. New York: Basic Books.

Bennett, A., Knox, J.D.E. and Morrison, A.T. (1978). Difficulties in consultations reported by doctors in general practice. *Journal of the Royal College of General Practitioners*, **28**, 646–651.

Bennett, P. and Murphy, S. (1997). *Psychology and Health Promotion*. Buckingham, UK: Open University.

Bergin, A. and Strupp, H. (1972). *Changing Frontiers in the Science of Psychotherapy*. Chicago: Aldine.

Bernstein, D.A. and Borkovec, T.D. (1973). *Progressive Relaxation Training*. Champaign, IL: Research Press.

Beutler, L.E., Engle, D., Mohr, D. *et al.* (1991). Predictors of differential and self-directed psychotherapeutic procedures. *Journal of Consulting and Clinical Psychology*, **59**, 333–340.

Beutler, L., Williams, R.E. and Wakefield, P.J. (1993). Obstacles to disseminating applied psychological science. *Applied and Preventative Psychology*, **2**, 53–58.

Beutler, L., Machado, P. and Neufeldt, S. (1994). Therapist variables. In A. Bergin and S. Garfield (Eds), *Handbook of Psychotherapy and Behavior Change* (4th edn, pp. 229–269). New York: Wiley.

Beutler, L., Kim, E.J., Davison, E. *et al.* (1996). Research contributions to improving managed health care outcomes. *Psychotherapy*, **33**, 197–206.

Bibb, J. and Chambless, D.L. (1986). Alcohol use and abuse among diagnosed agoraphobics. *Behaviour Research and Therapy*, **24**, 49–58.

Biber, B. and Alkin, T. (1999). Panic disorder subtypes: differential responses to CO_2 challenge. *American Journal of Psychiatry*, **165**, 739–744.

Billings, A.G. and Moos, R.H. (1981). The role of coping resources and social resources in attenuating the stress of life events. *Journal of Behavioral Medicine*, **4**, 139–157.

Blashfield, R.K. (1990). Comorbidity and classification. In J.D. Maser and C.R. Cloniger (Eds), *Comorbidity of Mood and Anxiety Disorders* (pp. 61–82). Washington, DC: American Psychiatric Press.

Blatt, S.J., Sanislow, C.A., Zuroff, D.C. and Pilkonis, P.A. (1996). Characteristics of effective therapists: further analysis of data from the NIMH Treatment of Depression Collaborative Research Program. *Journal of Consulting and Clinical Psychology*, **64**, 1276–1284.

Blowers, C., Cobb, J. and Mathews, A.M. (1987). Generalised anxiety disorder: a controlled treatment study. *Behaviour Research and Therapy*, **25**, 493–502.

Boot, D., Gillies, P., Fenelon, J. *et al.* (1994). Evaluation of the short-term impact of counselling in general practice. *Patient Education and Counselling*, **24**, 78–89.

Bootzin, R.R. and Nicassio, P.M. (1978). Behavioral treatments for insomnia. In M. Herson, R.M. Eisler and P.M. Miller (Eds). *Progress in Behavior Modification* (vol. 6). New York: Academic Press.

Borkovec, T.D. (1994). The nature, functions and origins of worry. In G.C.L. Davey and F. Tallis (Eds), *Worry: Perspectives on Theory, Assessment and Treatment*. Chichester: Wiley.

Borkovec, T.D. and Costello, E. (1993). Efficacy of applied relaxation and cognitive–behavioral therapy in the treatment of generalized anxiety disorder. *Journal of Consulting and Clinical Psychology*, **61**, 611–619.

Borkovec, T.D. and Whisman, M.A. (1996). Psychosocial treatments for generalized anxiety disorder. In M. Mavissakalian and R.F. Prien (Eds), *Long-Term Treatment of Anxiety Disorders*. (pp. 171–199). Washington, DC: American Psychiatric Press.

Borkovec, T.D., Abel, J.L. and Newman, H. (1995). Effects of psychotherapy on comorbid conditions in generalized anxiety disorder. *Journal of Consulting and Clinical Psychology*, **63**, 479–483.

Botella, C. and Garcia-Palacios, A. (1999). The possibility of reducing therapist contact and total length of therapy in the treatment of panic disorder. *Behavioural and Cognitive Psychotherapy*, **27**, 231–247.

Bowen, R.C., Cipywnyk, D., D'Arcy, C. and Keegan, D. (1984). Alcoholism, anxiety disorders, and agoraphobia. *Alcoholism: Clinical and Experimental Research*, **8**, 48–50.

Boyd, J.H. (1986). Use of mental health services for the treatment of panic disorder. *American Journal of Psychiatry*, **143**, 1569–1574

Bradley, B.P., Mogg, K., Millar, N. and White, J. (1995). Selective processing of negative information: effects of clinical anxiety, concurrent depression and awareness. *Journal of Abnormal Psychology*, **104**, 532–536.

Brawman-Mintzer, O., Lydiard, R.B., Emmanual, N. *et al.* (1993). Psychiatric comorbidity in patients with generalized anxiety disorder. *American Journal of Psychiatry*, **150**, 1216–1218.

Bridgewood, A., Malbon, G., Lader, D. and Matheson, J. (1996). *Health in England 1995: What People Know, What People Think, What People Do*. London: Office for National Statistics.

Brown, G.W. (1992). Life events and social support: possibilities for primary prevention. In R.Jenkins, J.Newton and R.Young (Eds), *The Prevention of Anxiety and
Depression* (pp. 22–32). London: HMSO.

Brown, G.W. and Harris, T.O. (1978). *Social Origins of Depression*. London: Tavistock.

Brown, J.S.L., Cochrane, R., Mack C.F. *et al.* (1998). Comparison of effectiveness of
large scale stress workshops with small stress/anxiety management training
groups. *Behavioural and Cognitive Psychotherapy*, **26**, 219–236.

Brown, T.A. (1996). Validity of the DSM-III-R and DSM-IV classification systems for
anxiety disorders. In R. Rapee (Ed.), *Current Controversies in the Anxiety Disorders*
(pp. 21–45). New York: Guilford Press.

Brown, T.A. (1998). The relationship between obsessive-compulsive disorder and
other anxiety-based disorders. In R.P Swinson, M.M. Antony, S. Rachman and
M.A. Richter (Eds), *Obsessive–Compulsive Disorder* (pp. 207–228). London: Guilford
Press.

Brown, T.A., and Barlow, D.H. (1992). Comorbidity among anxiety disorders: implications for treatment and DSM-IV. *Journal of Consulting and Clinical Psychology*,
60, 835–844.

Brown, T.A. and Barlow, D.H. (1995). Long-term outcome in cognitive–behavioral
treatment of panic disorder: clinical predictors and alternative strategies for assessment. *Journal of Consulting and Clinical Psychology*, **63**, 754–765.

Brown, T.A., DiNardo, P.A. and Barlow, D.H. (1994). *The Anxiety Disorders Interview
Schedule for DSM-IV (Current Episode)*. San Antonio, TX: Psychological Corporation.

Brown, T.A., Anthony, M.M. and Barlow, D.H. (1995). Diagnostic comorbidity in
panic disorder: effect on treatment outcome and course of comorbid diagnoses
following treatment. *Journal of Consulting and Clinical Psychology*, **63**, 408–418.

Brown, T.A., Chorpita, B.F. and Barlow, D.H. (1998). Structural relationships among
dimensions of the DSM-IV anxiety and mood disorders of negative affect, positive
affect, and autonomic arousal. *Journal of Abnormal Psychology*, **107**, 179–192.

Brownescombe-Heller, M, (1994). The rise and demise of the walk-in clinic. *Clinical
Psychology Forum*, **66**, 21–23.

Burbach, F.R. (1997). The efficacy of physical activity interventions within mental
health services: anxiety and depressive disorders. *Journal of Mental Health*, **6**, 543–
566.

Butcher, P. and de Clive-Lowe, S. (1985). Strategies for living: teaching psychological
self-help as adult education. *British Journal of Medical Psychology*, **58**, 275–283.

Butler, G. and Anastasiades, P. (1988). Predicting response to anxiety management in
patients with generalized anxiety disorder. *Behaviour Research and Therapy*, **26**, 531–
534.

Butler, G. and Booth, R.G. (1991). Developing psychological treatments for gener-
alized anxiety disorder. In R.M. Rapee and D.H. Barlow (Eds), *Chronic Anxiety:
Generalized Anxiety Disorder and Mixed Anxiety–Depression* (pp. 187–209). New York:
Guilford Press.

Butler, G., Gelder, M., Hibbert, G. *et al.* (1987). Anxiety management: developing
effective strategies, *Behaviour Research and Therapy*, **25**, 517–522.

Butler, G, Fennell, M., Robson, P. and Gelder, M. (1991). Comparison of behavior
therapy and cognitive behavior therapy in the treatment of generalized anxiety
disorder. *Journal of Consulting and Clinical Psychology*, **59**, 167–175.

Calhoun, K.S., Moras, K., Pilkonis, P.A. and Rehm, L.P. (1998). Empirically supported
treatments: implications for training. *Journal of Consulting and Clinical Psychology*,
66, 151–162.

Campbell, L. (1996). The treatment outcome pursuit: a mandate for the clinician and
researcher working alliance. *Psychotherapy*, **33**, 190–196.

Campbell, T., Blake, N. and Rankin, H. (1993). Anxiety management courses in
clinical practice: an evaluation. *Clinical Psychology Forum*, **59**, 18–22.

Cape, J. and Parham, A. (1998). Relationship between practice counselling and referral to out-patient psychiatry and clinical psychology. *British Journal of General Practice*, **48**, 1477–1480.

Castonguay, L.G., Goldfried, M.R., Wiser, S. *et al.* (1996). Predicting the effect of cognitive therapy for depression: a study of unique and common factors. *Journal of Consulting and Clinical Psychology*, **64**, 497–504.

Castro, J. (1993, 31 May). What price mental health? *Time*, 59–60.

Catalan, J., Gath, D.H., Anastasiades, P. *et al.* (1991). Evaluation of a brief psychological treatment for emotional disorders in primary care. *Psychological Medicine*, **21**, 1013–1018.

Chambless, D.L. and Gillis, M. (1993). Cognitive therapy of anxiety disorders. *Journal of Consulting and Clinical Psychology*, **61**, 248–260.

Chambless, D.L. and Goldstein, A.J. (Eds) (1988). *Agoraphobia*, New York: Wiley–Interscience.

Chambless, D.L. and Hollon, S.D. (1998). Defining empirically supported therapies. *Journal of Consulting and Clinical Psychology*, **66**, 7–18.

Chambless, D.L., Cherney, J., Caputo, G.C. and Rheinstein, B.J.G. (1987). Anxiety disorders and alcoholism: a study with inpatient alcoholics. *Journal of Anxiety Disorders*, **1**, 29–40.

Chambless, D.L., Renneberg, B., Goldstein, A. and Gracely, E.J. (1992). MCMI-diagnosed personality disorders among agoraphobic out-patients: prevelance and relationship to severity and treatment outcome. *Journal of Anxiety Disorders*, **6**, 193–211.

Charlesworth, K. (1996). *Are Managers Under Stress? A Survey of Management Morale.* London: Institute of Management.

Chorpita, B.F. and Barlow, D.H. (1998). The development of anxiety: the role of control in the early environment. *Psychological Bulletin*, **124**, 3–21.

Chorpita, B.F., Brown, T.A. and Barlow, D.H. (1998). Diagnostic reliability of the DSM-III-R anxiety disorders. *Behavior Modification*, **22**, 307–320.

Christensen, A. and Jacobson, N.S. (1994). Who (or what) can do psychotherapy: the status and challenge of nonprofessional therapies. *Psychological Science*, **5**, 8–14.

Clark, D.M. (1999). Anxiety disorders: why they persist and how to treat them. *Behaviour Research and Therapy*, **37**, S5–S27.

Clark, D.M. and Beck, A.T. (1988). Cognitive approaches. In C.G. Last and M. Herson (Eds), *Handbook of Anxiety Disorders*. New York: Pergamon.

Clark, D.M., Salkovskis, P.M., Hackman, A. *et al.* (1994). A comparison of cognitive therapy, applied relaxation and imipramine in the treatment of panic disorder. *British Journal of Psychiatry*, **164**, 759–769.

Clark, D.M., Salkovskis, P.M., Hackman, A. *et al.* (1999). Brief cognitive therapy for panic disorder: a randomized controlled trial. *Journal of Consulting and Clinical Psychology*, **67**, 583–589.

Clark, L.A. and Watson, D. (1991). Tripartite model of anxiety and depression: psychometric evidence and taxonomic implications. *Journal of Abnormal Psychology*, **100**, 316–336.

Clark, L.A., Watson, D. and Mineka, S. (1994). Temperament, personality, and the mood and anxiety disorders. *Journal of Abnormal Psychology*, **103**, 113-116.

Cohen, L.H. (1976). The research readership and information source reliance of clinical psychologists. *Professional Psychology*, **10**, 780–786.

Cohen, L., Sargent, M. and Sechrest, L. (1986). Use of psychotherapy research by professional psychologists. *American Psychologist*, **41**, 198–206.

Consumer Reports (1995). Mental health: Does therapy help? *Consumer Reports*, November, 734–739.

Corney, R. (1997). A counsellor in every general practice? Inaugural lecture, University of Greenwich, March.

Corney, R. and Murray, J. (1988). The characteristics of high and low attenders at two general practices. *Social Psychiatry and Psychiatric Epidemiology*, **23**, 39–49.

Corney, R., Ward, E. and Hammond, J. (1996). General practioners' use of mental health services: the impact of fundholding. Final report to the Department of Health.

Coryell, W., Endicott, J. and Winokur, G. (1992). Anxiety syndromes as epiphenomena of primary major depression: outcome and familial psychopathology. *American Journal of Psychiatry*, **149**, 100–107.

Coyne, J.C., Kessler, R.C., Tal, M. *et al.* (1987). Living with a depressed person. *Journal of Consulting and Clinical Psychology*, **55**, 347–352.

Crits-Christoph, P. (1992). The efficacy of brief dynamic psychotherapy: a meta-analysis. *American Journal of Psychiatry*, **149**, 151–158.

Croft-Jeffreys, C. and Wilkinson, G. (1989). Estimated costs of neurotic disorder in UK general practice 1995. *Psychological Medicine*, **19**, 549–558.

Cuijpers, P. (1998). A psychoeducational approach to the treatment of depression: a meta-analysis of Lewinsohn's 'Coping with depression' course. *Behavior Therapy*, **29**, 521–533.

Cummings, N.A. (1995). Behavioral health after managed care: the next golden opportunity for professional psychology. *Register Report*, **20**, 30–33.

Cureton, S. and Newnes, C. (1995). A survey of the practice of psychological therapies in an NHS Trust. *Clinical Psychology Forum*, **76**, 6–10.

Dadds, M.R., Spence, S.H., Holland, P.M. *et al.* (1997). Prevention and early intervention for anxiety disorders: a controlled trial. *Journal of Consulting and Clinical Psychology*, **65**, 627–635.

Day, C. and Wren, B. (1994). Journey to the centre of primary care: primary care psychology in perspective. *Clinical Psychology Forum*, **65**, 3–6.

DeRubeis, R.J. and Crits-Christoph, P. (1998). Empirically supported individual and group psychological treatments for adult mental disorders. *Journal of Consulting and Clinical Psychology*, **66**, 37–52.

DeRubeis, R.J., Gelfand, L.A., Tang, T.Z. and Simons, A.D. (1999). Medications versus cognitive behavior therapy for severely depressed outpatients: mega-analysis of four randomized trials. *American Journal of Psychiatry*, **156**, 1007–1013.

DiNardo, P.A. and Barlow, D.H. (1990). Syndrome and symptom comorbidity in the anxiety disorders. In J.D. Maser and C.R. Cloninger (Eds), *Comorbidity in Anxiety and Mood Disorders* (pp. 205–230). Washington, DC: American Psychiatric Press.

DiNardo, P.A., Barlow, D.H., Cerny, J. *et al.* (1985). *Anxiety Disorder Interview Schedule–Revised (ADIS-R)*. Albany: State University of New York.

DiNardo, P.A., Moras, K., Barlow, D.H. *et al.* (1993). Reliability of DSM-III-R anxiety disorder categories using the Anxiety Disorders Interview Schedule–Revised (ADIS-R). *Archives of General Psychiatry*, **50**, 251–256

DiNardo, P.A., Brown, T.A., and Barlow, D.H. (1994). *Anxiety Disorders Interview Schedule for DSM-IV (Lifetime Version)*. San Antonio, TX: Psychological Corporation.

Division of Clinical Psychology (1993). Report of the DCP survey of waiting lists in NHS clinical psychology services: 1992. *Clinical Psychology Forum*, **53**, 39–42.

Division of Clinical Psychology (1997). Clinical psychologists' caseloads and waiting lists : the DCP survey. *Clinical Psychology Forum*, **110**, 40–46.

Division of Clinical Psychology (1998). *Clinical Psychology Services in Primary Care*. Briefing paper no. 15. Leicester: British Psychological Society.

Dowell, A.C. and Biran, L.A. (1990). Problems in using the Hospital Anxiety and Depression Scale for screening patients in general practice. *British Journal of General Practice*, **40**, 27–28.

Dreesen, L., Arntz, A., Luttels, C. and Sallaerts, S. (1994). Personality disorders do not influence the results of cognitive behavior therapies for anxiety disorders. *Comprehensive Psychiatry*, **35**, 265–274.

Dupont, R.L., Shirobi, B.S., Rise, D. *et al.* (1993). The economic cost of anxiety disorders. Paper presented at the Anxiety Disorders Association Annual Meeting, Charleston, SC.

Durham, R.C. and Allan, T. (1993). Psychological treatment of generalised anxiety disorder: a review of the clinical significance of results in outcome studies since 1980. *British Journal of Psychiatry*, **163**, 19–26.

Durham, R.C., Murphy, T., Allan, T. *et al.* (1994). Cognitive therapy, analytic psychotherapy and anxiety management training for generalised anxiety disorder. *British Journal of Psychiatry*, **165**, 315–323.

Earll, L, and Kinsey, J. (1982). Clinical psychology in general practice: a controlled trial evaluation. *Journal of the Royal College of General Practitioners*, **32**, 32–37.

Eaton, W.W., Anthony, J.C., Romanski, A. *et al.* (1998). Onset and recovery from panic disorder in the Baltimore Epidemiologic Catchment Area follow-up. *British Journal of Psychiatry*, **173**, 501–507.

Eayrs, C., Rowan, D. and Harvey, P. (1984). Behavioural group training for anxiety management. *Behavioural Psychotherapy*, **12**, 117–129.

Eifert, G.H. (1996). More theory-driven and less diagnosis-based behavior therapy. *Journal of Behavior Therapy and Experimental Psychiatry*, **27**, 75–86.

Espie, C.A. and White, J. (1986a). The effectiveness of psychological intervention in primary care: a comparative analysis of outcome ratings. *Journal of the Royal College of General Practitioners*, **36**, 310–312.

Espie, C.A. and White, J. (1986b). Clinical psychology and general practice: a four year review. *Health Bulletin*, September, 266–273.

Evans, P., Clow, A, and Hucklebridge, F. (1997). Stress and the immune system. *The Psychologist*, **10**, 303–307.

Febbraro, G.A., Clum, G.A., Roodman, A.A. and Wright, J.H. (1999). The limits of bibliotherapy: a study of the differential effectiveness of self-administered interventions in individuals with panic attacks. *Behavior Therapy*, **30**, 209–222.

Feinstein, A.R. and Horwitz, R.I. (1997). Problems in the 'evidence' of 'evidence-based medicine'. *American Journal of Medicine*, **103**, 529–535.

Fifer, S.K., Mathias, S.D., Patrick, D.L. *et al.* (1994). Untreated anxiety among adult primary care patients in a health maintenance organisation. *Archives of General Psychiatry*, **51**, 740–750.

Fisher, P.L. and Durham, R.C. (1999). Recovery rates in generalized anxiety disorder following psychological therapy: an analysis of clinically significant change in the STAI-T across outcome studies since 1990. *Psychological Medicine*, **29**, 1425–1434.

Flesch, R. (1948). A new readability yardstick. *Journal of Abnormal Psychology*, **32**, 221–233

Fox, T. (1997). Giving clients information about non-attendance: does this reduce the number who 'fail to attend'? *Clinical Psychology Forum*, **110**, 20–24.

Frank, J.D. (1986). Therapeutic components shared by all psychotherapies. In J.H. Harvey and M.M. Parks (Eds) *Psychotherapy Research and Behavior Change*. Washington, DC: American Psychiatric Association.

Frank, J.D. and Frank, J.B. (1991). *Persuasion and Healing: A Comparative Study of Psychotherapy* (3rd edn). Baltimore: John Hopkins University Press.

Frank, R.G. and McGuire, T.G. (1994). Health reform and financing of mental health services: distributional issues. In R.W. Manderscheid and M.A. Sonnenscheim (Eds). *Mental Health US, 1994*. Washington, DC: Government Printing Office.

Friedli, K. and King, M. (1996). Counselling in general practice: a review. *Primary Care Psychiatry*, **2**, 205–216.

Friedli, K., King, M.B., Lloyd, M. and Horder, J. (1997). Randomised controlled assessment of non-directive psychotherapy versus routine general practitioner care. *Lancet*, **350**, 1662–1665.

Garfield, S.L. (1995). *Psychotherapy: An Eclectic–Integrative Approach*. New York: Wiley.

Garssen, B., Buikhuisen, M. and van Dyke, R. (1996). Hyperventilation and panic attacks. *American Journal of Psychiatry*, **153**, 513–518.

Geekie, J. (1995). Preliminary evaluation of one way of managing a waiting list. *Clinical Psychology Forum*, **85**, 33–35

Ginsberg, G., Marks, I. and Waters, H (1984). Cost benefit analysis of a controlled trial of nurse therapy for neurosis in primary care. *Psychological Medicine*, **14**, 683–690.

Gloaguen, V., Cottraux, J., Cucherat, M. *et al.* (1998). A meta-analysis of the effects of cognitive therapy in depressed patients. *Journal of Affective Disorders*, **49**, 59–72.

Goisman, R.M., Rogers, M.P., Steketee, G.S. *et al.* (1993). Utilization of behavioral methods in a multi-center anxiety disorders clinic. *Journal of Clinical Psychiatry*, **54**, 213–218.

Goldberg, D. and Huxley, P. (1992). Common Mental Disorders: A Biopsychological Approach. Routledge: London.

Goldberg, D. and Williams, P. (1988). *A User's Guide to the General Health Questionnaire*. Windsor, UK: NFER-Nelson.

Goldberg, D., Jackson, G., Gator, R. *et al.* (1996). The treatment of common mental disorders by a community team based in primary care: a cost-effectiveness study. *Psychological Medicine*, **26**, 487–492.

Goldfried, M.R. and Wolfe, B.E. (1998). Towards a more clinically valid approach to therapy research. *Journal of Consulting and Clinical Psychology*, **66**, 143–150.

Gortner, E.T., Gollan, J.K., Dobson, K.S. and Jacobson, N.S. (1998). Cognitive–behavioral treatment for depression: relapse prevention. *Journal of Consulting and Clinical Psychology*, **66**, 377–384.

Gould, R.A. and Clum, G.A. (1993). A meta-analysis of self-help treatment approaches. *Clinical Psychology Review*, **13**, 169–186.

Gould, R.A., Clum, G.A. and Shapiro, D. (1993). The use of bibliotherapy in the treatment of panic: a preliminary investigation. *Behavior Therapy*, **24**, 241–252.

Gourney, K. and Brooking, J. (1994). Community psychiatric nurses in primary health care. *British Journal of Psychiatry*, **165**, 231–238.

Gray, A. and White, J. (1998). Can large scale anxiety management groups be regarded as true therapy? *Clinical Psychology Forum*, **115**, 30–33.

Greenberg, P.E., Sisitsky, M.A., Kessler, R.C. *et al.* (1999). The economic burden of anxiety disorders in the 1990s. *Journal of Clinical Psychiatry*, **60**, 427–435.

Griffiths, T. (1985). Clinical psychology in primary health care. In F. Watts (Ed.), *New Developments in Clinical Psychology* (pp. 221–233). Leicester: British Psychological Society Books.

Grilo, C.M., Money, R., Barlow, D.H. *et al.* (1998). Pretreatment patient factors predicting attrition from a multicenter randomized controlled treatment study for panic disorder. *Comprehensive Psychiatry*, **39**, 323–332.

Grunebaum, M., Luber, P., Callahan, M. *et al.* (1996). Predictors of missed appointments for psychiatric consultations in a primary care clinic. *Psychiatric Services*, **47**, 848–852.

Harvey, I., Nelson, S.J., Lyons, R.A. *et al.* (1998). A randomized controlled trial and economic evaluation of counselling in primary care. *British Journal of General Practice*, **48**, 1043–1048.

Hassall, C. and Stilwell, J.A. (1977). Family doctor support for patients on a psychiatric case register. *Journal of the Royal College of General Practitioners*, **27**, 605–608.

Hayes, S.C. (1998). Building a useful relationship between 'applied' and 'basic' science in behavior therapy. *Behavior Therapist*, **21** (June), 109–112.

Hayes, S.C., Barlow, D.H. and Nelson-Gray, R.O. (1999). *The Scientist Practioner: Research and Accountability in the Age of Managed Care* (2nd edn). Boston: Allyn & Bacon.

Hayward, P. and Bright, J.A. (1997). Stigma and mental illness: a review and critique. *Journal of Mental Health*, **6**, 345–354.

Heide, F.J. and Borkovec, T.D. (1984). Relaxation-induced anxiety: mechanisms and theoretical implications. *Behaviour Research and Therapy*, **22**, 1–12.

Heimberg, R.G., Salzman, D.G., Holt, C.S. and Blendell, K.A. (1993). Cognitive–behavioral treatment for social phobia: effectiveness at five-year follow-up. *Cognitive Therapy and Research*, **17**, 325–339.

Herlihy, J., Bennett, P. and Killick, S. (1998). Self-help: a better way of coping with waiting lists. *Clinical Psychology Forum*, **119**, 5–8.

Herz, M.I. and Melville, C. (1980). Relapse in schizophrenia. *American Journal of Psychiatry*, **137**, 801–805.

Heurtin-Roberts, S., Snowden, L. and Miller, L. (1997). Expressions of anxiety in African Americans: ethnography and the epidemiological catchment area studies. *Culture, Medicine and Psychiatry*, **21**, 337–363.

Hickey, P. (1998). DSM and behavior therapy. *Behavior Therapist*, **21**, 43–55

Hoehn-Saric, R., McLeod, D.R. and Zimmerli, W.D. (1989). Somatic manifestations in women with generalized anxiety disorder: psychophysiological responses to psychological stress. *Archives of General Psychiatry*, **46**, 1113–1119.

Horvarth, A.O., Gaston, L. and Luborsky, L. (1993). The therapeutic alliance and its measures. In N.E. Miller, L. Luborsky, J.P. Barber and J.P. Docherty (Eds), *Psychodynamic Treatment Research: A Handbook for Clinical Practice*. New York: Basic Books.

Hoshmand, L.T. and Polkinghorne, D.E. (1992). Redefining the science–practice relationship and professional training. *American Psychologist*, **47**, 55–66.

Howard, K.I., Moras, K., Brill, P.L. *et al.* (1996). Evaluation of psychotherapy: efficacy, effectiveness and patient progress. *American Psychologist*, **51**, 1059–1064.

Hughes, I. (1995). Why do they stop coming? Reasons for therapy termination by adult clinical psychology clients. *Clinical Psychology Forum*, **81**, 7–11.

Hughes, I. (1997). Can you keep from crying by considering things? Some arguments against cognitive therapy for depression. *Clinical Psychology Forum*, **104**, 23–27.

Information and Statistics Division, National Health Service in Scotland (1998). *Deprivation and Health in Scotland*. NHS: Edinburgh.

Jacobson, N.S. and Christensen, A. (1996). Studying the effectiveness of psychotherapy: how well can clinical trials do the job? *American Psychologist*, **51**, 1031–1039.

Jacobson, N.S. and Gortner, E.T. (2000). Can depression be de-medicalized in the 21st century? Scientific revolutions, counter-revolutions and the magnetic field of normal science. *Behaviour Research and Therapy*, **38**, 74–80.

Jacobson, N.S. and Hollon, S.D. (1996). Cognitive–behavior therapy versus pharmacotherapy: now that the jury's returned its verdict, it's time to present the rest of the evidence. *Journal of Consulting and Clinical Psychology*, **64**, 74–80.

Jacobson, N.S. and Truax, P. (1991). Clinical significance: a statistical approach to defining meaningful change in psychotherapy research. *Journal of Consulting and Clinical Psychology*, **59**, 12–19.

Jabobson, N.S., Dobson, K.S., Truax, P.A. *et al.* (1996). A component analysis of cognitive–behavioral treatment for depression. *Journal of Consulting and Clinical Psychology*, **64**, 295–304.

Jannoun, L., McDowell, I. and Catalan, J. (1981). Behavioural treatment of anxiety in general practice. *The Practitioner*, **225**, 58–62.

Jannoun, L., Oppenheimer, C. and Gelder, M. (1982). A self-help treatment program for anxiety state patients. *Behavior Therapy*, **13**, 103–111.

Jarvis, T.J., Tebbutt, J. and Mattick, R.P. (1995). *Treatment Approaches for Alcohol and Drug Dependence*. Chichester: Wiley.

Jayakody, R., Danziger, S. and Kessler, R.C. (1998). Early-onset psychiatric disorders and male socioeconomic status. *Social Science Research*, **27**, 371–387.

Jenkins, R. (1985). Minor psychiatric disorder in employed young men and women and its contributions to sickness absence. *British Journal of Industrial Medicine*, **42**, 147–154.

Jenkins, R. (1998). Policy framework and research in England, 1990–1995. In R. Jenkins and T.B. Ustun (Eds). *Preventing Mental Illness: Mental Health Promotion in Primary Care*. Chichester: Wiley.

Jenkins, R. and Ustun, B.T. (Eds). (1998). *Preventing mental illness: Mental Health Promotion in Primary Care*. Chichester: Wiley.

Jenkins, R., Bebbington, P., Brugha, T.S. *et al.* (1998). The British psychiatric morbidity survey. *British Journal of Psychiatry*, **173**, 4–7.

Jerrom, D.W.A., Simpson, R.J., Barber, J.H. and Pemberton, D.A. (1986). General practioners' satisfaction with a primary care clinical psychology service. *Journal of the Royal College of General Practitioners*, **36**, 310–312.

Johnston, M. (1978). The work of a clinical psychologist in primary care. *Journal of the Royal College of General Practioners*, **28**, 661–667.

Jones, A. (1998). 'What's the bloody point?' more thoughts on fraudulent identity. *Clinical Psychology Forum*, **112**, 3–9.

Jones, L. and Lodge, A. (1991). A survey of psychiatric patients: views of outpatient clinic facilities. *Health Bulletin*, **49**, 320–328.

Jones, R.S.P. (1994). Research in clinical psychology: one trial aversion learning? *Clinical Psychology Forum*, **66**, 13–15.

Judd, L.L., Kessler, R.C., Paulus, M.P. *et al.* (1998). Comorbidity as a fundamental feature of generalized anxiety disorders: results from the National Comorbidity Study (NCS). *Acta Psychiatrica Scandinavica*, **98** (Suppl. 393), 6–11.

Jupp, H. and Dudley, M. (1984). Group cognitive/anxiety management. *Journal of Advanced Nursing*, **9**, 573–580.

Karno, M., Hough, R.I., Burnam, A. *et al.* (1987). Lifetime prevalence of specific psychiatric disorders among mexican americans and non-hispanic whites in Los Angeles. *Archives of General Psychiatry*, **44**, 695–701.

Katerndahl, D.A. and Realini, J.P. (1995). Where do panic attacks sufferers seek care? *Journal of Family Practice*, **40**, 237–243.

Katon, W. (1984). Panic disorder and somatization: review of 55 cases. *American Journal of Medicine*, **77**, 101–106.

Katon, W., Vitaliano, P.P., Russo, J. *et al.* (1987). Panic disorder: spectrum of severity and somatization. *Journal of Nervous and Mental Disease*, **175**, 12–19.

Kendall, P.C. and Clarkin, J.F. (1992). Introduction to the special section: comorbidity and treatment implications. *Journal of Consulting and Clinical Psychology*, **60**, 833–834.

Kendler, K.S. (1993). Twin studies of psychiatric illness: current status and future directions. *Archives of General Psychiatry*, **50**, 905–915.

Kendler, K.S. (1996). Major depression and generalised anxiety disorder: same genes, (partly) different environments—revisited. *British Journal of Psychiatry*, **168** (Suppl. 30), 68–75.

Kessler, R.C. (1997). The prevalence of psychiatric morbidity. In S. Wetzler and W.C. Sanderson (Eds). *Treatment Strategies for Patients with Psychiatric Morbidity* (pp. 23–48). New York: Wiley.

Kessler, R.C. (1999). The challenge for mental illness advocacy groups in the 21st century. Paper presented at the Gamian (Global Alliance of Mental Illness Advocacy Networks) International Meeting, New York, April.

Kessler, R.C. and Forthofer, M.S. (1999). The effects of psychiatric disorders on family formation and stability. In M.J. Cox and J. Brooks-Gunn (Eds), *Conflict and Cohesion in Families*. (pp. 301–320). Hillsdale, NJ: Erlbaum.

Kessler, R.C. and Frank, R.G. (1997). The impact of psychiatric disorders on work loss days. *Psychological Medicine*, **27**, 861–873.

Kessler, R.C. and Price, R.H. (1993). Primary prevention of secondary disorders: a proposal and agenda. *American Journal of Community Psychology*, **21**, 607–633.

Kessler, R.C., House, J.S. and Turner, J.B. (1987a). Unemployment and health in a community sample. *Journal of Health and Social Behavior*, **28**, 51–59.

Kessler, R.C., Turner, J.B. and House, J.S. (1987b). Intervening processes in the relationship between unemployment and health. *Psychological Medicine*, **17**, 949–961.

Kessler, R.C., McGonagle, K.A., Zhao, S. *et al.* (1994). Lifetime and 12 month prevalence of DSM-III-R psychiatric disorders in the United States. *Archives of General Psychiatry*, **51**, 8–19.

Kessler, R.C., Foster, C.L., Saunders, W.B. and Stang, P.E. (1995). Social consequences of psychiatric disorders. I: Educational attainment. *American Journal of Psychiatry*, **152**, 1026–1023.

Kessler, R.C., Nelson, C.B., McGonagle, K.A. *et al.* (1996). Comorbidity of DSM-III-R major depressive disorder in the general population: results from the US National Comorbidity Survey. *British Journal of Psychiatry*, **168** (Suppl. 30), 17–30.

Kessler, R.C., Frank, R.G., Edlung, M. *et al.* (1997a). Differences in the use of psychiatric outpatient services between the United States and Ontario. *New England Journal of Medicine*, **336**, 551–557.

Kessler, R.C., Berglund, P.A., Foster, C.L. *et al.* (1997b). Social consequences of psychiatric disorders. II: Teenage parenthood. *American Journal of Psychiatry*, **154**, 1405–1411.

Kessler, R.C., Crum, R.M., Warner, L.A. *et al.* (1997c). Lifetime co-occurrence of DSM-III-R alcohol abuse and dependence with other psychiatric disorders in the National Comorbidity Survey. *Archives of General Psychiatry*, **54**, 313–321.

Kessler, R.C., Walters, E.E. and Forthofer, M.S. (1998). The social consequences of psychiatric disorders. III: Probability of marital stability. *American Journal of Psychiatry*, **155**, 1092–1096.

Kessler, R.C., Olfson, M. and Berglund, P.A. (1999a). Patterns and predictors of treatment contact after first onset of psychiatric disorders. *American Journal of Psychiatry*, **155**, 62–69.

Kessler, R.C., Zhao, S., Katz, S.J. *et al.* (1999b). Past-year use of out-patient services for psychiatric problems in the National Comorbidity Survey. *American Journal of Psychiatry*, **155**, 115–123.

Kessler, R.C., Wittchen, H.-U., Stein, M. and Walters, E.E. (1999c). Lifetime co-morbidities between social phobia and mood disorders in the US National Comorbidity Survey. *Journal of Clinical Psychiatry*, **29**, 555–567.

King, M. (1997). Brief psychotherapy in general practice: how do we measure outcome? *British Journal of General Practice*, March, 136–137.

King, M. and Friedli, K. (1996). Counselling in general practice: a review. *Primary Care Psychiatry*, **2**, 205–216.

Kingdon, D., Tyrer, P., Seivewright, N. *et al.* (1996). The Nottingham study of neurotic disorder: influence of cognitive therapists on outcome. *British Journal of Psychiatry*, **169**, 93–97.

Klass, E.T., DiNardo, P.A. and Barlow, D.H. (1989). DSM-III-R personality diagnoses in anxiety disorder patients. *Comprehensive Psychiatry*, **30**, 251–258.

Klein, D.F. and Ross, D.C. (1993). Reanalysis of the National Institute of Mental Health Treatment of Depression Collaborative Research Program General Effectiveness Report. *Neuropsychopharmocology*, **8**, 241–251.

Koksal, F. and Power, K.G. (1990). Four systems anxiety questionnaire (FSAQ): a self-report measure of somatic, cognitive, behavioural and feeling components. *Journal of Personality Assessment*, **54**, 534–544.

Krueger, R.F., Caspi, A., Moffitt. T.E. and Silva, P.A. (1998). The structure and stability of common mental disorders (DSM-III-R): a longitudinal–epidemiological study. *Journal of Abnormal Psychology*, **107**, 216–227.

Krupnick, L.J., Sotsky, S.M., Simmens, S. *et al.* (1996). The role of the therapeutic alliance in psychotherapy and pharmacotherapy outcome: findings in the National Institute of Mental Health Collaborative Research Program. *Journal of Consulting and Clinical Psychology*, **64**, 532–539.

Lader, M.H. (1998). The nature and duration of treatment for GAD. *Acta Psychiatrica Scandinavia*, **98** (Suppl. 393), 109–117.

Lang, P.J. (1978). Anxiety: towards a psychophysiological definition. In H.S. Akiskal and W.H. Webb (Eds), *Diagnosis: Exploration of Biological Predictors*. New York: Spectrum.

Lehrer, P.M. and Woolfolk, R.L. (1993). *Principles and Practice of Stress Management*. New York: Guilford Press.

Lewinsohn, P.M., Munoz, R.F., Youngren, M.A. and Zeiss, A.M. (1986). *Control your Depression*. New York: Prentice Hall.

Ley, P. (1977). Psychological studies of doctor–patient communication. In S. Rachman (Ed.), *Contributions to Medical Psychology* (Vol. 1). Pergamon: Oxford.

Lidren, D.M., Watkins, P.L., Gould, R.A. *et al.* (1994). A comparison of bibliotherapy and group therapy in the treatment of panic disorder. *Journal of Consulting and Clinical Psychology*, **62**, 865–869.

Lindsay, W.R., Gamsu, C.V., McLaughlin, E. *et al.* (1987). A controlled trial of treatment for generalised anxiety. *British Journal of Clinical Psychology*, **26**, 3–15.

Lloyd, K.R. and Jenkins, R. (1995). Chronic depression and anxiety in primary care: approaches to liaison. *Advances in Psychiatric Treatment*, **1**, 192–198.

Lloyd, K.R., Jenkins, R. and Mann, A. (1996). Long term outcome of patients with neurotic illness in general practice. *British Medical Journal*, **313**, 26–28.

Lohr, J.M., Tolin, D.F. and Lilienfeld, S.O. (1998). Efficacy of eye movement desensitization and reprocessing: implications for behavior therapy. *Behavior Therapy*, **29**, 123–156.

Luborsky, L. and Digeur, L. (1993). A 'wild card' in comparative psychotherapy studies: the researcher's therapeutic allegiences. Paper presented at the meeting of the Society for Psychotherapy Research, Pitsburgh, PA, June.

Luborsky, L., Singer, B. and Luborsky, L. (1975). Comparative studies of psychotherapies: is it true that 'Everybody has won and all must have prizes?' *Archives of General Psychiatry*, **32**, 995–1008.

Luborsky, L., McLellan, A.T., Diguer, L. *et al.* (1997). The psychotherapist matters: comparison of outcomes across twenty-two therapists and seven patient samples. *Clinical Psychology: Science and Practice*, **4**, 53–64.

Lydiard, R.B., Brawman-Mintzer, O. and Ballenger, J.C. (1996). Recent developments in the psychopharmacology of anxiety disorders. *Journal of Consulting and Clinical Psychology*, **64**, 660–668.

Madden, S. and Hinks, M. (1987). Appointment keeping with clinical psychologists. *Clinical Psychology Forum*, **10**, 15–18.

Mann, A.H., Jenkins, R. and Belsey, E. (1981). The 12 month outcome of patients neurotic disorder in general practice. *Psychological Medicine*, **11**, 535–550.

Marks, I.M. (1985). Controlled trial of psychiatric nurse therapists in primary care. *British Medical Journal*, **290**, 1181–1184.

Marsland, D.W., Wood, M., and Mayo, F. (1976). Content of family practice: a data bank of patient care, curriculum, and research in family practice: 526 196 patient problems. *Journal of Family Practice*, **3**, 25–68.

Mathews, A. and McLeod, C. (1986). Discrimination of threat cues without awareness in anxiety states. *Journal of Abnormal Psychology*, **95**, 131–138.

Mauri, M., Sarno, N., Rossi, V.M. *et al.* (1992). Personality disorders associated with generalized anxiety, panic and recurrent depressive disorders. *Journal of Personality Disorders*, **6**, 162–167.

Mavissakalian, M.R., Hamann, M.S., Haidar, S.A. and de Groot, C.M. (1995). Correlates of DSM-III personality in generalized anxiety disorder. *Journal of Anxiety Disorders*, **9**, 103–115.

McAuliffe, E. and MacLachlan, M. (1992). Consumers' views of mental health services: the good, the bad and some suggestions for improvements. *Clinical Psychology Forum*, **47**, 16–19.

McCaskill, N.D. and McCaskill, A. (1983). Preparing patients for psychotherapy. *British Journal of Social and Clinical Psychology*, **2**, 80–84.

McLean, P.D., Woody, S., Taylor, S. and Koch, W.J. (1998). Comorbid panic disorder and major depression: implications for cognitive–behavioral therapy. *Journal of Consulting and Clinical Psychology*, **66**, 240–247.

McLeod, J. (1992). The general practitioner's role. In M. Sheldon (Ed.), *Counselling in General Practice*. London: RCGP Enterprises.

McPherson, F.M. (1998). Outpatient waiting lists: what are our responsibilites? *Clinical Psychology Forum*, **119**, 3–4.

McPherson, F.M., Watson, P.J. and Taylor, V.J. (1996). Audit of an adult mental health outpatient clinical psychology service. *Clinical Psychology Forum*, **98**, 26–28

Meichenbaum, D. (1985). *Stress Inoculation Training*. New York: Pergamon.

Merikangas, K.R., Eaton, J., Eaton, J. *et al.* (1996). Comorbidity and boundaries of affective disorders with anxiety disorders and substance misuse: results of an international task force. *British Journal of Psychiatry*, **168**, (Suppl. 30), 58–67.

Milne, D. and Paxton, R. (1998). A psychological re-analysis of the scientist–practitioner model. *Clinical Psychology and Psychotherapy*, **5**, 216–230.

Milne, D. and Souter, K. (1988). A re-evaluation of the clinical psychologist in general practice. *Journal of the Royal College of General Practitioners*, **38**, 457–460.

Milne, D., Britton, P. and Wilkinson, I. (1990). The scientist–practitioner in practice. *Clinical Psychology Forum*, **30**, 27–30.

Mogg, K., Bradley, B.P., Millar, N. and White, J. (1995). A follow-up study of cognitive bias in generalized anxiety disorder. *Behaviour Research and Therapy*, **33**, 927–935

Moorey, H. and Soni, S.D. (1994). Anxiety symptoms in stable chronic schizophrenics. *Journal of Mental Health*, **3**, 257–262.

Moras, K. and Barlow, D.H. (1992). Dimensional approaches to diagnosis and the problem of anxiety and depression. In W. Fiegenbaum, A. Ehlers, J. Margraf and I. Florin (Eds), *Perspectives and Promises of Clinical Psychology* (pp. 23–37). New York: Plenum Press.

Morrow-Bradley, C. and Elliott, R. (1986). Utilization of psychotherapy research by practising psychotherapists. *American Psychologist*, **41**, 188–197.

Mostofsky, A. and Barlow, D.H. (2000). *The Management of Stress and Anxiety in Medical Disorders*. Boston, MA: Allyn & Bacon.

Mynors-Wallis, L.M., Gath, D.H., Lloyd-Thomas, A.R. *et al.* (1995). Randomised controlled trial comparing problem solving treatment with amitryptyline and placebo for major depression in primary care. *British Medical Journal*, **310**, 441–445.

Mynors-Wallis, L., Davies, I., Gray, A. *et al.* (1997). A randomised controlled trial and cost analysis of problem solving treatment for emotional disorders given by community nurses in primary care. *British Journal of Psychiatry*, **170**, 113–119.

Newnes, C. (1993). A further note on waiting lists. *Clinical Psychology Forum*, **53**, 33–35.

Newton, J. (1988). *Preventing Mental Illness*. London: Routledge.

Norcross, J.C. and Goldfried, M.R. (Eds), (1992). *Handbook of Psychotherapy Integration*. New York: Basic Books.

Norton, G.R., Harrison, B., Hauch, J. and Rhodes, L. (1985). Characteristics of people with infrequent panic attacks. *Journal of Abnormal Psychology*, **94**, 216–221.

Oei, T.P.S. and Shuttleworth, G.J. (1996). Specific and non-specific factors in psychotherapy: a case for cognitive therapy for depression. *Clinical Psychology Review*, **16**, 83–103.

Oldham, J.M., Skodal, A.E., Kellam, H.D. *et al.* (1995). Comorbidity of Axis I and Axis II disorders. *American Journal of Psychiatry*, **152**, 571–578.

Olfson, M., Broadhead, E., Weissman, M.M. *et al.* (1996). Subthreshold psychiatric symptoms in a primary care group practice. *Archives of General Psychiatry*, **53**, 880–886.

Olfson, M., Kessler, R.C., Berglund, P.A. and Lin, E. (1998). Psychiatric disorder onset and first treatment contact in the United States and Ontario. *American Journal of Psychiatry*, **155**, 1415–1422.

Orford, J. (1992). *Community psychology: Theory and Practice*. Chichester: Wiley.

Orlinsky, D.E. and Howard, K.I. (1986). Process and outcome in psychotherapy. In S.L. Garfield and A.E. Bergin (Eds), *Handbook of Psychotherapy and Behavior Change* (3rd edn). New York: Wiley.

Ormrod, J. (1995). Short and long-term effectiveness of group anxiety management training. *Behavioural and Cognitive Psychotherapy*, **23**, 63–70.

Ost, L-G. (1989a). One-session treatment for specific phobias. *Behaviour Research and Therapy*, **27**, 1–7.

Ost, L.-G. (1989b). A maintenance program for behavioural treatment for anxiety disorders. *Behaviour Research and Therapy*, **27**, 123–130.

Otto, M.W., Peneva, S.J., Pollack, R.A. and Smoller, J.W. (1995). Cognitive–behavioral and pharmacologic perspectives on the treatment of posttraumatic stress disorder. In M.H. Pollack, M.W. Otto and J.F. Rosenbaum (Eds), *Challenges in Psychiatric Treatment: Pharmacologic Strategies*. New York: Guilford Press.

Paul, G.L. (1967). Outcome research in psychotherapy. *Journal of Consulting Psychology*, **31**, 109–118.

Paykel, E.S. (1991). Depression in women. *British Journal of Psychiatry*, **158** (Suppl. 10), 22–29.

Persons, J.B. (1986). The advantages of studying psychological phenomena rather than psychiatric diagnoses. *American Psychologist*, **41**, 1252–1260.

Persons, J.B. (1994). Why don't my patients do as well as the ones in the outcome studies? *Behavior Therapist*, **17**, 60.

Pini, S., Goldstein, R.B., Wickramaratne, P.J. and Weissman, M.M. (1994). Phenomenology of panic disorder and major depression in a family study. *Journal of Affective Disorders*, **30**, 257–272.

Powell, T.J. (1987). Anxiety management groups in clinical practice: a preliminary report. *Behavioural Psychotherapy*, **15**, 181–187.

Powell, T.J. and Enright, S.J. (1990). *Anxiety and Stress Management*. London: Routledge.

Power, K.G., Simpson, R.J., Swanson, V. and Wallace, L.A. (1990). Controlled comparisons of pharmacological and psychological treatment of generalised anxiety disorder in primary care. *British Journal of General Practice*, **40**, 289–294.

Prochaska, J.O. and Norcross, J.C. (1983). Contemporary psychotherapists: a national survey of characteristics, practices, orientations, and attitudes. *Psychotherapy: Theory, Research and Practice*, **20**, 161–173.

Rachman, S. (1978). Human fears: a three systems analysis. *Scandanavian Journal of Behaviour Therapy*, **7**, 237–245.

Rachman, S.J. and Wilson, G.T. (1980). *The Effects of Psychological Therapy*. New York: Pergamon.

Rapee, R.M. (1991a). Psychological factors involved in generalized anxiety. In R.M. Rapee and D.H. Barlow (Eds), *Chronic Anxiety, Generalized Anxiety Disorder and Mixed Anxiety Depression* (pp. 1–28). New York: Guilford Press.

Rapee, R.M. (1991b). Generalized anxiety disorder: a review of clinical features and theoretical concepts. *Clinical Psychology Review*, **11**, 419–440.

Raw, S.D. (1993). Does psychotherapy research teach us anything about psychotherapy? *Behavior Therapist*, **16**, 75–77.

Regier, D.A., Narrow, W.E., Rae, D.S. *et al.* (1993). The deFacto US mental and addictive disorders service system: epidemiologic catchment area prospective 1 year prevalence rates of disorders and services. *Archives of General Psychiatry*, **50**, 85–94.

Robertson, S. and Sheldon, M. (1992). Separating assessment and treatment in everyday practice. *Clinical Psychology Forum*, **43**, 33–35.

Robins, L.N. and Regier, D.A. (1991). *Psychiatric Disorders in America: The Epidemiologic Catchment Area Study*. New York: Free Press.

Robson, M.H., France, R. and Bland, M. (1984). Clinical psychology in primary care: controlled clinical and economic evaluation. *British Medical Journal*, **288**, 1805–1808.

Rohde, P., Lewinsohn, P.M. and Seeley, J.R. (1991). Comorbidity of unipolar depression. II. Comorbidity with other mental disorders in adolescents and adults. *Journal of Abnormal Psychology*, **100**, 214–222.

Rosen, G.M., Lohr, J.M., McNally, R.J. and Herbert, J.D. (1998). Power therapies, miraculous claims and the cures that fail. *Behavioural and Cognitive Psychotherapy*, **26**, 99–101.

Roth, A. and Fonagy, P. (1996). *What Works for Whom? A Critical Review of Psychotherapy Research*. London: Guilford Press.

Royal College of General Practitioners, Office of Population, Census and Surveys and Department of Health and Social Security (1986). *Studies on Medical and Population Subjects No. 36. Morbidity Statistics from General Practice, Third National Study, 1981–2*. RCGP, OPCS, DHSS: London.

Salkovskis, P.M. (1991). The importance of behaviour in the maintenance of anxiety and panic: a cognitive account. *Behavioural Psychotherapy*, **19**, 6–19.

Salkovskis, P.M. (1995). Demonstrating specific effects in cognitive and behavioural therapy. In M. Aveline and D.A. Shapiro (Eds), *Research Foundations for Psychotherapy Practice* (pp. 191–228). Chichester: Wiley.

Salmon, P., Stanley, B. and Milne, D. (1988). Psychological problems in general practice: two assumptions explored. *British Journal of Clinical Psychology*, **27**, 371–379.

Sanderson, W.C. and Barlow, D.H. (1990). A description of patients diagnosed with DSM-III-R generalized anxiety disorder. *Journal of Nervous and Mental Disease*, **178**, 588–591.

Sanderson, W.C. and Wetzler, S. (1991). Chronic anxiety and generalized anxiety disorder: issues in comorbidity. In R.M. Rapee and D.H. Barlow (Eds), *Chronic Anxiety, Generalized Anxiety Disorder and Mixed Anxiety Depression* (pp. 119–135). New York: Guilford Press.

Sanderson, W.C., DiNardo, P.A., Rapee, R.M. and Barlow, D.H. (1990). Syndrome comorbidity in patients diagnosed with a DSM-III-R anxiety disorder. *Journal of Abnormal Psychology*, **99**, 308–312.

Sanderson, W.C., Beck, A.T. and McGinn, L.K. (1994). Cognitive therapy for generalized anxiety disorder: significance of comorbid personality disorder. *Journal of Cognitive Psychotherapy*, **8**, 13–18.

Sartorius, N., Ustun, B., Lecrubier, Y. and Wittchen, H.U. (1996). Depression comorbidity with anxiety: results from the WHO study on psychological disorders in primary health care. *British Journal of Psychiatry*, **168** (Suppl. 30), 38–43.

Scheibe, G. and Albus, M. (1994). Prospective follow-up study lasting two years in patients with panic disorder with and without depressive disorders. *European Archives of Psychiatry and Neurological Science*, **244**, 39–44.

Schiff, S.B. and Glassman, S.M. (1969). Large and small group therapy in a state mental health center. *International Journal of Group Psychotherapy*, **19**, 150–157.

Scogin, F., Jamison, C. and Davis, N. (1990). Two year follow-up of bibliotherapy for depression in older adults. *Journal of Consulting and Clinical Psychology*, **58**, 665–667.

Scott, A.I.F. and Freeman, C.P.L. (1992). Edinburgh primary care depression study: treatment outcome, patient satisfaction, and cost after 16 weeks. *British Medical Journal*, **304**, 883–887.

Scott, M.J. and Stradling, S.G. (1990). Group cognitive therapy for depression produces clinically significant reliable change in community based settings. *Behavioural Psychotherapy*, **18**, 1–19.

Scott, M.J. and Stradling, S.G. (1997). Client compliance with exposure treatments for posttraumatic stress disorder. *Journal of Traumatic Stress*, **10**, 523–526.

Scott, M.J., Stradling, S.G. and Greenfield, T.A. (1995). The efficacy of brief cognitive therapy programmes for anxiety and depression, and the relevance of a personality disorder diagnosis. Paper presented at the World Congress of Behavioural and Cognitive Therapies, Copenhagen, July.

Seager, M., Scales, K., Jacobson, R., Orrell, M. and Baker, M. (1995). New psychology referral system: the reaction of GPs. *Clinical Psychology Forum*, **83**, 12–14.

Seligman, M. (1993). An interview with Martin Seligman. *Behavior Therapist*, **16**, 261–265.

Seligman, M. (1995). The effectiveness of psychotherapy: the Consumers Reports study. *American Psychologist*, **50**, 965–974.

Seligman, M. (1998). Why therapy works. *American Psychological Association Monitor*, **29**(12), 3.

Shadish, W.R., Matt, G.E., Navarro, A.M. *et al.* (1997). Evidence that therapy works in clinically representative conditions. *Journal of Consulting and Clinical Psychology*, **65**, 355–365.

Shah, A. (1992). The burden of psychiatric disorder in primary care. *International Review of Psychiatry*, **4**, 243–250.

Shapiro, D.A. and Shapiro, D. (1982). Meta-analysis of comparative therapy outcome studies: a replication and refinement. *Psychological Bulletin*, **92**, 581–604.

Shapiro, F. (1995). *Eye Movement Desensitization and Reprocessing: Basic Principles, Protocols and Procedures*. New York: Guilford Press.

Sharp, D. and Morell, D. (1989). The psychiatry of general practice. In P. Williams, G. Wilkinson and K. Rawnsley (Eds), *Scientific Approaches to Epidemiological Psychiatry*. London, Routledge.

Sharp, D.M., Power, K.G., Simpson, R.J. *et al.* (1997). Global measures of outcome in a controlled comparison of pharmacological and psychological treatment of panic disorder and agoraphobia in primary care. *British Journal of General Practice*, **47**, 150–155.

Shea, M.T., Elkin, I., Imber, S. *et al.* (1992). Course of depressive symptoms over follow-up: findings from the National Institute of Mental Health Treatment of Depression Collaborative Research Program. *Archives of General Psychiatry*, **49**, 782–787.

Shear, M.K. and Schulberg, H.C. (1995). Anxiety disorders in primary care. *Bulletin of the Menninger Clinic*, **59**, A73–A85.

Shear, M.K., Schulberg, H.C. and Madonia, M. (1994a). Panic and generalized anxiety disorder in primary care. Paper presented at a meeting of the Association for Primary Care, Washington, DC, September.

Shear, M.K., Pilkonis, P.A., Cloitre, M. and Leon, A.C. (1994b). Cognitive behavioral treatment compared with nonprescriptive treatment of panic disorder. *Archives of General Psychiatry*, **51**, 395–401.

Shear, M.R., Cloitre, M. and Heckelman, L. (1995). Emotion-focused treatment for panic disorder: a brief dynamically informed therapy. In J.P. Barber and P. Crits-Cristoph (Eds), *Dynamic Therapies for Psychiatric Disorders (Axis-I)* (pp. 267–293). New York: Basic Books.

Shepherd, M. (1991). Primary care psychiatry: the case for action. *British Journal of General Practitioners*, **41**, 252–255.

Sherbourne, C.D., Wells, K.B., Meredith, L.S. *et al.* (1996). Comorbid anxiety disorder and the functioning and well-being of chronically ill patients of general medical providers. *Archives of General Psychiatry*, **53**, 889–895.

Skaife, K. and Spall, B. (1995). An independent approach to auditing psychology services for adult mental health clients. *Clinical Psychology Forum*, **77**, 14–18.

Sledge, W.H., Moras, K., Hartley, D. and Levine, M. (1990). Effect of time-limited psychotherapy on patient drop-out rates. *American Journal of Psychiatry*, **147**, 1341–1347.

Sloane, R.B., Staples, F.R., Cristol, A.H. *et al.* (1975). *Psychotherapy Versus Behaviour Therapy*. Cambridge, MA: Harvard University Press.

Smail, P., Stockwell, T., Canter, S. and Hodgeson, R. (1984). Alcohol dependence and phobic anxiety states. I. A prevalence study. *British Journal of Psychiatry*, **144**, 53–57.

Smith, M.L. and Glass, G.V. (1980). *The Benefits of Psychotherapy*. Baltimore, MD: Johns Hopkins University Press.

Snaith, R.P. (1992). Anxiety and panic disorder. *Current Opinion in Psychiatry*, **5**, 234–237.

Spitzer, R.L., Williams, J.B.W., Gibbon, M. and First, M.B. (1990). *Structured Clinical Interview for DSM-III-R: Personality Disorders (SCID-II)*. Washington, DC: American Psychiatric Press.

Startup, M. (1994). Dealing with waiting lists for adult mental health services. *Clinical Psychology Forum*, **68**, 5–9.

Street, L.L., Salman, E., Garfinkle, R. *et al.* (1997). Discriminating between generalized anxiety disorder and anxiety disorder not otherwise specified in a Hispanic population: is it only a matter of worry? *Depression and Anxiety*, **5**, 1–6.

Strosahl, K.D., Hayes, S.C., Bergan, J. and Romano, P. (1998). Assessing the field effectiveness of acceptance and commitment therapy: an example of the manipulated training research method. *Behavior Therapy*, **29**, 35–64.

Suinn, R.M. and Richardson, F. (1971). Anxiety Management Training: a non-specific behavior therapy program for anxiety control. *Behavior Therapy*, **2**, 498–510.

Swendsen, J.D., Merikangas, K.R., Canino, G.J. *et al.* (1998). The comorbidity of alcoholism and depressive disorders in four geographic communities. *Comprehensive Psychiatry*, **39**, 176–184.

Task Force on Promotion and Dissemination of Psychological Procedures (1995). Report and recommendations. *Clinical Psychologist*, **48**, 3–23.

Teasdale, J.D., Fennell, M.J., Hibbert, G.A. and Amies, P.L. (1984). Cognitive therapy for major depressive disorder in primary care. *British Journal of Psychiatry*, **144**, 400–406.

Telch, M.L., Lucas, J.A., Schmidt, N.B. *et al.* (1993). Group cognitive–behavioral treatment of panic disorder. *Behaviour Research and Therapy*, **31**, 279–287.

Teti, D.M., Lamb, M.E. and Elster, A.B. (1987). Long-range socioeconomic and marital consequences of adolescent marriage in three cohorts of adult males. *Journal of Marriage and the Family*, **49**, 499–506.

Thyer, B.A., Parrish, R.T., Himle, J. *et al.* (1986). Alcohol abuse among clinically anxious patients. *Behaviour Research and Therapy*, **24**, 357–359.

Tollefson, G.D., Luxenberg, M., Valentine, R. *et al.* (1991). An open label trial of alprazolam in comorbid irritable bowel syndrome and generalized anxiety disorder. *Journal of Clinical Psychiatry*, **52**, 502–508.

Trepka, C., Laing, I. and Smith, S. (1986). Group treatment of general practice anxiety problems. *Journal of the Royal College of General Practitioners*, **36**, 114–117.

Trethowen, W.H. (1977). *The Role of Psychologists in the Health Service*. London: HMSO.

Turner, S., Beidel, D.C., Spaulding, S.A. and Brown, J.M. (1995). The practice of behavior therapy: a national survey of cost and methods. *Behavior Therapist*, **18**, 1–4.

Turvey, T. (1997). Outcomes of an adult psychology service. Paper presented at the Annual Conference of the British Psychological Society, Edinburgh, April.

Tyrer, P., Seivewright, N., Ferguson, B. *et al.* (1993). The Nottingham study of neurotic disorder: effect of personality status on response to drug treatment, cognitive therapy and self-help over two years. *British Journal of Psychiatry*, **162**, 219–226.

Ustun, T.B. and Sartorius, N. (1995). *Mental Illness in General Health Care: An International Study*. Chichester: Wiley.

Weich, S. (1997). Prevention of the common mental disorders: a public health perspective. *Psychological Medicine*, **27**, 757–764.

Weissman, M.M. and Beck, A.T. (1978). Development and validation of the Dysfunctional Attitude Scale: a preliminary inverstigation. Paper presented at the meeting of the American Educational Research Association, Toronto.

Weisz, J.R., Weiss, B. and Donnenberg, G.R. (1992). Effectiveness of psychotherapy with children and adolescents: a meta-analysis for clinicians. *Journal of Consulting and Clinical Psychology*, **55**, 542–549.

Wells, A. (1997). *Cognitive Therapy of Anxiety Disorders: A Practice Manual and Conceptual Guide*. Chichester: Wiley.

Westbrook, D. (1991). Can therapists predict length of treatment from referral letters? A pilot study. *Behavioural Psychotherapy*, **19**, 377–382.

Westbrook, D. (1993). Cutting waiting lists by cutting treatment: outcomes and pitfalls. Paper presented at the Annual Conference of the European Congress of Behaviour and Cognitive Therapy, London, September.

Westbrook, D. (1995). Patient and therapist views of different waiting list procedures. *Behavioural and Cognitive Psychotherapy*, **23**, 169–176.

Westbrook, D. and Hill, L. (1998). The long-term outcome of cognitive behaviour therapy for adults in routine clinical practice. *Behaviour Research and Therapy*, **36**, 635–643.

White, J. (1992). Use of the media and public lectures to publicise stress. In D. Trent (Ed.), *Promotion of Mental Health* (Vol. 1). Bristol: Avebury Press.

White, J. (1993a). 'Straight from the horse's mouth'. *Clinical Psychology Forum*, **53**, 20–22.

White, J. (1993b). Subconscious retraining: A placebo strategy for generalized anxiety disorder. *Behavioural Psychotherapy*, **21**, 161–164.

White, J. (1995a). Stresspac: a self-help anxiety management package: a controlled outcome study. *Behavioural and Cognitive Psychotherapy*, **23**, 89–107.

White, J. (1995b). 'Stress Control': a controlled comparative investigation of large group therapy for generalized anxiety disorder: eight year follow-up. Paper presented at the World Congress of Behavioural and Cognitive Therapies, Copenhagen.

White, J. (1995c). An analysis of components in large group didactic therapy: 'Stress Control'. *Clinical Psychology Forum*, **76**, 11–13.

White, J. (1997a). *Stresspac*. London: Psychological Corporation.

White, J. (1997b). Cognitive–behavioural treatment of GAD: a comparison of patients with and without an additional Axis-II personality disorder. Paper presented at the Annual Association for Advancement of Behavior Therapy Convention, Miami Beach, November.

White, J. (1997c). 'Stress Control' large group therapy: implications for managed care systems. *Depression and Anxiety*, **5**, 43–45.

White, J. (1998a). 'Stress Control' large group therapy for generalized anxiety disorder: two year follow-up. *Behavioural and Cognitive Psychotherapy*, **26**, 237–245.

White, J. (1998b). An Advice Clinic in primary care. *Clinical Psychology Forum*, **113**, 9–12.

White, J. (1998c). 'Stresspac': three year follow-up of a controlled trial of a self-help package for the anxiety disorders. *Behavioural and Cognitive Psychotherapy*, **26**, 133–141.

White, J. (1998d). How can we improve primary care psychology? Paper presented at the Division of Clinical Psychology (Scotland) Conference, Glasgow, November.

White, J. and Keenan, M. (1990). 'Stress Control': a pilot study of large group therapy for generalized anxiety disorder. *Behavioural and Cognitive Psychotherapy*, **20**, 97–114.

White, J. Keenan, M. and Brooks, N. (1992). 'Stress Control': a controlled comparative investigation of large group therapy for generalized anxiety disorder. *Behavioural and Cognitive Psychotherapy*, **20**, 97–114.

White, J., Brooks, N. and Keenan, M. (1995). Stress Control: a controlled comparative investigation of large group therapy for generalized anxiety disorder: process of change. *Clinical Psychology and Psychotherapy*, **2**, 86–97.

White, J., Jones, R. and McGarry, E. (1999). Cognitive–behavioural computer therapy for the anxiety disorders in primary care. Paper presented at the Annual Conference of the British Psychological Society, Belfast, April.

White, J., Jones, R. and McGarry, E. (in press). Cognitive–behavioural computer therapy for the anxiety disorders in primary care. *Journal of Mental Health*.

Wilkinson, R.G. (1992). Income distribution and life expectancy. *British Medical Journal*, **304**, 165–168.

Wilkinson, R.G. (1996). *Unhealthy Societies*. London: Routledge.

Wittchen, H.-U., and Essau, C.A. (1989). Comorbidity of anxiety disorders and depression: does it affect course and outcome? *Psychiatry and Psychobiology*, **4**, 315–323.

Wittchen, H.U., Zhao, S., Kessler, R.C. and Eaton, W.W. (1994). DSM-III-R generalized anxiety disorder in the National Comorbidity Survey. *Archives of General Psychiatry*, **51**, 355–364.

Wolfe, B. (1994). Adapting psychotherapy outcome research to clinical reality. *Society for the Exploration of Psychotherapy Integration Newsletter* (June), 160–166.

World Health Organization (1992). *The Tenth Revision of the International Classification of Diseases and Related Health Problems (ICD-10)*. Geneva: WHO.

Yalom, I.D. (1975). *Theory and Practice of Group Psychotherapy*. New York: Basic Books.

Zigmond, A.S. and Snaith, R.P. (1983). The Hospital Anxiety and Depression Scale. *Acta Psychiatrica Scandinavica*, **67**, 361–370.

Zinbarg, R.E. and Barlow, D.H. (1996). Structure of anxiety and the anxiety disorders: a hierarchical model. *Journal of Abnormal Psychology*, **105**, 181–193.

Zinbarg, R.E., Barlow, D.H., Liebowitz, M. *et al.* (1994). The DSM-IV trial for mixed anxiety–depression. *American Journal of Psychiatry*, **151**, 1153–1162.

Zubin, J. (1978). But is it good for science? *Clinical Psychology*, **31**, 5–7.

INDEX

Page numbers in *italics* refer to tables; references to 'courses' or 'sessions' are to 'Stress Control' courses or sessions.

actions
  behavioural anxiety 137, 162–74
  depression 195, 197
  panic attacks 178–80, 183
advertising of sessions 76
aerobic exercise 113, 200
age factors
  age at onset 16
  teenage marriage 17
  teenage parenthood 16
agoraphobia
  comorbidity 7, 8, 9, 10, 51, 66
  diagnosis 12
  early intervention 51
  flexibility of CBT 70
  prevalence *4*
  'Stress Control' 89, 216
alcohol use 9–10, 106
alternative therapy 112
antidepressant medication 47, 112, 136, 200
Anxiety Disorder Interview Schedule 77
anxiety management training 47, 48
assessment interviews 77–8
  assessors 76–7, 88–9
  common questions 82–5
  introduction to course 78–82
  key messages 86–8
  need for 88
attendance 42–3, 72, 77, 119
avoidance 112–13, 167, 168

behavioural therapy 44, 45, 46
behaviours 137, 162–74
  depression 195, 197
  panic attacks 178–80, 183

bibliotherapy 91–3, 216–17
  see also self-help manual
body
  anxiety effects 138, 141–50
  depression 195, 200
  panic attacks 178–83
breathing 114, 180, 182–3, 184
British Psychiatric Morbidity Survey 4–5, 15

caffeine 170
CD-ROM 'Stresspac' 222
challenging thoughts 155–62
clinical effectiveness 35, 36–7
  primary care studies 43–50
  'Stress Control' 218
clinical efficacy 35, 36
  see also research studies
clinical efficiency 35, 36–7
  'Stress Control' 63, 70–1, 74, 218–20, *220*
clinical practice–research gap *see* research studies
clinical psychology services 39, 45–6
  see also primary health care, mental health care within; 'Stress Control'
cognitions 137, 151–62
  depression 195, 196–7
  panic attacks 178–80, 183
  pre-attentive bias 218
community mental health teams 44
community nurses 44
community psychiatric nurses 43–4
comorbidity of disorders 7–11
  early intervention 50–1

comorbidity of disorders (*cont.*)
  'Stress Control' 67–8, 215–16, 218
  structure of disorders 64–7
  treatment outcomes 27–8, 29, 66–7,
    215–16, 218
  vulnerability factors 26
computerised 'Stresspac' 222
coping strategies 73–4, 126, 168, 170
counselling 45, 47
cultural factors 18, 71–2, 73

depressive disorders
  comorbidity 8–9, 10, 27–8, 29, 51, 66–7
  diagnostic problems 12
  early intervention 51
  prevalence 5, 6, 7
  primary care 44, 49
  research–practice gap 27–8, 29, 32, 34
  social costs 14–15
  'Stress Control' 67, 191–200, 222
  structure of disorders 66–7
describing stress 104–5
diagnostic issues
  comorbidity studies 8, 26
  DSM system 24–5, 26
  and prevalence 3–4, 5
  primary care 12
  structure of disorders 64–9
diaries 106, 125
distraction techniques 113, 118
divorce 17
DSM system 24–5, 26

early-onset disorders 16, 17
economic costs 13–14, 63, 74
economic factors 14, 15, 17–18, 29–30
educational factors 16
employment 13, 15, 17
exercise 113, 200
exposure techniques 167

family members 89, 92, 113
friends 89, 92, 113

general practitioners (GPs)
  as assessors 88–9
  communication with 119
  patient interaction 90
  perceptions of anxiety 11
  referrals from 76, 88–9
  see also primary health care, mental
    health care within
generalised anxiety disorder (GAD)
  comorbidity 7–8, 9, 10–11
    structure of disorders 65, 66–7

treatment outcomes 27, 29, 66–7,
    215–16, 218
  vulnerability factors 26
DSM diagnostic criteria 24
economic costs 14
prevalence 4, 5, 6
research studies
  comparative trials 31–2, 218
  patient representativeness 28–30
  in primary care 47, 48–9
  'Stress Control' 215–16, 218
  time factors 35
genetic factors 9, 26
goal setting 106
group size 71, 119–21
group therapy 47–50
  see also 'Stress Control'

handouts of quotations 102–4, 217
hierarchical model 64–5
homework assignments 124–5, 127
hyperventilation 180, 182–3, 184

individual therapy 47, 60–1
  with 'Stress Control' 68–9
  'Stress Control' compared 220–1
information provision 90
  bibliotherapy 91–3
  learning about stress 101–4, 132–40
  research evidence 216–17
  self-help manual 94–100
insomnia 185–91

learning about stress 101–4, 131–40

marriage 16–17
medical conditions 68
medication 47, 112, 136, 200
mood disorders
  comorbidity 8–9, 10, 11
    early intervention 51
    'Stress Control' 67
    structure of disorders 66–7
    treatment outcomes 27–8, 29, 66–7
  comparative trials 32
  diagnostic problems 12
  prevalence 5, 6, 7
  see also depressive disorders
music during sessions 118
myths about stress 135–7

obsessive-compulsive disorder (OCD) 7,
  67
onset of disorders 15–16, 17, 50–1
outcome studies *see* research studies

panic attacks, treatment 174–85, 216
panic disorder (PD)
  bibliotherapy 91
  comorbidity 7–8, 9, 10
    early intervention 51
    'Stress Control' 69, 216
    structure of disorders 65, 66
    treatment outcomes 27–8
    vulnerability factors 26
  diagnosis in primary care 12, 13
  flexibility of CBT 70
  prevalence 4, 5, 6
  primary care 48–9
  'Stress Control' 69, 216
panic disorder with agoraphobia (PDA)
  comorbidity 7, 8, 9, 51
  diagnosis 12
  flexibility of CBT 70
  'Stress Control' 216
parenthood 16
partners 89, 92, 113
patient–therapist relationships 33–5, 73
person-centred counselling 45
personal disclosure 71–2
personality disorders 10–11, 27, 29
  'Stress Control' 67–8, 215–16, 218
phobia
  comorbidity 11
  prevalence 4
  'Stress Control' 67
  see also agoraphobia; social phobia
post-traumatic stress disorder
  diagnosis 12
  prevalence 4
  treatment outcomes 30, 216
power therapies 112
practice–research gap see research
  studies
pre-attentive bias 218
pre-course preparation 91–2, 100, 101–14
prevalence of disorders 3–7, 4
prevention of disorders 50–1, 61–2
primary health care
  access to services 38–9
  consultation rates 11–12, 13
  diagnostic problems 12
  economic costs 13
  mental health care within 41
    complexity of therapy 42
    multi-level services 51, 52
    patient attendance 42–3
    problems of 'failure' 41
    service interactivity 50–2
    treatment effectiveness 43–50
    treatment innovations 43, 49–50

waiting lists 40–1
  see also 'Stress Control'
  prevalence of disorders 5–7
problem solving 44, 170
progressive muscular relaxation 144,
  145–9
psychiatrists 44
psychosocial factors 15–17, 30, 68, 72
psychotic disorders 69

quick control techniques 113–14
quotations from sufferers 102–4

rapid control techniques 113–14
reassurance 112
referrals 76, 88–9
relapse prevention 61–2, 93
relaxation 144, 145–9
research studies
  gap with practice 20–4
    closing the gap 35–7
    comorbidity effects 25–8, 29
    comparative trials 30–3
    exclusion criteria 28–9
    non-specific variables 33
    patient representativeness 28–30
    social factors 17–18, 29–30
    therapist–patient factors 33–5
    time factors 35
  in primary care 43–50
  'Stress Control' 211–22

satellite therapies 222–3
scientist–practitioners 36–7
seating arrangements 116–17
self-assessment forms 104–6
self-help, bibliotherapy 91–3
self-help course 221–2
self-help manual 94–100, 216–17
  learning about stress 101–4
service provision see primary health
  care, mental health care within
setting goals 106
short-term techniques 113–14
sleep problems 185–91
slides 123
social factors
  economic costs 13–14
  and psychological 15–17, 30, 68, 72
  research design 17–18, 29–30
  social costs 14–15, 17
social phobia
  comorbidity 7–8, 9, 10, 11
  economic costs 14
  prevalence 4, 5

social phobia (*cont.*)
  'Stress Control' 89, 216
social support 61
somatics 138, 141–50
  depression 195, 200
  panic attacks 178–83
spouses 89, 92, 113
stimulus control 187, 188, 190–1
'Stress Control' 57–9
  behavioural anxiety 162–74
  cognitive anxiety 151–62, 218
  course materials 90–100
  depression 191–200, 222
  developments 221–3
  diagnostic issues 64–9
  end of the course 203–7
  insomnia 185–91
  learning about stress 101–4, 131–40
  linking the techniques 201–3
  panic attacks 174–85
  pre-attentive bias 218
  preparation by students 91–2, 100,
    101–14
  rationale for 59–64
  repeating the course 206
  research evidence 211–22
  running a session 115–27
  satellite therapies 222–3
  setting up courses 76–89
  somatic anxiety 141–50
  therapy issues 69–75
  as true therapy 217
Stress Inoculation Training 161
stress management courses 49–50
  see also 'Stress Control'
'Stresspac' 221–2
  course materials *see* written material

TAB model 137–8
  depression 194–5

panic attacks 178–80
targeting stress 105–6
teachers, number of 74–5
teaching aids 123–4
teaching style 121–2
teenage marriage 17
teenage parenthood 16
therapist–patient relationships 33–5,
  73
thoughts
  cognitive anxiety 137, 151–62, 218
  depression 195, 196–7
  panic attacks 178–80, 183
time factors
  multi-level services 52
  'Stress Control' sessions 74, 118, 124,
    218–20
  treatment outcomes 35
tone of sessions 118
treatment outcome studies *see* research
  studies

unemployment 15, 17

venues for courses 115–16, 117
videos 118, 124
vulnerability factors 26

waiting lists 40–1
work 13, 15, 17
written material 90
  bibliotherapy 91–3
  diaries 106
  handouts of quotations 102–4,
    217
  self-assessment forms 104–6
  self-help course 221–2
  self-help manual 94–100, 101–4,
    216–17
  therapist manual 93

Index compiled by Liz Granger